PLAIN ENGLISH

by Susie Fisher

To the Amish

You are my mother
  You are my root
You're the one who bore me
  I hate the pain I caused you

You ask me to say
  my needs don't count
I'm just a blob in a sea of faces
  one like the rest

  Snowflakes all the same…

It's all tangled up inside me
      the good, the bad and the in-between
      oh especially the in-between
But I can't say it's all a shade of gray

  I need some truth
  Just a little truth…

Color, what is color
      Is it when my heart is breaking
      Because I got kicked again
For being sweet
  For trusting
      For believing love reigns
  It's a hard world

You're right to be separate
  You warned me
    I didn't listen
      No, I didn't listen…

If freedom comes with the price
   to turn my back on you
Individuality is a joke
   we're loners out here
I miss you, my mother tree
    Your caring heart
        Your humility
                You gave me my start

Can I do it
Can I say you're a fraud?

Part I

Chapter 1

M y earliest memory of school is shoe envy. Those shiny black patent-leather shoes Jane and Sally wore! I could not have cared less about their brother Dick—he was beside the point—and the dog Spot was cute, of course, and it was lovely that he could run.

But those darling little shoes the girls had on, with the little straps across the front! The second thing I envied was their white socks.

I, on the other hand, wore thick black stockings and horrid black shoes. It didn't help that two of my classmates, Linda and Lena Petersheim, twins and Amish like I was, were allowed to wear white stockings. And Mrs. Leatherman, our ancient teacher who walked with a limp and had a black tooth and iron-gray curls, didn't pick on them like she did on me.

When my mother told her that I was coming home every day for the first few weeks of second grade and saying that "I was bored and knew everything," she skipped me to third grade and that was when the trouble really began. She made me help her teach the other children, which I didn't mind, but what did hurt was the day we had our "races" outside and when I stepped up with the second graders she said with a vicious twinge in her voice, "Susie, you're a third grader now!" Of course, I lagged way behind the much larger third graders because I was petite to start with.

Mrs. Leatherman also seemed to derive a great deal of pleasure from when I stumbled over the word "perfumery" one day. For Christmas that year she gave me this vile-smelling perfume with a card that made a great joke out of it, the one word she had tossed at me that I couldn't quite manage.

However, it wasn't all bad—the school yard was surrounded on two sides by an apple orchard and behind the school was a small area where Linda and Lena and I ate our lunches. I usually had a bologna sandwich and something else rather unspectacular and, of course, the twins seemed to always have better lunches than I had.

My other great fantasy during this time was "finger rings." I imagined that one day I would own my very own box of finger rings, and I'm not talking about a small box, either. I wanted a large cardboard box full of them.

At home I couldn't indulge in fantasies much.

There was no end to the work, ever.

We had to clean the house thoroughly every single Saturday. Even working in my room wasn't a pleasure, because I wanted to dawdle and daydream a bit, but the minute my mother heard that my footsteps had stilled, she screamed up the stairs for me to get back to work.

In the summertime, we also had to mow the yard and trim it by hand, and work in the garden, which I really hated. The string beans especially seemed to mutate into gobs and gobs of endless work and I didn't even like them that much. The strawberries and peas were better; at least one could nibble now and then to ease the pain.

When I was old enough to read and in my Nancy Drew phase, I'd stash one of those fabulous books behind the flour canister in the kitchen and sneak a paragraph or two when Mom wasn't looking.

The worst room to clean was the formal living room. It simply had no soul. There was a china cabinet full of dishes no one ever touched and they looked like prisoners behind that glass. The pillows on the rocking chairs looked starved for feathers. The green shade at the window looked too morbid for words. Naturally, I chose that room to desecrate when I was four years old.

Amish females are never, ever supposed to cut their hair.

What did I do? Cut mine, and I did it in a spirit of great calm. I pulled a small brown padded bench into the room. Then I traipsed to the medicine cabinet in the bathroom and gathered together all Dad's wonderful, mysterious grooming tools: hair scissors, shaving cream, razor, and shaving brush. The brush was my favorite out of all the tools because it had such nice, plump bristles, in stark contrast to the starved pillows on the rocking chairs, I suppose.

Once I had placed the items neatly side by side on the bench, I picked up the scissors and snip! went the front hair that my mother had rolled into what Amish mothers called "bobbies"—they took bread-bag twisties and rolled their little girls' hair tightly around them. Didn't do much for my forehead, but it sure made cutting my hair easier.

Oh, my goodness. Lightning struck, and thunder rocked the house that day.

And every time we went to church for quite a while after that, my mother complained that it looked like she was taking an English child to church with her. (The Amish call *all* outsiders English, regardless of their nationality.)

I felt indifferent about that. The joy had been in the snipping, and bangs or bobbies, I was too young to care.

There was another hair episode when I was six years old. My hair was by then long enough to roll back tightly at the sides. One morning I was sitting on the bathroom countertop and my mother had just finished doing my hair in the acceptable Amish fashion, which is to say, tight and uncomfortable.

She stepped back, frowned, and put her hands on her hips.

"I can't make you look Amish!" she said.

3

I felt a little taken aback. *Was there something wrong with me?* But then I ran off to play and forgot all about it.

By the time I was twelve, I realized that being Amish was no laughing matter. The men made all the rules, and the women obeyed them. It seemed odd to me, for example, that the males were allowed to have buttons on their shirts and pants, but we females were not allowed, after a certain age, to have buttons on *anything*, but rather had to use straight pins to keep our dresses, capes, and aprons together. Also, we used pins to secure our prayer coverings on our heads. I always thought the hats the boys wore were so much more carefree, somehow. They didn't pin them down but rather tossed them off when they were inside. In summer they wore straw hats, dashing things that looked like they were made for fun times and in winter, black hats that Mom and we girls brushed with vigor so they'd be nice again for Sunday.

I didn't mind being a girl, really, in spite of the straight pins because the one thing I thought more horrible than anything else in the whole Amish culture were the *beards*. At least we girls didn't have to grow those when we were married!

Mom and Dad always looked very serious and rather heavy-hearted after the biannual council meeting, when the preachers stated all the rules. I wasn't allowed to attend—not that I wanted to!—because I was not yet a baptized member of the church. But Dad especially always got stricter after that meeting, probably because he felt guilty about all his smart ways to get around the rules of the Amish church. Which made me mad, because if a guy has brains, like my Dad surely did, why shouldn't he use them?

One of the kind things he did for my mother was rig up a light that was both lovely and practical. It hung on the cabinet

4

right above where we washed the dishes. I could tell my mom considered it romantic for her husband to do that for her. I mean, what with not being able to buy jewelry or that sort of thing for his wife, what is an Amish husband supposed to do to show his love? Well, what my dad did was try to make life easier on my mother, which I thought was very sweet, and I could tell she did, too. So one night there we were, washing and drying dishes with that pretty gas light beaming down on us like it knew how unusual it was for Amish females to wash dishes with all that glorious light shining down, when into our driveway clopped a horse carrying a couple of mean preachers in a buggy, both of them sporting stern expressions and evil-looking beards, the kind of beards that brooked no nonsense, romantic or otherwise, from its church members. (Even though gas lights were allowed, I guess they didn't like how conveniently located and pretty that one was!)

Even though I was just a little girl when it happened, I could sense my father's grief when he took that light down from its perfect nesting place.

I would find out later just how extensive the rules really were at those council meetings. They covered *everything*, not just how you dressed, even though God knows that was bad enough. There were also rules about farm equipment, which didn't apply to us because we didn't farm, but I had to wonder— did God really *care* about things like tractors, and if the wheels on the buggies were rubber or not? Apparently they thought so, because rubber tires were strictly forbidden.

Also, God seemed to make an exception for odd things, according to the Amish. Take electricity, for example. We couldn't have it in the house, but they allowed my father his power tools in the cabinet shop, because he powered everything with a giant diesel instead of getting it from an electric company. I guess the Lord was pleased that we had to suffer a little for that electricity. That diesel scared the living daylights out of me. It was loud, and smelled vile, and seemed to shake the whole room it was housed in.

I also learned quickly that not all Amish families were the same. We seemed to be troublemakers, frankly. The preachers frowned on us constantly. They visited my parents *every year* to try to persuade them to send us schoolchildren to an Amish school rather than to the Mennonite one we attended. I guess they were concerned we would be influenced by the kids at the school, who had modern conveniences and didn't dress as plainly as we Amish did.

My siblings and I were scared when the preachers showed up, because we loved our school. One night I heard Mom and Dad talking, and they agreed we were getting a better education at the Mennonite school (most of the Mennonite teachers had college degrees while the Amish teachers were only allowed an eighth grade education). My parents especially loved that we had music class at our school. I could sing alto, soprano, and high tenor by the time I was twelve and they thought that fabulous, and some of my other siblings could harmonize too.

However, my mother worried terribly what her siblings, the Esh side of the family, thought of us children. I hated the feeling of her gaze on me at our big family gatherings. She had a look on her face that was a mix of sadness and shame, like she could tell I wasn't quite the Amish girl I should be, inside or out.

Chapter 2

Bird-in-Hand, Pennsylvania, is a small town located about six miles east of the city of Lancaster and is about an hour and a half west of Philadelphia. It is a pretty town, and as you drive along the one main road, Route 340, you'll see fields and some livestock, and if you're lucky you'll see a horse-drawn buggy or two. There is also a restaurant, an inn, a farmers market, a hardware store, and some other miscellaneous shops.

Our house, the one I grew up in, is visible from Route 340. It's one of those solid-looking red-brick houses, the kind that are built to last, and we moved there when I was three years old.

My father is an expert cabinetmaker and has two big buildings where he creates his masterpieces with the help of two of my brothers. One building is where they do all the sawing and all that, and it smells deliciously of sawdust. They do the staining and finishing in another building, and it smells very strongly and not so pleasantly of paint. It is also houses a small showroom and an office.

My favorite thing, though, is not the house or the cabinet shops but rather what surrounds them: glorious fields, with rich brown earth turned up in early spring, fields that even as a child calmed and soothed my soul. In one field the farmer usually planted corn that grew tall and proud before it was hacked down in the fall. Across the road from our house the farmer had cows that grazed in the field and I loved the whole scene, the green of the field, the black and white of the cows, and the blue, blue sky.

Up the road from our house was a farm where we got our milk. This Amish family was very plain, much stricter than we were, and they looked at us with pitying despair—or at least that's how it felt to me. Their daughters helped my mother with the weekly cleaning and such when we children were small and those girls frightened me a little, and yet I found them fascinating, too. Even the way they breathed seemed pious to me.

Our other close neighbors were two English families. One of them had a couple of "hippie" sons and nothing terrified me more as a child than seeing those longhaired men roar past on their motorcycles.

I was always a little ambiguous about our house. I liked the outside—the red bricks, the yard, the trees, the small (by Amish standards) garden, the flowerbeds.

The inside sort of overwhelmed me. There was an enormous kitchen/sitting area, with miles of cabinets, as befitted a cabinetmaker's abode. My parents' bedroom was on the first floor, as was the formal living room, the one I disliked so much, and a bathroom. Upstairs there were four bedrooms and another bathroom, and we had a large attic and even larger basement, with a storage area for canned goods and potatoes and the like.

We used propane gas lights so there was always a rather unpleasant, vague smell of gas, and for some reason I didn't think that house really *liked* me. The only room in the whole house that really embraced me was the pantry. We had a lovely disheveled pantry, with rows and rows of shelves and a darling window that looked out over the cornfield, and it was usually my job to clean and rearrange and try to bring some order to that room, but she—for our pantry was surely a cheerful soul with rosy cheeks and a cap placed all askew over messy curls— always seemed to wink at me and say "Sure, dearie, go ahead, but we both know it's only a matter of time before things are a mess again."

My escape from all the work at home was school. The one-room public school taught by Mrs. Leatherman, the one I had attended as a first- and third-grader, had been sold and now my siblings and I attended Weavertown Mennonite School. Oh, how I loved that school—it had *electric lights*! On rainy days, when our house in Bird-in-Hand would be gloomy and dark all day, I was happy to escape to school, engrossed in books in a room lit by that magical force brought to us courtesy of Thomas Edison.

The Mennonite school was a mile from our house off a country road. My favorite teacher, Emma Ruth Hostetter, encouraged my creativity and we had the most marvelous conversations in class. She allowed us students our flights of fancy and when we veered off the subject she went right with us. It was a glorious two years—fifth and sixth grade—with her.

After school, though, came the one-mile trek home, where I was usually put to work right away.

I am Susie, the third child. I have an older brother Steve, and an older sister, Annie. We oldest children had to work the hardest, of course, and while my brother Steve helped Dad in the shop, my sister Annie and I were required not only to help with the cooking, cleaning, and upkeep of the yard and garden, but also help take care of the younger children. I have five younger siblings—Ruth Ann, Levi, Sally, Junior, and Mervin. I loved taking care of the younger children, but it always seemed to me that that house just demanded and demanded of me. S*et the table...sweep the floor...iron the clothes...wash the dishes...*with very little breathing room.

Chapter 3

Church was the bane of my existence in those days. We only had it every other Sunday, and the week before "Church Sunday" I dreaded it terribly but never said a word to anyone about how I felt.

It was torture for me to sit three hours on a hard bench listening to a sermon by a couple of bearded men speaking mostly in German, which I didn't fully understand. We spoke Pennsylvania Dutch at home, which was a German dialect, but in church they spoke and read mostly "High German" as they called it, and while I would learn to read it later, as a child I was able to understand very little of it.

My cousin Barbie sat next to me, and we raised a little quiet hell together. I'd whisper to her, "What do you think they'd do if I'd get up and scream?" and she'd giggle and then I'd giggle and I was really afraid one day out of sheer, frantic boredom I'd actually do it—scream at the top of my lungs. It became almost an obsession.

Summers were a little easier. Then church would be held in someone's barn and I always loved the delicious smell emanating from the hay bales that were usually stacked in close proximity to where the benches were placed. We were also allowed to go to church barefoot in the summer, which I loved, but otherwise we had to wear our Sunday shoes to church.

One Saturday morning when I was nine years old, Mom and Dad presented me with a new pair of shoes. Usually Saturday mornings were loud with children running around and people cleaning and Dad working in the shop, which meant the diesel was running, but for some reason that day it was quiet and it was just the three of us.

"Shoes!" I thought with great delight as I ran to my dad's brown recliner and squirmed into its cavernous depths.

I opened the lid.

Lifted the tissue paper.

Staring up at me was the ugliest shoe I'd ever seen. It was black with rubber soles, black shoe strings, and a round toe.

We hated each other on sight.

I picked it up, and almost of its own volition, my arm pitched it as hard as it could across the room. The shoe landed in front of the gas stove with an outraged thump.

The room went completely silent.

I was not in the habit of rebelling like that; usually I was sweet, obedient, and amenable, at least on the outside, which is probably why my parents froze with shock. Before they could recover and punish me, I grabbed the shoe and ran up to my room where I hurled it and its loathsome mate under the bed.

My other major act of rebellion in my childhood years had a similar paralyzing effect on my parents.

I was in the seventh grade. Gone was my beloved Miss Hostetter and I now had a be-pimpled, red-faced, bearded horror of a teacher, Mr. Sauder.

He attended the "River Brethren" church, a group I'm a little vague about. They own cars and have electricity, but their beards rivaled the Amish married men's in their untrimmed glory, and Mr. Sauder's was an almost unbelievable shade of red, an unfortunate combination with his red complexion and even redder pimples.

The seventh, eighth, and ninth graders all shared one school room and there were maybe twenty-five of us. On the other side of the wall were the third and fourth graders taught by a mean woman named Miss Gingerich. Oh, she pretended, did Miss G. I never had her as a teacher, but I did not trust her—I felt that behind that jovial exterior was the heart of a cruel woman.

One day after music class she told poor Mr. Sauder that none of us had been singing.

Hello? Really? I loved to sing and certainly *had* been singing, as had many of my classmates.

Well, Mr. Sauder punished us by telling us that we couldn't have recess, or a lunch break, for three days. We had to eat at our desks and if we wanted to go to the bathroom we had to ask.

By the second day I seethed with rage. *The injustice*! So I announced to my stunned classmates that I was going home, in the middle of the day. I grabbed my lunchbox, stalked out the door, and ran most of the way home.

That night Mr. Sauder held a conference with Mom and Dad in the kitchen while I cowered in the living room waiting for the consequences.

No one said a word to me. Not one.

Until the next day, when Mr. Sauder bleated a weak apology to me and after that, we tolerated each other a little better.

Chapter 4

M y childhood was not all work and bad shoes and church and longing for things I could not have. There were good things too.

My siblings and I were crazy about the water and every summer my parents took us somewhere swimming. One of those places was Mt. Gretna, a lake an hour or so north of where we lived.

My mother would pack watermelon and other good things in a gigantic cooler and off we'd go, usually with some driver Dad had hired at the time to work in the cabinet shop.

My mother always wore the same bathing suit, year after year—she'd come out of Mt. Gretna's changing room, blinking in the sun with a rather bashful look on her face. Her dark hair was still rolled back into a bun, but she wore no covering on her head and her swimsuit was a bleached turquoise blue splashed with white flowers.

My father also wore the same mustard-colored swim trunks every year. His skin looked very white and his abdomen was taut—Dad has been the same weight as long as I can remember, probably because he is the most "perfect eater" on the planet, I am certain. He has portion size down to a science, never diets, and does everything in moderation except ice cream. The man does love a good bowl of ice cream.

Oh, the thrill of that sparkling water! Even my parents enjoyed the water, and my mother, who swam like a fish, would jump off the high dive way out at the deep side of the lake. Dad would splash around with us at the shallow side and occasionally even carry us around on his shoulders and toss us into the water while we giggled with delight.

Afterwards we'd chow down on watermelon and sandwiches and finally, sleepy and happy, head down the road and stop somewhere for ice cream cones. I could never eat all of mine, so I'd hand it to my father to finish and promptly fall asleep with my head nestled against his shoulder.

The other special pleasure was riding to Lancaster City on the bus with my mother. Sometimes it was just the two of us. First we'd go to Central Market, where we'd visit an Amish maiden lady who was a friend of my parents. She'd greet us in that bright, artificial way she had, while she waited on customers and sold them meats and cheeses and the like. Then Mom and I would go to Woolworth's, and I ached a little when we walked past the pretty shoes, but, of course, I knew better than to say anything and tried to be happy just looking.

One day we missed the bus home and my mother shrugged her shoulders and laughed. "Des macht sich," she said. (Pennsylvania Dutch for "This will work out.") Those were my favorite times with my mother—when she was laughing and carefree. She looked so pretty that way, and I think she was as happy as I was to escape the confines of that house in Bird-in-Hand now and then.

Mom was also good about letting us get new dresses for special occasions, like the beginning of the school year or the annual Christmas program. How I enjoyed shopping on those occasions! I loved the smell of fabric and wandered happily around the store, touching the bolts of cloth like they were almost sacred.

Mom usually allowed us to wear colors that skirted the edge of decorum, Amish-rules-wise—we didn't always have to wear dark colors and my very favorite dress was a pale lilac cotton that had a *matching apron* instead of the usual black one! I felt so special in that outfit, and when Miss Hostetter complimented me the first day I wore it, my joy was complete.

14

My sister Annie and I had some good times and I was ecstatic when a couple from Buena Vista, Virginia, Maynard and Nannie Green, for whom my father had installed cabinets after a flood had ravaged their home, took the two of us to Virginia to visit them when I was ten years old.

Virginia! How I loved her! The majestic views on Skyline Drive and the gentle energy the whole state seemed to exude...Annie and I snickered over the "Virginia is for Lovers" bumper stickers and little did I know one day that sweet state would be my home!

Another special occasion was when I was twelve years old and was chosen to go to Florida along with my sister Sally and my brother Junior. Why we three, I don't know, but a van-full of us went: my parents, we three children, my Uncle Aaron (my mother's brother), his wife Betty, and a few of their children.

Our drivers were a lovely Mennonite couple and on the way down south, they took a photograph of us all. I remember thinking how different and carefree my parents seemed on that vacation.

How can I recount the joys of that trip? The orange blossoms in particular, their scent...the beautiful women in their colorful long gowns at Cyprus Gardens...the palm trees and warm Florida sunshine...and finally, the Ringling Museum. I wandered outside alone and found the rose garden where they grew lavender-colored roses! I was enchanted. And later, the Ringling Bros. Barnum and Bailey Circus, which overwhelmed me somewhat but I thought the tigers magnificent.

Christmas was always a highlight of my childhood. My mother did such a beautiful job of making it magical for us. We didn't have a Christmas tree because there was no electricity for lights, but that did not stop us from celebrating in style.

The baking began weeks prior. My aunts, my mother's three sisters—Sally, Anna Mary, and Lydia—would come and the four women would bake up a storm. We kids helped, too, and they let us cut the dough into shapes for sand tarts. We made bells and Santa Clauses and Christmas trees and the like and then we'd sprinkle them with red and green sugar.

At some point we usually had a get-together with the Eshes, my mother's side of the family. Mom had twelve siblings so as you can imagine this event was a *huge* affair.

(I'm told when I was two years old I stood on a table and sang Jolly Old St. Nicholas for the uncles and aunts, and wouldn't sing it again until they threw some pennies my way. A fine commercial sense it showed and I'm proud of myself!)

We cousins had a splendid time together and sometimes at the Christmas get-togethers we made up plays and performed them for the uncles and aunts, who laughed and clapped with a good deal of tolerant amusement.

My grandparents on my mother's side were a mixed bag. My grandfather gave Santa a run for his money, with his pure-white beard and twinkling brown eyes. He usually kept candy on hand for us kids, not a kind I liked really—it was this too-sweet orange-marshmallow stuff—but I appreciated the gesture nevertheless.

My grandmother, Annie, seemed a very unhappy woman to me. She was overweight and seemed tired a lot, and no wonder, after raising all those kids? She loved to read and I think my creative streak is very much from this side of the family. Poor Grandma Esh! She probably wasn't cut out to do the hardcore cleaning and the like that is demanded of Amish women.

Anyway—back to Christmas: the weeks preceding dragged endlessly! Finally, Christmas Eve, and I usually couldn't go to sleep for hours wondering what Christmas morning would bring, and I'm quite sure the Baby Jesus did not occupy too much space in my brain during those tense anticipatory moments.

Finally, Christmas morning!

We lined up by age, oldest to youngest, and then we filed into the kitchen in an orderly fashion to the table where our presents were stacked. Our gifts were not wrapped, but there was a paper plate at each place with our names written at the top and there were oranges and nuts and chocolates on each plate.

Candles were everywhere, which drove my father nuts because he was worried about fire, but my mother insisted and she looked so lovely in the candlelight, her face alight with happiness as she watched us exclaim over our presents.

My favorite of all the presents I received was a doll I named Carol. She had the most beautiful blond hair, and blue eyes, and wore a red velvet outfit…and best of all, she had the most darling little white socks and black patent-leather shoes just like Sally and Jane's in my first grade reader! Carol and I took one look at each other and said, "Oh, but I do so *love* you!"

Chapter 5

I only remember one spanking. I'm sure I got more of them but this one was so unfair I seethed at the injustice of it.

One afternoon my brother Steve chased me around and around the basement and, as little girls are wont to do when their brothers are chasing them, I was screaming.

Next thing I knew my mother, whose nap had been interrupted by my screams, yanked my arm and dragged me to my father's shop where he…

I draw a veil over what happened there. It is too painful to recount.

We all feared Dad more than Mom because while he didn't say much, when he did we *listened.* One day he asked who had put a wet toothbrush in his baking soda—he used baking soda to brush his teeth sometimes—and I stood at the washbasin with him as he looked at me with accusing eyes.

I said it wasn't me, but I think it might have been. It is the only time I remember lying to either of my parents, but I was far too afraid of the consequences to tell the truth.

Another time I was trying to joke with Dad when he cracked me over the head with his knuckle.

My mother had cooked a meal for Dad's workers and their wives, and one of them was a handsome man named Melvin Kauffman. He was "Beachy Amish" (Beachy Amish are sort of a cross between Amish and Mennonite. Not as "fancy" as the Mennonites, but they allow cars and electricity and don't dress quite as plainly as the Amish). Mel owned a truck that he used to deliver Dad's cabinets. Apparently he said "thank you" a lot and I had heard my parents joking about it. So I was standing at the refrigerator and said to my dad, "Do you think Mel will say thank you when we hand him the mashed potatoes?"

I laughed as I said it, hoping Dad would share in the joke, but instead he frowned and cracked me one.

However, he wasn't always like that; he could be tender and caring, too, like the time we went to the dentist together when I was ten years old. We had this dentist named Dr. Appleyard. He would yank open our jaws and glare inside like he hated teeth and especially children's teeth more than anything in the world. I trace my hatred of any sound resembling a dentist's drill back to that irascible fiend.

For some reason that Saturday morning Dad and I were the only ones there and afterwards we walked across the street to an ice cream place where, oh glorious day! Dad bought me a root beer float! Dad didn't say anything like, "I'm sorry that was such a bad experience, sweetheart." Rather, there was something about the tender way he settled me on the barstool that told me more about how he felt than his words could have.

I don't have a single recollection of being hugged as a child or told I was loved. (I asked my mother once if she loved me and she said "Yes, if you're good.") However, Dad would tuck the blankets around us at night, and again, the caring was more in the way he performed that simple task than if he had said, "Good night, Susie, I love you." Considering how I tortured Dad with my "why" questions, he did a good job with me, I think. One night after supper when I was seven years old, Dad was sitting on a rocking chair reading the newspaper. I sat down on the floor next to him.

"Dad," I said, "why are there no Amish missionaries?"

Probably wondering why he couldn't have a child in the house who asked easy questions like Where do babies come from, Dad turned that dull shade of red he always turned when I came up with stuff like this.

He looked off to the distance and said, "Well, the forefathers...it's just not the way we do things..." and turned back to the solace of the newspaper.

Those forefathers! I always pictured them as a group hidden by a grayish fog, except for one red-faced bearded thug in suspenders waving his fist and yelling, "It's just not the way we do things!"

I stalked away feeling thwarted and frustrated. *The forefathers! The way we do things!* did not satisfy my insatiable search for answers.

The crowning humiliation of my young life was on a "bike hike." What *possessed* me to attempt to join my classmates, most of whom were Mennonites and tough cookies who had been riding bikes since they were little kids, I do not know. I didn't even have a bike, nor did I really know how to ride one!

But I wanted to go along, and someone said they had an extra bike. Well, this extra bike turned out to be very small. It was a detestable thing, with little wheels and a sneering look about it, but I hiked up my skirt and alighted.

Sparing my tender audience the painful details, let's just say I could not begin to keep up no matter how furiously I pedaled, and finally, I gave up and rode home while they continued on their merry way.

I had another bike incident and one that nearly took my life. I was fourteen years old and out of school, and once a week I pedaled a couple of miles to a nearby farm where an Amish couple, Sam and Sarah Beiler, lived. We Amish weren't allowed to have bicycles, but for some reason we acquired this beat-up black bike, and I loved it. It was just my size and I enjoyed the ride through Bird-in-Hand, past the restaurant and market, and to the Beilers' beautiful farm.

Sam and Sarah were more loving than any Amish I knew. They treated me more like an honored guest than the hired help, and we often sat around the picnic table after lunch and laughed and talked together.

One day on my way home, a construction crew was working on the road and one of those big roller-type monstrosities was in front of me. I waited because a car was coming the other way and I could not pass. Suddenly the driver threw the machine into reverse and I jumped off my bike and landed in the ditch.

The driver ran right over the bike and flattened it beyond repair.

He helped me out of the ditch, and while he did not say much I could tell by his red face and the tears in his eyes that it had shaken him to the core. He walked home with me, and my parents, who were busy as usual, barely acknowledged the incident, but that sweet man's kindness and concern touches me to this day.

Sometimes on Sundays Dad would hitch up Joe, our horse, and we'd head to Georgetown, which is in Bart Township, about ten miles south of where we lived. My mother grew up on a farm there and it was where my grandparents and many of my uncles and aunts and cousins still lived.

It was a beautiful drive. The horse found it a bit difficult though and there was one mile-long hill he particularly struggled with, so we children usually got out and walked to lighten the load a little.

While I enjoyed playing with my cousins, I didn't like the feel of Georgetown much because it had a severe, depressed feeling about it. Bird-in-Hand was a buxom, cheerful soul who welcomed friends and strangers with equal graciousness, but Georgetown was her thin, puritanical cousin who seldom smiled.

21

My grandparents' house depressed me in the *extreme.*
Sundays of course we didn't have to work but on any other day
of the week when we visited, we girls were immediately put to
work. No hugs, no smiles for the grandchildren—just get in
there and work, girls!

My grandfather sold meats and cheeses at a market in
Somerville, New Jersey, so there was always a lot of that sort of
thing around and to this day I rarely eat sausage because I can
picture it in one of those big black frying pans with cold white
grease at the bottom. *Gross!*

That house just refused to warm up to me. It made my
home place look like a sweetheart in comparison. It always
seemed to be cold no matter what time of year, and it smelled
musty and rather dank.

My grandmother braided rugs and she'd sit at her sewing
machine, lips pursed, sewing.

One day I was working in the yard, which seemed
impossible to beautify no matter what I did, and I suddenly had
the thought—I wonder what hell is like? As much as a burn on
the hand hurts, what would it feel like to burn forever and ever?

My father's side of the family, on the other hand, was a
happier, cozier, lot. My uncle Amos Fisher, my dear friend
Barbie's father, was a fantastic guy who let the occasional swear
word slip, which always made my cousin Barbie and me giggle.

They lived close to us, also in Bird-in-Hand. Amos was
a plumber and they had a few acres of land along with a small
chicken house and barn. We'd play in the hay and Barbie's
brother Benuel would tease us and sing "The Battle of New
Orleans" at the top of his voice:

In 1814 we took a little trip
Along with Colonel Jackson

down the mighty Mississip.
We took a little bacon
an' we took a little beans
And we caught the bloody British
at the town of New Orleans.

Barbie's mother, Anna, was a sweet rather nervous woman with a great laugh. They always had a lot of good food in the house and on Sundays we ate like royalty after our hours of play outdoors.

Speaking of good food! My father and mother made what I am convinced is the best ice cream on the planet. To this day I sneer at ice cream in the freezer section of the grocery store because my taste buds just can't *forget,* you know?

Since we got all our milk from our plain neighbor Junie's, it was very fresh and not ruined by super-pasteurization and all that. Mom would take fresh cream and some other magical ingredients—to this day I don't know what they are and don't want to, it would spoil the magic—and then Dad would take the tall metal canister to the shop where he had rigged a way to have a motor turn the handle so we didn't have to turn it by hand, and bam! He pulled the paddle out of the wooden vat that had been packed with ice and salt, put it on a plate and handed it to us kids, and we dug into the ice cream with greedy spoons.

My mother instilled within me a love of nature, or maybe it was just naturally there in both of us. She'd say, "There's a beautiful sunset tonight!" and entreated us kids to join her, so we'd run out behind the paint shop to where the sun was setting in the west over our neighbor's field and drink in the glorious sight.

Sometimes in the very early morning, she and I looked up at the stars together when I got up to help her hang clothes on the line. "That's the big dipper, Susie," she'd say and I'd look up at the sky, thrilled with the stars and happy for the rare shared moment with my mother.

Chapter 6

W
hen I was six years old, my Grandmother Fisher came to live with us for a while.

One of the great regrets of my life is that I did not have the opportunity to get to know her better. I was named after her, although she had the far more interesting name of Susanna, while I was plain "Susie."

She gave birth to my father when she was in her early forties. She was in her twenties when she married my grandfather, who was twenty-plus years older and a widower, and an Amish preacher to boot. He died in a freak accident when my father was fourteen years old—he tripped on the attic stairs while preparing for church—so she was left a widow in her fifties.

From what I can gather she was an attractive woman and had quite a vivid personality. She spoke English a lot even though it was considered more correct to speak Pennsylvania Dutch.

One day she and her children were sitting around the table chattering away in English when she looked out the window and saw her husband coming toward the house. She said, "Shut up, kids, here comes the preacher!"

She had a generous nature, too. In those days hobos, or tramps as they were sometimes called, would occasionally stop by farms looking for work and a meal. Well, Susanna not only cooked them a fantastic meal but also presented them with ice cream for dessert. The story goes that after stuffing himself to the gills one of them rocked back and forth with his hands on his stomach and said, "My stomach is frozen! My stomach is frozen!"

Here's one of my favorite stories about Grandma Susanna: an Amish biddy wrote my grandmother a letter before my uncle Amos was to be married that ran something along the lines of "Now that Amos is getting married, isn't it time those pockets come off his shirts?" (I guess it was considered *hoch mood*, or pride, to have a pocket on one's shirt.)

Anyway, Susanna fired back: "Maybe you could take the material from those pockets and use it to lengthen the hems on your daughter's dresses."

Go, Grandma!

I have a feeling she needed her space too, just one more trait we share, and excessive noise bothered her. She still lived on the home farm after her husband died, but had her own living quarters on the other side of the farmhouse where my uncle Levi and his wife and many children lived.

One day her grandsons were playing in the yard outside her window, apparently making a huge racket. She opened the window and shouted, "Be quiet, you sons of bitches!"

Now you know. I get it honestly.

But sadly, by the time she came to live with us, she was eighty years old and bedridden. My one memory—and I shall always treasure it—is of her taking my small hand in her wrinkled one. She said, "You're my namesake, Susie," and then she gave me a vase of flowers. It was a simple arrangement of tiny artificial flowers in a small vase covered by tinfoil. I felt there was something significant about that moment, and I was very proud that we shared the same name, even if hers was fancier than mine.

I don't remember much about her funeral except for two things: some adult with a strong morbid streak held me up to the casket and insisted I touch Grandma's face. It was cold, and hard, and I'm angry at that sick, twisted adult, whoever she was, because I still recoil at the memory of the feel of death under my small fingers.

But even stronger than that memory was later that night when we had evening prayers. As I knelt next to my father, he put his arm around my shoulders and I saw him cry for the first time in my life.

Chapter 7

Age fourteen was a significant year for me. My brother Steve was by then seventeen and the coolest guy ever, I thought. He wore his blond hair parted to one side and didn't look Amish *at all.* He got a car, a green Dodge Charger that purred when he drove it down the road, and when he deigned to give me a ride in it, I thought it just the most amazing thing ever.

My sister Annie was only a year younger than Steve and was now sixteen, so she was allowed to date and such. She looked so pretty when she dressed up to go out. She had huge brown eyes and a sort of stately way of carrying herself.

Then Steve purchased a radio—*forbidden!* One night when my parents were away, he, Annie and I gathered around that battery-powered wonder and listened with what I am sure were guilty yet delighted expressions on our faces. But when we heard the clip clop of the horse's hooves in the driveway, we ran to hide the radio in Steve's closet.

And so whenever our parents were gone, out came the radio and we listened to the Beatles, Creedence Clearwater Revival, Elton John...one of my favorite songs was Crocodile Rock, maybe because my name was in it—*I remember when rock was young, me and Susie had so much fun*—but also because I thought Elton John had the *sexiest* voice!

After listening to all that rock 'n roll music, Steve bought a guitar and taught himself how to play it.

We hosted some fantastic parties. Our house was ideal for entertaining and my parents had a busy social life of their own, so we kids often had the place to ourselves for the weekend.

We had a spacious basement where we played ping pong and shuffleboard, and the boys drank beer and smoked copious amounts of cigarettes so that by the end of the weekend we had to open every window in the house, no matter what time of year, to air out the place before my parents returned. Steve and his buddies gathered up the beer cans and there were usually several bagsful.

We had added to our musical repertoire a record player by that time, and I loved the sound of the needle when it hit the black vinyl disc.

There were two boys in my life at that time, and they were as different as night and day. I guess you could say I had a good boy and a bad boy interested in me, and what more could a teenage girl ask for?

I was not yet sixteen so I could not officially date, but my group of girlfriends and I were allowed to get together on the odd Sunday afternoon and the boys invariably found us.

There was a main group of four of us friends. Naomi was a pretty girl with dark hair, big brown eyes, and a superior air about her; my cousin Barbie, who had never lost her famous giggle; and then there was Hannah, who was thin and wiry. I did not like Hannah much because she had a sarcastic way about her and she and I never bonded.

There were other girls, too, but we four were the core group because we were all close in age: Naomi's birthday was in March, mine was in May, Barbie's in June, and Hannah's in July, so we would start *rumspringa* (running around) at the same time. It was imperative that you had one girlfriend who was your "best" friend and the two of you would start the whole *rumspringa* thing together (more on that later).

That experience would prove to be shattering for me, but at the moment my innocence was intact and while I did not always feel I fit in with the other girls, I enjoyed elements of our camaraderie nevertheless.

Hannah's brother Junior was the "bad boy" who was interested in me. He was handsome with dark eyes and hair and had what I thought of as a sophisticated way about him. He phoned me sometimes and I'd dash out to the phone booth outside our house (we weren't allowed to have one in the house so we kept it outside, and my father rigged a bell so we could hear it ring).

I was a little ambivalent about Junior. I liked him on one hand, and it gave me a certain thrill when I saw him or talked to him. But there was a part of me that didn't trust all that sophisticated charm.

Eli was the other boy who liked me. He was sandy-haired and had a kind way about him.

In reality, the boy I was most attracted to was neither of these two but rather a boy who I think was also interested in me but never did anything about it, maybe because he was Junior's best friend. His name was Henry and he was, in hindsight, just my type: intelligent, with a dry sense of humor and a somewhat sardonic view of the world. Then something killed my relationship with Junior and I'm still a little angry with my sister Annie about it. Why she did it, I don't know, but one night Junior called me on the phone. He was sixteen by that time and had a car, and Annie pretended to be me and told him I would go to the hop with him and Henry. This was forbidden, of course, since I was only fifteen at the time. She did not even bother to tell me what she had done, so the following Saturday night I was icing chocolate cupcakes for Sunday company when I heard a car come in the driveway.

Junior and Henry! Two of the hottest guys in my world! And there I was, with icing on my apron.

Junior seemed so excited to see me and I could not understand what he meant when he said, "Are you ready to go?"

"Go where?" I said, puzzled, and the look of disappointment on his face when we finally sorted out the mess still haunts me.

Chapter 8

My education came to a crashing halt when I was fourteen years old. I was lucky—I got ninth grade while most Amish children stop at the eighth. (By law, we had to stay in school until we were fourteen, and because I had skipped second grade I now got an extra year of learning.)

I bade Weavertown Mennonite School a heartbroken goodbye. That last day of school stands out in my mind as one of the saddest days of my life. No more cheerful electric lights, no more school friends...there were eight of us, four boys and four girls, and we had known each other since the fourth grade. None of them was Old Order Amish so I knew I would not see much, if anything, of them after school was over.

The downside of being educated at the Mennonite School was that I always felt a little different from my Amish friends, who had all been educated at Amish schools. Or maybe I just didn't fit in, period, and it had nothing to do with where I went to school, I don't know.

Regardless, I missed school terribly.

There was an emptiness not just in my mind but also in my soul, not that I could have articulated it at the time. Suddenly it felt that life had only two dimensions: work, work, and more work; and my teenage friends.

My soul craved color and art and my mind, learning; but for Amish girls neither is considered important. You don't need higher education or art to marry and have babies.

So I worked. I decorated cakes, for one thing, an activity forced on me by my mother. Not content to saddle me with learning how to make quilts, an activity I loathed with all

32

my heart and soul—cutting all those little pieces and sewing them together was tedious and horrible—she also promised my cousin Emma I'd decorate a cake for her to take to a wedding.

(Amish weddings are always held on Tuesdays and Thursdays. Why, you ask? Heck, I don't know. But Amish brides do not have one big decorated wedding cake; friends of the bride bring individual wedding cakes decorated with flowers and words such as "Congratulations Aaron and Sadie.")

When I was in the eighth grade a woman, an unbelievably smug type who had, incidentally, also taught me how to make quilts—came to school to give us girls a crash course on how to decorate cakes.

I was hopeless. My faint distaste for pansies can be traced back to that first class, because we had to make icing pansies out of yellow and purple icing. That greasy gooey icing went everywhere except where it was supposed to and my pansies ended up looking like a couple of black eyes the morning after a beating rather than flowers of the field.

But my mother felt I was talented enough to do a real cake for a real wedding and so! I did it. The icing had some cake crumbs in it but overall, for my first real effort, I guess it was somewhat passable. Or maybe Emma was just being kind. She was my cousin, my Uncle Levi Fisher's daughter, and I had always adored her because when I was a little girl she gave me the best birthday present I had ever received: a blue bathing suit with a white ruffle and a candy necklace. I was speechless with delight.

My cake decorating business took off and I branched out and made "sunset cakes"—cakes I decorated with sunset scenes that I created out of icing and then added palm trees and the like. The brides and their friends just loved 'em and I had almost more business than I could handle.

I made cakes in a lot of different shapes, hearts and the like, but one day someone asked me to make a cake in the shape of a chicken house because the groom built chicken houses for a living.

Well! I ask you! I almost despaired over that one. I think the chickens ate all the pansies (just kidding).

I also worked at a greenhouse, again at my mother's behest. It was my job to pick out the best geraniums and petunias and the like and place them in flats. I liked the good smell of soil and the feel of the sun on my face as it shone through the glass panes, but I always felt rather small and inadequate next to the other workers.

One day Barry, a tall, good-looking man who delivered the plants to various local stores, asked me if I wanted a ride on his motorcycle.

Well! Did I! I was long past my childhood fear of motorcycles and was thrilled when he carefully placed the helmet over my white prayer covering. I scooted up behind him and shyly wrapped my arms around his waist. We must have made quite a picture as we roared down the road and finally came to a screeching halt in my parents' driveway.

He stopped the motorcycle and hopped off, and when he removed my helmet and fixed my prayer covering for me, I thought for a brief moment he was going to kiss me. I thanked him for the ride and he looked at me with a tender expression, and then rode off with a wave of his hand.

I also worked for my grandfather at a market in New Jersey, a job I despised more than I can possibly describe.

Grandpa employed a driver named Harry, who drove a horrible black truck with a leaky exhaust pipe, so the interior always smelled like exhaust fumes. I have a sensitive nose and the smell of the fumes at 4:30 a.m., which is when they picked me up, was almost more than I could bear. Then there was

Harry himself, who wore tight brown polyester pants and very thick black-rimmed glasses. He was usually gnawing on a gigantic piece of ring bologna, and while the other girls didn't seem fazed, I huddled in a corner of the truck and prayed I wouldn't throw up.

Then we'd stop at various places picking things up, baked goods and cheeses and the like, but the *very worst* was when we picked up the lunchmeats and sausage and scrapple and other "delicacies." We had to help load the truck so I did my best, trying not to smell the meat, but what really, finally, put me over the edge, for some reason, was the greasy smell of soup some of the girls bought at the vending machine there. Almost like clockwork, try valiantly as I may to suppress it, about twenty minutes after that stop Harry had to pull over so I could throw up, and then we kept going to Somerville where customers were already jostling against each other waiting for us.

Grandfather yelled at me the most, I guess because I was his granddaughter. "Susie! Customers!" he shouted as if I wasn't already weighing and wrapping and making change for all I was worth. Gone was the candy-dispensing Santa look-alike and there sat as mean a slave driver as you'd find anywhere. I hated that whole scene, and when we got back to Lancaster County around midnight I felt drained not just physically but also mentally and emotionally, only to start the whole dreadful process again a week later.

Better were my jobs in Bird-in-Hand. I worked at a snack bar at the Farmers Market a couple of days a week, serving hamburgers and sodas and dipping ice cream for the tourists, and while it made my biceps ache, it was cake compared to working for Grandfather.

I also worked in the laundry at Bird-in-Hand Motor Inn, folding endless stacks of towels and sheets. A bit mind-numbing, but it was okay.

I babysat occasionally for my mother's "Amway lady" named Carol and her husband John. Carol was so lovely! She had flawless skin and blue eyes and wore the prettiest clothes. My sister Ruth Ann and I babysat for their three boys, who were good kids but bundles of energy, and one memorable Saturday afternoon, someone left the screen door open and a goat sauntered in the door! Ruth and I scrambled on top of the dining room table and screamed while the three boys chased the goat around and around the table and finally, outside.

Our heart rates had finally slowed down somewhat when in dashed a German Shepherd! It was not John and Carol's and thus a stranger and untrustworthy. Ruth Ann and I scrambled back up on the table in a flash. More screaming by us, more chasing by the boys, and finally, peace, or as close as it got in that household, reigned.

Then one day Carol showed us how to use makeup! A little discreet foundation, a little blusher, a little mascara. Not enough to really be noticeable, but just enough to thrill. We even played with a little pale-blue eye shadow but of course, could not wear it at home. We bought some of that fabulous makeup and also some skincare—cleanser, toner, and moisturizer.

I gave my parents ninety percent of what I earned, and saved as much as I could from the remaining ten percent. The understanding was that one day when I married they would then help with the purchasing of the furniture and that sort of thing. My father had opened savings accounts in all our names but he controlled them, so I had to give my money to him to bank.

Then my dear friends, Sam and Sarah Beiler for whom I was still working one day a week, moved to another county. I helped them on moving day, and even rode in the cab of the huge tractor trailer truck that carried all their goods! In spite of that excitement, it was a very sad day for me and I felt bereft without their precious friendship.

There was one disturbing incident that I did not tell anyone, not even my parents, about. One day a salesman came to our house selling Bibles and Bible story books. He wore these awful brown pants that were a little too short for him and there was something about his expression I did not like.

I was sitting in a chair looking at one of the books, when my mother left the room to get her pocketbook. Suddenly his hands were all over me, touching my breasts through my dress. It was horrible and happened so fast I went into semi-shock.

However, in spite of those few unhappy incidents and how much I missed school, my fourteenth and fifteenth years were happy ones.

A good thing, considering what happened when I turned sixteen.

Chapter 9

I would like to slay dead the misconception that is out there about that enigmatic word *rumspringa*.

This erroneous rumor or whatever you call it states that Amish parents allow their teenagers their bout of freedom or as some would say, wild-oats-sowing. "Go!" these liberal-minded parents allegedly say to their kids. "Sure, we raised you to be Amish, which is to say don't drive a car, don't have electricity, and dress in a way that would please the most particular Moses coming down the mountain with the Ten Commandments.

"But now we want you to toss that all out the window and be English for a while. Do the opposite! Start up that hot rod! Drink! Buy fancy clothes! And then, dear, when you've finished, *choose*: Amish or English."

Please, people. Please!

While it's true that Amish kids have more freedom when they turn sixteen and run around (rumspringa means simply that, running around), to my knowledge no Amish parents have *ever* had that kind of a conversation with their offspring.

I know mine didn't.

It is, however, true that there was a startling and perhaps unhealthy, psychologically speaking, contrast from age fifteen to sixteen. Suddenly we were exposed to things we had never heard of before, let alone experienced.

When I turned sixteen, my friends threw a big party for me. Forty or so kids, boys and girls alike, showed up and we played volleyball on the macadam outside my dad's shop. I felt pretty and popular that night, the last time I would feel that way in a long while, the popular part at least—although when you're rejected as much as I was you don't feel very pretty after a while either.

It all started when Naomi, the girlfriend who was supposed to be my best friend, instead chose this girl Esther to take my place. None of us had heard of her before. The four of us—Naomi, Barbie, Hannah and I—had had our plans all worked out and when Esther popped up out of her loathsome trap, I was out of luck.

Esther was attractive, with clear skin, green eyes, and dark hair. She wasn't very bright, but that was beside the point—when you're sixteen no one cares how smart you are, right?

We girls ran around in pairs, so it was beyond awkward when, on my first Saturday night as a sixteen-year-old, this dude pulled into my parents' driveway in a hideous van—it was 1977, after all—with his friend in the front seat and Esther and Naomi in the back.

I had dressed carefully for the occasion. Your first weekend of rumspringa is a very big deal, so I showered and put on a very little discreet makeup, and put up my hair while the gas light hissed beside my head.

I wore a lovely lavender dress and the color did nice things for my complexion. But I felt sick inside...I knew, deep down, the night would be a disaster, and I was right.

Nevertheless, I climbed into the van next to where Esther and Naomi were giggling and flirting with the guys in front. The driver was nicknamed Happy Jack—I have no idea why—and to this day I don't know his real name.

The boys announced we were going to see a movie, and while a part of me was excited, the other part was nervous because I had never seen a movie in my life.

Lancaster sported its own drive-in theater at that time so as we pulled up to the ticket window, Happy Jack yelled back at us girls to "stay down"—I didn't know why until he drove away and they all laughed uproariously that the five of us were going to watch a movie but had only paid for two tickets, which made me feel troubled and guilty.

I sat in a corner of the van and watched while the huge screen lit up with images.

There was a good deal of violence and I felt sick and shocked as I tried to absorb it all. It made matters worse that Naomi and Esther seemed so much more sophisticated than I was and were completely unfazed by it all.

I was quiet on the way home, and when they dropped me off I felt like the most gauche sixteen-year-old on the planet.

The next weekend they picked me up again, with different boys this time, and we went to a hop.

It was May, and a beautiful spring night. Cars were parked in the field and on the grass, and as we girls made our way to the barn, suddenly the band struck up the first note.

That music thrilled me, positively *thrilled* me. It was my brother Steve's band and they were fabulous...my cousin Mel played the drums, my brother was the lead guitarist, and there were also a base guitarist and rhythm guitarist.

They played some of the great 70's music of that day—Bachman Turner Overdrive, Beatles, Eagles...with a little Willie Nelson "Blue Eyes Cryin' in the Rain" tossed in as a slow song, when whatever boy you were dancing with at the time took the liberty to take you in his arms and dance cheek to cheek, so to speak.

My thrill didn't last long, however, because the girls lined up in pairs and when Naomi and Esther and I headed to the front of the barn where the band was playing to start dancing, I felt like disappearing, permanently.

The other girls looked at me pityingly—*who let her in?*—and kept dancing until the boys cut in. But the boys were my salvation, because they seemed to have no problem with me. I am sure they had no idea how heroic they appeared to me when they showed me even the slightest attention. A far departure from age fourteen and fifteen, when I took their interest as a matter of course.

Soon my cousin Barbie turned sixteen, and for a few weeks before Hannah started running around, she and I were paired up together. But I could feel the change in Barbie—at that point I was a pariah, and she did not attempt to hide her knowledge of that.

Then two boys asked Barbie and me on a double date. My date's name was Dave and he was thin, blond, and very sexy. He was the lead guitarist for another one of our bands and they played harder stuff than Steve's band did. Dave showed me a book he had, songs from the band KISS, and I thought those long tongues wretched, just wretched. But I found Dave's guitar playing very attractive.

It was considered a matter of course in that era for Amish boys and girls to sleep together (but not have sex, God forbid!). Things have changed now, I understand, and it is not as common a practice, but at that time our parents turned a collective blind eye.

So Dave and I, and Barbie and her date, went to a party and then Dave drove me to his parents' farm in his souped-up blue Chevy, with Foreigner "Feels like the First Time" blaring from the excellent speakers.

The farmhouse was dark, so Dave lit a kerosene lamp and we crept up the stairs to his room. I felt shy as I took off my rose-colored dress and crawled into bed next to him clad only in my slip.

41

We kissed—and what a feeling! Dave was expert, extremely so, and gone were my hurts and fears of what the other girls thought of me. I kissed that boy right back and discovered what a gift kissing is!

Then in July Hannah turned sixteen and life became hell again. Amazing how when you're a teenager the whole world is colored by what your social life is like—if your friends turn on you, nothing else matters. And while I did not contemplate suicide, I can see why teenagers who deal with the kind of rejection I encountered sometimes consider ending their lives rather than live with that kind of pain.

One very hot Saturday night in August, we were all at a hop and Esther, Naomi, Barbie, and Hannah took their places in front of the band to dance, and every other girl in the place had someone to dance with, except me. My sister Annie was at that hop too but she had her own set of friends and was also dating someone, so she was no help either.

To make matters worse I was wearing brown, this horrid brown dress with a matching cape and black apron.

The whole barn was rocking out, and the sweet smell of hay mingled with the sour stench of beer and acrid cigarette smoke filled the air, but I felt that I was standing in a circle where no sound or air or human touch could reach me.

I stood there alone in the middle of the barn, feeling invisible and yet horribly alive because every cell in my being hurt. Girls danced on either side of me but no one noticed me, no one talked to me. Even the boys did not come to my rescue that night, and that moment, standing in isolation in my ugly brown dress, stands out in my mind as the loneliest I have ever felt in my life.

My reprieve was the weekends I had a date with Dave and I truly do not know what I would have done without him.

One night his band was playing at a VFW camp outside Lancaster County. I loved watching him set up with the rest of the group and when he picked up his guitar to play, *well!* Hot, if you know what I mean.

Once a year or so the guys rented the VFW pavilion and things usually got wilder there because we didn't have to worry about anyone's parents or the state of the barn, etc.

That night was no exception and around midnight someone yelled, "Cops!" The band stopped playing and Dave grabbed my hand and said, "Run!" We dashed to his car and tore out the driveway, and while some of the boys were arrested for underage drinking, we escaped unscathed.

That September a new girl, Annie Lapp, turned sixteen and everyone considered it a perfect solution that the two of us would be friends. I didn't know Annie very well, but she was a cheerful soul who stood 4'11", if that, in her stocking feet, and she had thick ankles and a big smile. We had little in common and I doubt she was any more thrilled about our being tossed together than I was, but we did our best. My favorite recollection of Annie is sitting in the back of some guy's car on a Sunday afternoon belting out Fleetwood Mac's "Second Hand News" at the top of our lungs.

Dave and I still dated but not as frequently, and then another boy asked me out.

My brother Steve had a lot of great friends and they often stayed at our house overnight. I loved cooking breakfast—still do, actually, there's something about the whole egg thing that turns me on, cooking-wise—anyway, I made beautiful over-light eggs and bacon and toast and orange juice for them and one day one of them asked me out.

His name was Sol and he was a different type, personality-wise, for me. He was tall and handsome, with a shy grin and a muscular body. His thick dark hair was cut beautifully—all the boys in our group had English haircuts but his was done by a master, because it had that movie star thing going on.

One Sunday afternoon he drove me to Ricketts Glen, a Pennsylvania state park with beautiful waterfalls. I wore a red dress and white sneakers to hike in, and while I knew I wasn't in love with Sol or anything like it, I enjoyed the day very much.

The most romantic thing he did was pick me up and carry me across a bridge. I felt very small and feminine and breathless!

We went out a few more times, and I hope Sol's memories of those dates are as happy as mine are.

I also had a small crush on Jake, one of Steve's other friends. Jake appealed to me because he seemed to have this innate sense of kindness about him and of course, it didn't hurt that he was *hot!*

One day I decided to surprise my brother Steve with a birthday party. He played ice hockey as did a lot of his pals, and I consider the cake I decorated for him one of my masterpieces—I found a small set of plastic hockey players and even a set of nets, and I made the top of the cake an ice rink.

I cooked dinner for the boys and then presented the *pièce de résistance*—the cake!

Steve told me later never ever to do that again, he *hated* surprises, but I enjoyed it, especially the accolades from his cool friends.

Church continued to be a chore because there was such a dichotomy between weekends and what the preachers said. They chastised us for our wild behavior and warned us about the evils of drink and rock music and too-short dresses and the like, and sometimes my tender conscience felt like it was split in two. On one hand I wanted to do what was right, whatever that was according to the Amish church, but on the other, how could I? I despaired sometimes as I pondered just how good was good enough: just how long did one's dress have to be to please God and the bishops? How large the prayer covering, how plain the hair?

I had memorized a lot of Bible verses at Weavertown Mennonite School, but none of them was any help. The Bible did not address the specifics, so most of the time I walked around feeling, spiritually, like a terrible failure.

And soon I would be expected to "join church"— seventeen was the typical age for girls to join, which meant that if I made that solemn commitment I could be punished for bad behavior by being required to confess my failures in front of the church or worse, be excommunicated.

Chapter 10

T he day I joined the Amish church stands out in my mind as the most oppressive of all the days I have lived on this beleaguered planet.

There I was, in my white organdy cape and apron and demure blue dress. The bishop sprinkled water on my head in the name of the Father, the Son, and the Holy Ghost and said, "Do you promise to stay with the Amish church for the rest of your life?"

As I said yes I felt the spiritual equivalent of a concrete block crashing down on my head. I knew I was doing the right thing in my parents' eyes and the church's eyes, but why didn't I feel settled inside?

I continued the whole wild-weekend thing but suddenly it felt much scarier because now the preachers had a whip they held over my head, i.e., I was now a member of the Amish church and as such could be called upon to confess or—horrors!—be shunned.

The other kids in my gang seemed oblivious, though. Even though some of the other girls had also been baptized, they didn't seem to care one way or the other. However, my conscience continued to feel ripped in two. I had promised to stay with the Amish church and obey its rules but there I was, still listening to rock music, still getting around in cars, still dressing in a manner not exactly approved of by the bishops.

I became more and more confused, and then one fateful day I read a religious pamphlet about how the one thing God will not forgive is when you sin against the Holy Spirit. The pamphlet called it the "unforgivable sin" and I became convinced I had committed it.

I lay in bed at night, feeling cut off from God, and very cold and alone.

Finally I shared my fear with my brother Steve and he looked worried, which in hindsight I can understand. He thought I had lost my mind. And then my parents found out what I was thinking and all hell broke loose.

Dad said to me one night, "While straight is the gate and narrow is the way that leads to life, there's such a thing as making the path *too* narrow."

Mom rushed me to this quack doctor, who in my opinion was the mother of all quacks, and actually looked sort of like a duck come to think of it. She had a very large mouth and a fat behind that waddled when she walked. She took a sample of my hair and supposedly had it analyzed, and then declared I was in need of her expensive vitamins. Sheesh!

Then I stopped getting my period, perhaps as a result of residual trauma from when I turned sixteen or the mental stress I was under or both, I don't know, but it worried my parents and they took me to the hospital.

I stayed for a few days while they ran some tests, and one evening, to my great surprise, Omar, the older brother of my old nemesis Naomi, came to visit me. While I appreciated his thoughtfulness I was also a little confused as to why he bothered, since I didn't know him very well, but what I felt as clearly as if he had spoken the words was an apology for his sister's behavior.

Then the doctor prescribed some sort of drug and I got my period and was allowed to go back home.

Alas, my mind was less amenable. It stubbornly refused to agree that everything was fine, so my parents' next step was to take me to a psychiatrist in Lancaster City. All I remember of that visit was a cold, cluttered room with shelves and shelves full of horrid books that looked liked they hated human touch.

The psychiatrist was tall and thin and bespectacled. I have not from that day to this felt that anyone was less interested in what I had to say. There I was, a teenaged Amish girl who had led the ultimate sheltered life, and I'm sure he wondered what the hell kind of problem I thought I had that warranted wasting his valuable time.

His face did not change expression as I haltingly tried to tell him what was wrong. It did not go over well and I felt almost physically ill with embarrassment sitting in that hard-backed chair trying to explain things to a man who looked a thousand miles away.

He dashed off a prescription and handed it to my anxious mother who had been hovering in the waiting room.

I shudder now when I think about how irresponsible he was by prescribing the drug lithium that I understand is used to treat manic depression, which I most certainly did not have. Needless to say it had a profoundly negative effect on me to the point where I really *did* feel crazy and my parents were, I think, terrified and ashamed that they might have a mentally ill daughter on their hands.

I eventually stopped taking the lithium and kept my thoughts and my feelings to myself, and slowly, lost the idea that I had committed the unforgivable sin. However, the internal storm that was brewing slinked into a corner, grumbling, biding its time.

Chapter 11

That fall my sister Annie married her boyfriend Ben. She was nineteen years old and I felt bereft as I contemplated life without her at home. She and I were not as close as we had been as children because she spent so much time with Ben, but still, I adored her, and knew I would feel her absence keenly.

The wedding was held in my dad's shop and, as is typical for Amish weddings, there were no flowers, no music, no long white gown, no exchange of rings, no plans for a lavish honeymoon, no *now you may kiss the bride*. Just a ceremony that felt similar to a church service except there was a lot of talk about Adam and Eve and it Not being good for man to be alone, and when the divine moment came the preacher called the couple up front and in the presence of their attendants—I was one—they exchanged some simple vows and were pronounced husband and wife. And then they sat back down until the service was over.

Annie, as well as I and her other bridesmaid, wore blue dresses. My sister wore a white cape and apron and that was the only difference in her appearance as the bride, while the other bridesmaid and I wore blue capes and black aprons. Ben and the two groomsmen were wearing exactly what they wore to church—white shirts, black pants and black jackets.

So Annie left home to start her new life, and by winter of my seventeenth year I no longer cared much about my friends nor did they care about me. I stayed home a lot on weekends, much to the dismay of my parents who considered it unhealthy. Finally on New Years Day, 1978, things came to a head.

No one was at home except me. It was cold outside, but bright sunlight streamed through the window as I sat on the sofa reading the Bible. As I read, the thought came: if I needed to be Amish to please God, what was the purpose of Jesus' death on the cross? Suddenly I accepted the truth that I could never be good enough and that is why Jesus, who was faultless, had carried all my sins at the cross. On that sunny New Year's Day I believed, and cried, and repented.

The joy I experienced in the days that followed is indescribable...to think that I could, finally and forever, be at peace in my heart and my conscience was sweet indeed. Soon after that experience, I met another Amish girl, Lizzie, who was a few years older than I was and shared my beliefs.

Lizzie was heavyset and quiet, with hazel eyes and brown hair. She knew some members of the Reubenite church, an offshoot of the Amish, whose members still dressed plain but had cars and electricity. Their teenagers didn't go to hops or drink or listen to rock music; rather, their activities of choice were Bible studies, suppers and singings.

How to describe that stint with the Reubenites? The word that comes to mind is "sterile." It lacked authenticity for me in some troubling yet guilt-producing way. There I was, with teenagers who supposedly believed the way I did, and yet I found it to be stifling and rather cold. The Bible study groups were okay, but the suppers bored me and singing hymns "a cappella" had its limits. (Like the Amish, the Reubenites did not allow musical instruments.)

Besides, I did not really fit in with those kids, either. I was still, after all, Old Order Amish, while they were not and the distinction was an important one. So I floundered along, in between two worlds—the Old Order Amish and the New Order Amish. Then one night my father came in to the kitchen where I was washing dishes.

"Susie, the preachers are here to see you," he said.

Even though it was a warm summer night, I shivered as I walked with my father to his office.

There they stood—two bearded preachers with strained expressions.

"We hear you're attending Bible study groups," the first one said.

"That's not our way," the other one said in a harsh tone of voice.

I felt crushed in mind and spirit as I stood in that small room with those two men who exuded authoritarian energy out of their very pores. I realized then that nothing I could do would please the Amish preachers—not then, not ever. They constantly admonished us young people in church services about the dangers of "mixing with the world," i.e. going around in cars and dancing and that sort of thing, but on the other hand neither did they want us to study the Bible for ourselves. What—were they afraid if we delved too deeply we'd find out what they were teaching was wrong?

"I'm not supposed to go dancing and now I'm not allowed to go to Bible study either? What do you want us young people to *do*?" I said as tears streamed down my face.

They didn't answer that question.

When they left, my father patted my shoulder and I felt his compassion more strongly than if he had said the words.

My comfort during those several years was my younger sister Ruth Ann. I was now nineteen and she was just turning sixteen, and she felt as uncomfortable with her group of friends as I had, so we found alternative ways to have fun. One of our great pleasures, music-wise, was listening to Amy Grant, who had recorded her now-famous album "My Father's Eyes" in 1979. That song, and "Lay Down the Burden of your Heart" often brought tears to my eyes as Ruth Ann and I listened to

Amy's beautiful songs on the cassette player we kept hidden in the closet.

Then a woman who was an occasional taxi driver for the Amish invited us to a service at Victory Chapel in Atglen, Pennsylvania. I'm sure she had no idea how fateful an event that would prove to be in my life, and Ruth Ann's too.

I will never forget walking into that church. It hugged me to its heart, that sweet place with its red carpet and wooden pews, and welcome oozed out of her to my wounded soul. I don't remember a single word of the sermon, but I know I cried off and on throughout the message.

Had our parents known what we were up to, I'm sure they would have freaked out on a magnificent scale, but I think they were so relieved I was at least getting out of the house now and then on weekends that they turned a blind eye.

They would have been even more horrified had they witnessed the scene in my bedroom one night.

As I knelt beside my bed to pray, prayer covering firmly pinned to my head, I was startled to hear these words from a quiet place inside me: "I can hear you without that thing pinned to your head."

I was so taken aback I stayed frozen in place for a second or two but then I stood up and with trembling fingers removed the straight pins that secured the prayer covering to my head. I placed it on the dresser and then, feeling resolute, knelt back down to pray, and great peace descended as I felt connected to God in a new, freeing way as I poured out my heart to him.

The next morning, I pinned my prayer covering to my head as usual, but in my heart I knew it no longer mattered, and that something in my heart had forever shifted and changed.

The other event of spiritual significance happened at an unlikely place and time. I worked for my uncle at market one day a week, where he sold meats, cheeses, and baked goods like my grandfather had, and I was arranging loaves of bread on the counter when a woman walked up to me. She was slender with a thin face and bright eyes, and there was something alive and attractive about her. She bought some bread and then said, "Have you ever heard of the baptism of the Holy Spirit?"

It felt as natural as if she'd said, "It's cold out today, isn't it?"

I don't recall feeling a bit surprised by the question. I shook my head no, and she said, "May I pray for you?" and I said yes.

There I was, an Amish teenager in a green dress and white apron, and this lovely, lovely woman took the time to care enough to pray for me. *Thank you, dear lady, wherever you are...*

Nothing changed, not then anyway; she smiled her goodbye, picked up her bread, and I went back to selling goodies to customers avid for Amish fare.

But that night in my bedroom, to my great surprise, I discovered I had a new prayer language. I, Susie E. Fisher, spoke in tongues! But again, it didn't feel like a dramatic event—it just *was*, and it is a gift I am grateful for to this day.

It is a greatly misunderstood gift and usually associated with kooks. But from my perspective, it is a brilliant gift from God—when we don't know how to pray, he can pray it for us. Wonderful!

Yet another event shaped my life that year. Ruth Ann joined me in several more surreptitious visits to Victory Chapel. One night a family from Virginia sang and we were enchanted. The father preached the sermon and while his style was a little too flamboyant for my taste, I loved the music and Ruth Ann and I were thrilled when their daughters, teenagers about our age, invited us to visit them in Virginia sometime.

I doubt they expected us to take them up on it but we found someone to take us and wrote to let them know we were coming.

Ruth Ann and I dressed as prettily as our Amish wardrobes allowed. We were both experts by this time at applying the barest hint of makeup with great effect—amazing what a little mascara and blusher can do for a girl—and we both had a variety of pastel-colored dresses in hues of pink, peach, lavender, pale blue and the like. We chose our favorites and with great excitement packed for the trip.

We received a bleak welcome. Actually, it wasn't a welcome at all—no one was home but the door was open and our driver, who had plans of his own, was kind enough to stay until finally, anxious hours later, the family showed up.

However, they seemed very different from the glamorous entertainers we had seen on stage at Victory Chapel. There was a heavy, depressed air about the mother and two girls, and the father was just *weird.* (We would find out later he had, ahem, *issues*, which explained a lot, but at the time we were bewildered and disquieted at the lack of warmth we felt.)

Our driver left and promised to pick us up at the end of the weekend, and there Ruth Ann and I were, stuck with a Southern evangelical family who were probably as confused about what to do with us as we were with them.

Worse, at church services the next day, the father introduced us to the congregation and said some scandalous things about the Amish that were not true at all and made much of how we were saved and all that. We were too polite to address it, but later that night in the spare room Ruth Ann and I shared I said to her, "What was that all about?"

"I don't know," she said. "What is wrong with him?"

The next afternoon the girls decided to dress Ruth Ann and me "English." Even though my Amish girlfriends had occasionally dressed in jeans and the like, I never had, and I was nervous about the whole thing, but we agreed to their scheme. They found dresses that fit us, modest but feminine and frilly, and they took quite a time styling our hair. Ruth Ann's was easier because she has thick hair while mine is fine and takes a bit of handling, but after some bouts with the curling iron it succumbed and it curled around my shoulders like theirs did and I find it hard to describe, even now, how it felt—a delicious happiness tinged with sadness that, like Cinderella at the ball, it would only last for a short while and then, back to the ashes, so to speak.

As we took off our finery several hours later, I said to Ruth Ann, "Well, I guess this is the last time I'll dress this way until I get to heaven."

Chapter 12

M y family's universe, as we knew it, shook to its foundations when my sister Annie and her husband Ben left the Amish to join the Reubenite church.

Mom *freaked.* Her eldest daughter, excommunicated! The horror could be no greater, and she chose me as her favorite outlet on whom to heap all her venom and despair. She rehashed stories I'd heard before as a child about the terrible things that happened to people who left the Amish. The worst one was about this Amish man who declared to his foes that "if I am wrong for leaving the Amish, when I am dead and buried, there will be snakes in my grave."

Yup, you guessed it—he passed away, and sure enough, snakes haunted his grave.

Ugh! I had always doubted the truth of that story but the way my mother said it, with ghoulish relish, was awful.

Ben and Annie's departure from the Old Order Amish left quite a pall on our household, so Ruth Ann and I became even more creative in how we handled our jaunts to places like Victory Chapel. And we continued to glean great comfort from the music we listened to on our cassette player.

I was worried about the younger children at that time. Mom seemed to be more and more obsessed with keeping us all in line, i.e. in the Amish church, and while I had long played nurturer to my younger siblings, welcoming them home from school with hugs and snacks so they wouldn't suffer as I had as a child when I was put to work the minute I walked in the door, I took my role even more seriously during that terrible time.

And while I hadn't spent much time with my sister Annie since she had gotten married, I was now banished from seeing her altogether, which made us both very sad indeed.

So life jogged along rather uncomfortably. I was still working hard at market and the laundry at Bird-in-Hand Motel and baking and decorating cakes in the fall for weddings. I also babysat one night a week for the children of a Bible study group, English couples who attended the same church as our Amway lady Carol.

Little did I know how fateful that insignificant job would turn out to be.

Then my old boyfriend Dave, the KISS fan of the narrow face and expert kissing skills, came back into my life. He had settled down quite a lot—he was no longer playing in the band and wanted to reconnect with me, he said.

I felt torn. I liked him, had always liked him, but was it enough to date him again? Since he wasn't yet a member of the church, he still had a car, and one night he took me out to dinner. I felt confused, and a little guilty too. It was wonderful after such a long dearth to have a man in my life again, but I knew, deep in my heart, I did not love him. However, it was good to have a social life and we got together with friends, others who were no longer fully in the Amish scene but not quite out either. We played volleyball and other games, and ate supper together and so forth.

Lizzie and I continued our friendship as well, and I would probably have stayed in that comfortable place had not a nagging sense of *something* continued to bubble, like a volcano in the cradle, slurping up formula, growing steadily more capable of expression at a massive scale.

The first drops of lava appeared quite out of the blue in July of my 20th year. I woke up one morning, and, as clearly as I had heard, *"You don't need to wear that thing on your head for me to hear you,"* I heard, *"Break up with Dave."*

I shut myself in the upstairs bathroom and cried for a while. I didn't argue, didn't even question it—I knew it was exactly what I needed to do, but it was hard. Dave had been my security, a gap to fill the loneliness of my days. I was 20 years old, marriageable in Amish terms. What would I do now? Life without him would be very empty, with nothing to fill the void but a lot of work. Even the occasional "rebellious" outings with Ruth Ann would not be enough to slake my thirst for excitement and romance and adventure. And while Dave didn't rock my world, I liked him very much, had always liked him. But finally the tears subsided, and I said "yes" in my heart.

When he came to see me the following Saturday night, we sat in his car and talked for a while. I was quiet and finally he asked what was wrong.

"Dave, I can't see you anymore," I said.

He looked shocked, and then terribly hurt.

"Why not?" he said, and I stumbled around, not remotely sophisticated enough to do the whole "it's not you it's me" routine, and I thought my heart would break when he started to cry.

We said our goodbyes, his blue eyes still filled with tears, and as I gently shut the car door, I felt like I was saying farewell to my last and final security.

A few weeks later I was picking up toys in the basement of the couple's house where I babysat for the parents who attended the Bible study. Dan, a successful businessman who had left the Amish years before and led the group along with his wife, came downstairs to check on my progress. I expected him to take me home as he usually did when the kids were gone but instead he stayed to chat.

"Susie, have you ever thought about leaving the Amish?" he said.

I was so startled I dropped the red toy car I was holding. "No," I said. "The Bible says you should obey your parents."

"Just think about it," Dan said.

I walked upstairs in a daze and went to the bathroom to wash my hands and try to compose myself. I stared at my reflection in the mirror. Twenty years old, and I had had this same face in varying stages all my life, so why did it look so different to me suddenly?

My eyes, just a normal old brown, looked back at me.

The words fell out of my mouth: "You're going to leave the Amish," I said to my strange new reflection, and she sparkled back at me like she had been waiting to hear those words for a very long time.

Part II

Chapter 13

The following Sunday my parents left for church in the horse and buggy, expecting me to follow by foot.

I spent a long, uncomfortable morning in the old home place. The house knew I was up to no good, of course, and the clock ticked like a warning bomb, ready to explode when I finally heard our horse, Joe, clop his dutiful way into the driveway.

The younger children ran into the warm July sunshine to play while my parents, with concerned looks on their faces, shepherded me into the living room.

"Where were you, Susie?" my dad asked. He looked especially darling that day, dapper and elegant in his good Sunday clothes—white shirt, black pants and vest, and shoes polished to a respectful shine.

The expression on my mother's face scared me and I didn't like the look in her eyes so I looked down and muttered, "I'm leaving the Amish church."

The scene that ensued haunts me to this day.

Dad's face turned red and he looked as though I had slapped him, hard. Mom yammered on and on; I don't think I heard a single word she said...all I felt was this howling sense of sadness and shame that I had hurt my parents in a way I could never fix, never heal, never *explain.*

The weeks that followed were a particular kind of hell for me. My mother cornered me every chance she had, her words stinging like needles on bare skin, drawing blood with every venomous word.

She threatened, she cajoled, she begged, and then started all over again. Finally in desperation I called my sister Annie and she said she and Ben would pick me up that night, and we agreed on a time.

After I had washed the supper dishes I ran upstairs and was pulling clothes off hangers with shaking hands, when suddenly Mom ripped the closet door open, grabbed a hanger off the clothes rod and beat me with it, slamming it against my body over and over again. I held my arms over my face and could not find the words to ask her to stop.

Needless to say, I did not leave home that night, and the lectures increased in amount and fury. I wanted to talk to Dan, the Bible study leader, about what was happening but felt intimidated and far too shy to call him. Finally one August afternoon, after a particularly violent conversation with my mother, I sneaked to the phone booth and dialed his number.

"Answer, Answer," I begged, and sure enough, he picked up.

"Dan!" I said, and stumbled over my words as I explained what was going on.

"I'm close by and I'll pick you up," he said calmly. "Meet me in the lobby of the Bird-in-Hand Motel."

I didn't even have time to say goodbye because suddenly the door opened and there was my mother, holding a thick piece of wood from my father's shop in her hand with a crazed look in her eyes.

I was trapped in a smaller space than the closet this time and had no place to go. She slammed 2 x 4 against my wrist several times and before she could hit me again, somehow I wrenched away from her grasp and raced inside the house, grabbed a black plastic garbage bag from the kitchen, ran upstairs and threw a few clothes and fifty bucks into it, and dashed out the back door and down the road. I felt like the very demons of hell were after me as I raced down the hill, and when one of my black Sunday shoes fell out of the bag, I didn't bother to pick it up.

I crossed Route 340 and gasped my way into the small motel lobby, my face a sweaty, flushed, mess. When Dan showed up a few minutes later, I wanted to burst into tears but avoided it with extreme effort. He settled me into the passenger seat of his car and the air conditioning blew cool air onto my overheated face. Dan, bless him, didn't say much as he drove down the road.

"I'm taking you to Frank and Wendy Nettle's, one of the couples in the Bible study—you remember them, right?"

I nodded. I didn't know them well, only that they were a young couple with two small children.

"They could use some help on the farm, and you can stay there until you find a place of your own," he said, and I nodded, too drained to speak.

The farm was spectacular. It was one of those well-kept farms that bedazzled tourists, and was every bit as pleasing to the eye as the neighboring farms run by the Amish.

The house intimidated me a little, though, as did Wendy, its chatelaine. She showed a lot of teeth when she smiled but somehow that smile didn't quite reach her eyes. She had decorated the house in a rather cold, farmhouse-chic style, and my room and I loathed each other on sight. The carpet was purple and the antique furniture, to my untrained eye, looked stiff and uncomfortable. It sneered at me and the white doilies reminded me uncomfortably of what I had left behind.

I called home to let my parents know I was okay, and had a tearful conversation with my sister Ruth Ann. We both knew she would be forbidden to have any contact with me and there was a jagged hole in my heart when I hung up the phone.

I settled into the Nettle household by helping with the laundry, cleaning, and occasionally taking care of the children; indeed, all the things I had done most of my life.

I missed Ruth Ann and my other siblings terribly, but I tried hard not to show that to the Nettles. I was grateful for their hospitality; however, I had some very bad nights in that cold purple room.

One day Wendy announced that she and one of her friends were taking me shopping and to get my hair done. I was already wearing some castoffs from one of her friends and was wearing my hair down. It hung around my face, not very flattering I am sure. So I said okay, sure, and was rather uncomfortable with the sophisticated Wendy and her friend, who I felt were laughing at me behind my back.

It's hard to forgive the woman who gave me my first haircut. It really is. She was pretty herself and *her* hair wasn't permed, so why did she do that to mine? Fine hair like mine should never, ever be permed, and yes, it was the 80's...but still.

I figured they were the experts, so there I sat, with this vile-smelling liquid seeping into my scalp and tight rollers digging into my head, while the three of them looked on in what I couldn't help but think was a slightly condescending manner.

I left that salon with a head full of horrid brown curls. Sheesh!

Next stop, Park City mall, and that day stands out in my mind as the worst shopping trip I have *ever* been on. A shame, isn't it? Twenty years of my life as an Amish girl, and you'd think I'd have deserved a fabulous makeover day, but nope!

The two women didn't even bother to hide their scorn as they handed me jeans and sweaters and the like through the dressing room door. I ended up with clothes that did not suit me and jeans that did not flatter my figure.

I kept track of what was spent and realized I desperately needed a job and a car—and fast—so I could move out of Frank and Wendy's.

Bless them, Frank and Wendy taught me how to drive in their blue Chevrolet Chevelle, and I sincerely thank them for that.

I got my driver's license and landed my first job as a waitress at a restaurant called "No Place Like Sam's" (now a Denny's) on Route 30. The manager hired me on the spot and I promptly developed a crush on the assistant manager, a handsome blue-eyed man who drove a loud red sports car.

Babs, the head waitress, trained me. She wore bright-blue eye shadow and had bleached blond hair. In between flirting with the truckers, she showed me how to make coffee and take orders and the rest of it, and I often caught her looking at me with this how-can-anyone-be-this-innocent stare. But she was kind, and I appreciated it very much.

I paid Wendy back for the clothes purchases and hair salon visit, and paid her rent out of my Styrofoam cup of waitress tips each week, and continued to help with the housework as much as I could.

On Sundays I went to church at Victory Chapel. Oh, how that sweet church soothed my soul! There was many a Sunday night when I ended up at the front of the church when the call for prayer came and sobbed out my hurt and culture shock and homesickness, and the red carpet didn't seem to mind my salty tears at all.

I joined the church youth group and the kids did their best, I am sure, but in the way of the young, they were often cruel without trying. One of the boys asked me out, actually several did, but the one I really liked, a boy who played guitar in the church band, was my favorite. Wayne wore a lot of khaki and had a smug smile, but I thought him wonderful, just wonderful. I became one of the backup singers so we were thrown together a lot; however, after our first date he seemed to just tolerate me.

My one salvation during those difficult days of adjustment was Julie Wheatley, a tall, glamorous girl with huge green eyes and a million-dollar smile. She took me under her wing, and when the pastor announced that he needed singers to accompany him to England to visit a church that had invited him to preach, I was thrilled when Julie and I were among those chosen.

My first jet ride! I was thrilled beyond measure and then…England!

We giggled at the guards' stoicism at Buckingham Palace, rode the double-decker buses, nibbled on Cadbury chocolate, shopped for dresses and yes, dutifully sang at the church services. But all too soon I was back at my waitress job and the dreariness at Frank and Wendy's.

They let me use their car to drive to work but I needed one of my own, and Dan knew a used car dealer who brought one to the farm for my inspection one icy winter day. It was a dear little car, the red of its paint long dulled, but that didn't matter. I waited impatiently for Dan and the dealer to stop their chattering and finally I couldn't wait any longer. I fired up the engine and off we went, and when I didn't kill myself or smash the car, she and I both agreed it was a good omen.

I didn't have any money to buy it so an old English friend of my parents, Jane Barge, loaned me the money. We arranged a payment plan and there I was! Wheels, at last!

Next stop—apartment hunting. I could afford very little on what I was making and finally I found this unbelievably tiny upstairs apartment with threadbare carpet and a bathroom so small I could barely turn around in it. The owners, a dour couple who looked like they bit into pennies to make sure they were real, agreed to let me have it at the asking price, and one fine day I sailed out of Frank and Wendy's with my few possessions in the trunk of my car, an independent woman at last.

One Saturday night a few weeks later, I was dressed to go out in a denim skirt and flowered top. I was walking toward my car when suddenly I felt like a mule had kicked me in the stomach. Coming down the driveway toward me were two Amish men, one a preacher and one a deacon, and even the horse wore a somber expression as he brought them closer and closer to where I was standing. I walked to the buggy on legs that felt like they had never been used before.

"Hello," I said.

The preacher I didn't like, a tall, thin man with a beard that looked like a fir tree with a lot of needles missing, said in Pennsylvania Dutch, "You know why we're here."

I nodded. Yes, I knew.

The deacon, who looked like an older, wearier version of Harrison Ford, said, "If you don't show up on Sunday to confess, you will be excommunicated." It looked like it hurt him to say the words.

(The electing of Amish preachers, and the hierarchy of the elite in power, is veiled in secrecy, even to me. Amish churches are divided into districts by geographic location, and each district has two preachers, a deacon, and a bishop. The bishop is the highest in authority, and the deacon's job is to collect alms twice a year and visit the erring members of the congregation to warn them of the consequences if they do not repent. He also reads passages of the Bible at the biweekly services. The two preachers, well—preach.

These men keep these posts until they die or are too sick or old to do their jobs, and then new ones are elected. They do not attend seminary or receive special education of any kind; rather, members of the congregation nominate them and when a man receives three or more nominations, he is then, along with the rest of the nominees, given a songbook to choose from and if it has "that" slip of paper in it, he is suddenly a preacher. There is a lot of weeping at these services and the women especially rally 'round the wife of the newest preacher. She is usually crying copiously because suddenly it means that she has to dress even plainer and be held to even higher standards than before.

Twice a year, before council meeting, all these men—the bishops, deacons, and preachers from all the districts—gather to discuss the rules they will announce to their respective congregations. The bishops preside over that meeting, and I confess I rather shuddered in horror at the thought of all those men concocting some stringent new rules to make us even more miserable. The purpose of those meetings was also to discuss how to handle any new technology that had cropped up since the last time they had met. Mobile phones are a current challenge—many of the Amish in Lancaster County have them—how tempting, and how delicious! Those handy little gadgets don't require electricity, one just has them. Not too long ago, I laughed heartily when my brother told me that my mother's cell phone rang during an Amish funeral. She'd forgotten to turn it off, and I admit I didn't feel too sorry for her!)

As I listened to the two men speak, I shivered at the picture their words concocted. I had attended one such service as a member and will never forget it to my dying day. After the regular church service, the children and non-members were dismissed and the preachers announced the name of the person to be excommunicated. There was oppression in the atmosphere that day, a sense of heaviness that weighed down on me like a heavy fist.

Then they said, "We deliver _____ to Satan, for the destruction of the flesh."

(I grieve as I write this. I hate the practice of shunning those who leave the Amish church, and often wonder what our Anabaptist ancestors would think about it all. Some of those courageous men and women died at the hands of the Catholic Church because they felt so strongly that children should not be baptized at infancy, but rather when they are old enough to make a conscious decision to serve God. How would they feel if they saw the Amish now? Would they support excommunicating someone just because he or she chose to worship in a different church, but still believed in Jesus? I think they would weep. And so do I.)

"I won't be there," I said to the two men.

They nodded, and the Harrison Ford look-alike clucked to the horse and they left me standing in the driveway, all thoughts of a lighthearted Saturday night with my friends gone.

I was still shaking when I made my way back up the stairs to my apartment. I gulped a glass of tepid water and the next day, I burned all my Amish clothes in the big trash barrel my landlord kept out back. Prayer coverings, dresses, capes, aprons, my remaining black Sunday shoe...all of it, up in a puff of smoke.

Chapter 14

My guardian angels were kept rather busy those first months after I left home.

One Wednesday night I was driving to Victory Chapel for their midweek service. It was one of those dark, gloomy nights and the roads in Atglen, where the church was located, were hilly and treacherous. Suddenly my windshield fogged up and I couldn't see a thing and the windshield wipers didn't help, so I prayed really hard and got there in one piece, shaken but intact.

I mentioned to someone at church how rough a drive it had been and explained why, and she looked at me with the strangest expression on her face and explained that there was this handy little gadget called the, um, *defroster.*

I also didn't know about getting the oil changed in one's car and when my old car started belching black smoke one Sunday when I was leaving the church premises, Wayne, the guitar player I had had a crush on, laughed and laughed and suggested I get the oil changed. I felt humiliated and looking back, I think it was nasty of him to be so demeaning about it. But I got my car serviced the next day.

My angels could have done a better job of cluing me in on some practical things, though, like how to hold a hair dryer properly when you're drying your hair, and you know that tag on your clothes? Girlfriend, that means it's the *back.* I think I had been out of the Amish for ten years before I heard that tidbit of information and probably wore some stuff backwards, tops and such, without realizing it.

Clothes shopping in general was not an immediate success. After that first awful shopping excursion with Wendy and her friend, I went to Park City Mall by myself one day. I stood in front of one of the department stores and felt absolutely paralyzed. So many choices! Where to start? I tried some things on and was so overwhelmed I ended up buying nothing at all.

I also shopped at Goodwill and other secondhand stores, and shudder when I think about some of the stuff I bought there. Money was tight so it was a plus to buy clothes cheaply, but still—that was no excuse for purchasing that hideous red knit pantsuit, was it?

Overall, I had no idea what I liked, clothing-wise, and given some of the atrocious fashions in the eighties I guess I can't be held completely responsible, but it still hurt when I heard that an English friend of my parents, who had seen me at the mall one day wearing a wretched bronze-colored dress and a small white cardigan (!), said, "Susie looked prettier Amish." I'm sure that was deserved, especially given my frizzy brown hair, but still, it cut deeply nevertheless.

I did myself well in nightgowns, though, thanks to a sweet Jewish couple I cleaned for every Wednesday. I had three jobs now—I still worked as a waitress at No Place Like Sam's and had graduated from nightshift to the morning shift, which I liked much better. I served the truckers eggs and bacon and coffee with a smile, happy I didn't have to deal with the inebriated post-bar crowd anymore.

I was also a hostess at a Mennonite-run resort and felt special in dress-up clothes and heels as I guided diners to their tables.

Then I had three cleaning jobs, one for a wealthy couple who had a big, beautiful house. Maggie was a trim woman who informed me that she liked the vacuum cleaner tracks to run evenly, not haphazardly, but otherwise she was fairly laidback and her house was always cheerful and a pleasure to clean. She left a crisp twenty-dollar bill on the counter for me every week and often I did not see her at all because she was usually gone by the time I got there.

Then there was this other house, a dark, brooding, disturbed house that I hated cleaning. It brooked no creativity in its cleaners and when the woman who owned it started asking me to do things like clean the oven, I quit. There are some things in life that are just not worth a few bucks to do, and cleaning someone's crusty oven is one of them.

Then there was my beloved Jewish couple. They lived in an apartment in Millersville, outside Lancaster City. They were both in their eighties and they always served me the same lunch, cottage cheese with bananas accompanied by a handful of Triscuits. And every so often the missus would look at me with a sweet expression and say to her husband, "Honey, why don't we give Susie a nightgown?" and he'd look at me pleadingly as if to say, "Please don't tell her she gave you one two weeks ago because she doesn't remember, okay?"

They had owned a lingerie factory which was now run by one of their sons, but they still had a lovely stash and sure enough, home I'd go not only with twenty bucks but also with a pink or blue or yellow nightgown.

However, it was exhausting work, and when I was "promoted" to a waitress position at the resort where I was hostess, I was happy because I earned more money as a server and could quit my job at No Place Like Sam's and work full-time at the resort.

One night the owner, a large Mennonite man, called the restaurant and asked to speak with me. He asked if I could bring him a bag of shrimp and a container of cocktail sauce to the house he shared with his equally large, plainly-dressed wife. I was a little surprised by the request—we waitresses did not usually make house calls and I found it odd that the owner had asked for me by name. However, I packed up the shrimp and cocktail sauce, as requested, and drove to his house.

I felt dirty in my white uniform and rubber-soled waitress shoes. I had worked ten long hours and as every server knows, after a while your very pores smell like food and your hair feels greasy and lank from those constant trips to the kitchen.

I rang the doorbell and waited, paper bag in hand.

I heard heavy footsteps and then there he was, all beaming joviality.

"Come in!" he said and I followed him into the kitchen and handed him the bag. His wife was nowhere in sight, and he took the bag from me and suddenly grabbed me and kissed me on the mouth, hard. I felt like I couldn't breathe as his wet, fleshy lips imprisoned my mouth. I clawed my way out of his grasp and ran to the door, too shocked to speak.

I never breathed a word about that incident to anyone, even though I should have, and tried to avoid him as much as I could after that.

Chapter 15

I wanted desperately to get out of the food industry and started scanning the want ads for office jobs. But who would hire me? I had done some basic secretarial work for my father, but that was it. However, I decided to try anyway. What did I have to lose but my pride? I applied to a few places and when an accounting firm called me to schedule an interview for a receptionist position, I bought a pale-pink business suit and off I went to an attractive old building in Lancaster City.

I met with the managing partner, a handsome man who wore the haggard expression of tax executives everywhere when April is approaching. He spent a half hour with me and offered me the job on the spot. Feeling dazed, I walked to my car and realized that At Last! my waitress days were over and maybe I could even quit my cleaning jobs.

How to describe my entrée into Corporate America? The firm for which I worked was the Lancaster office of one of the Big Eight accounting firms—it was in the days before Arthur Andersen dropped out of the picture and some of the mergers had not yet taken place.

I had taken some typing classes so I wasn't completely helpless in that department, but I was an extreme novice nonetheless. Most of the staff was male—good-looking guys who crushed the cliché that accountants are geeks. There were two females on the administrative staff, a raucous duo who took great pleasure in saying the F word in front of me to see how I'd react. I think (hope) I didn't give them the satisfaction of showing my surprise; however, it was true that I had not heard the word spoken out loud very often in my life and certainly not at work.

The managing partner continued to be kind to me and I am grateful to him to this day for his gentleness toward me in that hardboiled office setting.

I worked there for about a year until the head corporate office decided they no longer needed a Lancaster branch so we all had to find new jobs. I applied to a number of places, one of which was a local plumbing and heating company that was looking for an executive assistant to their president and CEO, and was both surprised and relieved when they offered me the job.

On our last day together at the accounting firm, the boss took us to lunch at his club and on the way back, gave me a ride in his red Porsche—a fitting goodbye present, indeed—and we all bade each other a rather sad goodbye.

Chapter 16

I liked my plumbing and heating CEO—he was good to me. But I became hungry for more, a hunger that would not go away until finally I relented and looked into the possibility of taking some college courses.

Deep down inside, I was terrified to even consider it. Sure, I had my high school equivalency diploma; I had taken care of that within the first year of leaving the Amish. However, most undergrads had four years of high school and what did I have? A ninth grade education, obtained at a small Mennonite school. But I choked down my fear and signed up for an evening class at Millersville University, a Pennsylvania state college.

My foray into the sacred halls of academe was marred by a dry cough and a strong sense of my total inability to compete or even keep up with the tough babies swarming their way toward class that first night. None of my ancestors had ever gotten a college degree or anything close to it, unless you went back to the pre-Amish days in which case you'd probably hit the Catholic strain of my ancestry, and who knows what those fine folks might not have learned in the course of their lives? But regardless, for the last 200-300 years, since the introduction of the Amish to the ancestral strain, to my knowledge there wasn't a college degree to be found on either side of my family tree. So who did I think I was, without so much as a high school education to my name? And if anyone thinks a GED brought any comfort, well, they could think again—I had passed the test with flying colors without studying, sure; but to this day there are gaps in my education so wide you could toss entire truckloads of furniture into them.

As I entered the classroom with the other students, I heard one girl ask another what her GPA was and I despaired because I didn't know what that acronym meant, but somehow I knew it mattered by the tense, clipped way the other girl answered.

Oh, yes. Susie E. Fisher felt about as small as it gets on that fine spring evening.

I slipped into a chair and reached for a Halls cough drop because my hack now felt like a giant mountain inside my throat, ready to embarrass me at the most inopportune moment.

And then He appeared and I fought the most insane need to laugh outright.

Conventional wisdom would label it suicide for an inexperienced Amish girl to sign up for COMM 100—a course on public speaking—as her first college class, but the Universe must have known that this professor, and only he, could have been the crown prince who would help me feel like a human worthy of learning rather than some ignorant outcast with no educational rights to speak of.

His clothes! This professor wore lime-green pants, a pea-green shirt, and a jacket with violent purple and brown checks. He had a full head of white hair and a matching beard, and all of this was enhanced by a mouth that easily turned up at the corners despite his advanced education.

My sense of humor trumped my terror. I relaxed a bit and tried not to a) giggle or b) cough.

I tore my gaze away from the professor's fascinating outfit and opened my textbook, and something in me sang— perhaps the fourteen-year-old girl who had thought that her education had come to an end?

I studied like mad for all the tests and quizzes, and spoke, publicly, like my life depended on it, because I knew I was out to prove I could do this, Amish past or not.

I got a 4.0 and was one of five students that term who won a prize from the university for a speech I gave. There were tears in my eyes at the awards ceremony when I walked up to the podium to accept it, and the proud look on my wonderful professor's face made it all worth while.

I also wanted to cry, but for a different reason, during another course I took.

I was sitting on my bed on a beautiful Saturday afternoon. I'd like to say a handsome, muscular man was in bed with me, but no: instead, sneering back at me was a painting by Pat Buckley Moss. I and the geese on Ms. Buckley Moss's painting were arguing with each other—did they, or did they not, have a Deep Meaning?

The professor of the English Composition course I was now taking instructed us to analyze a work of art, and I say this: if I ever paint (and I plan to), on the back of each painting will be "Do Not Analyze this Work of Art."

Anyway. The painting on my bed was lovely, if you like that sort of thing—a barn, sky, etc.—very bucolic. But the geese seemed to be the focal point and I could find no deep meaning in them *at all.*

I picked up my pen. Put it down again. Looked out my bedroom window at the blue sky and puffy clouds. And seethed with resentment that I had worked all week and here I was, analyzing things that were not meant to be analyzed when I could be outside in the sunshine.

"But what do you *mean?*" I said to the geese.

"We're geese, stupid, just geese," they replied.

This went on for another hour or two.

I finally wrote what had to be the lamest paper I've ever turned out. I hated disappointing the good professor, who had said I was his best student. But even for him, I couldn't analyze geese.

So I staggered along, and slowly gained more confidence. Work was going well; I was finally getting an education. Of course, I still made the odd blunder, like the time I attended a bridal shower for a Mennonite girl with whom I worked, and when she opened my gift—a sexy red negligee—the room went completely silent. There were some plainly-dressed Mennonite women at the shower and it seemed to me that they and their practical gifts—toasters, rolling pins, cookie sheets, and the like—turned up their collective noses at my offering. But still, aside from the occasional gaffe, for the first time since I had left home, I felt relatively settled and happy.

But there was a hole in my heart, and I knew what it was.

Chapter 17

I wanted to see my parents. I missed them terribly. The first time I had gone home after I left the Amish, to collect my birth certificate so I could apply for a passport, had been a disaster. My mother had screamed the entire time. She took one look at my cut hair, my denim skirt, and red blouse, and literally screamed, over and over again, until I fled the house with those terrible shrieks ringing in my ears.

Did I dare try again?

I trembled a fair amount at the thought of facing my mother again. But even worse than my fear of facing her was spending another Christmas without my family. That first Christmas alone, which I spent at the Nettle's in that cold purple bedroom, crying off and on throughout the day, was almost unbearable.

I prayed, and one day a quiet thought came: *Go and help your mother.*

So one Saturday morning I donned a long green dress and drove the few miles to Bird-in-Hand. When I walked through the front door and smelled the familiar propane-gas fumes from the gas lights, I shook inside but I stayed. My mother took one look at me and her face turned hard and cold. She started lecturing me but I didn't say a word...I knew where the bucket and soap were and I got down on my hands and knees and washed the kitchen floor, and gradually she stopped the acidic flow of her diatribe and went back to her work. When I was finished cleaning the kitchen, I went out to the garden and picked strawberries.

After I was finished, I hugged my mom and drove home. Two weeks later, I went back and folded the laundry, dusted the bedrooms, and cleaned the bathrooms.

A few months later my mother invited me to join her at the table for a cup of peppermint tea. The next time she asked me to stay for lunch and I am sure she will never know how I felt, sitting at that table with her and dad and my siblings, eating leftover meatloaf and mashed potatoes and peas and canned homemade applesauce.

Then she broke the shunning rules some more by asking me to take her to the store and such, and I stayed meek and sweet and grateful until one night when, quite by accident, I shook things up a little.

It was a grouchy December night. The Christmas shoppers at the mall where I had taken my mother to do some Christmas shopping had that harried look, the kind that said they were finding nothing on their lists and wanted to kick Santa and all his elves on their fat and skinny ankles, respectively.

My mother is one of those women who not only dillies but also dallies while shopping, and by the time she had accumulated her various things, I was in quite a state. Loaded down with her shopping bags, we finally headed to TGI Friday's for a bite to eat.

The hostess led us to our table and my mother placed her shawl and bonnet on the chair next to her. I threw my coat on the back of my chair and snapped open the menu. Our waitress walked up to us and smiled this "And what have we here?" smile and asked what we wanted to drink.

I hesitated. *Should I?* After trotting after my mother for several hours, I felt I deserved something special but didn't want to evoke a lecture, so I decided to order what else?—a strawberry daiquiri. Looks sweet, looks pretty, and my mother need never know it had that all-important ingredient so necessary to soothing black-sheep daughters carrying shopping bags for their Amish mothers.

The waitress wrote down my drink order and turned to my Amish mother, who said, "I'll have one too!"

Infinitesimal pause while the waitress and I exchanged glances.

"Does she know it's an alcoholic beverage?" her eyes queried.

"No," mine replied.

Her eyebrows lifted.

I nodded.

When the waitress returned and placed those pretty pink concoctions on the table, Mother practically inhaled hers and was, shall we say, slightly more gregarious than usual?

I, on the other hand, was sipping mine and sort of reeling. My mother had already broken Rule One (*Do not ride in a car with a shunned person if he or she is driving*) and Rule Two (*Do not eat with a shunned person*), but I felt we were inventing a new category altogether, i.e., do not drink alcoholic beverages with a shunned person. I'm sure the bishops never even thought of that rule.

So we ate our dinner, Mom happily, I a trifle guiltily, and then the waitress returned and asked me if I wanted another daiquiri.

"No, thank you," I said.

Mom quacked, "I will!"

Oh God.

She was getting happier by the minute, and if you'd like to tell *me* alcohol isn't a gift, you'll have a hard audience. On the way home she was nicer to me than she had been since I left the Amish church. Gone were our differences and we chattered like a couple of schoolgirls.

Later she told me that Dad mentioned she seemed "different" when she came home. She also said that she slept extra well. I kept my damn mouth shut, and then, of course, I had to corrupt my dad a little too. It was only fair.

He and I were sitting in his office one afternoon when he told me about the scheme he was hatching to go to Europe. The Amish are not allowed to step foot on planes, ever, so Dad, smart man that he is, decided: boat.

He frowned over the price of two tickets—one for him and one for my mother—to sail across the Atlantic on a humble little boat called the Queen Elizabeth 2, or as it is more commonly known, the QE2.

After I had also gulped a little about the price tag, I said, "Dad, believe me, if the bishops knew how worldly those cruise ships are, what with all the drinking, dancing, and gambling that goes on, they'd beg you to fly."

An expression of longing flitted across Dad's face because he loves to fly, and has actually done so several times. He's involved in disaster relief—helps in the aftermath of hurricanes and floods and the like—and the organization he belongs to, Mennonite Disaster Service, holds annual meetings in various parts of the country. Sometimes he flies to them. Discreetly, of course.

He tapped his pencil on his desk. "Well…I did check out the price of flights, and it would cost much less than traveling on the QE2 both ways…"

So then I, the ever-helpful daughter, said, "Couldn't you take the QE2 over and fly back? And you know, confess later?" (Can't you see it? A special airline for the Amish called Fly Now, Confess Later.)

He looked tempted, very tempted, but Amish won and he and Mom took the QE2 over, traipsed around Europe for a month with some tour group, and then, being the dutiful Amish they are, traveled the high seas back the way I am sure the bishops would have wanted them to: in Grand Luxury.

My dainty suggestion must have taken root, however, because some time later my parents boarded a jet and flew to Israel. It was my mother's first time on a plane and I thought it fabulous that if she was going to break the rules, to do it right, and what the heck! fly internationally instead of taking some lame trip to New Hampshire, not that there's anything wrong with that destination, of course.

They loved the whole trip, but then some Amish snitch found out they flew and tattled to the bishop. My parents were told: Fly again and you are both Excommunicated.

Chapter 18

My excommunicated sister Annie, or Anne as she liked to be called now, and her husband Ben left the Reubenite church and joined one that was similar to the one I attended. Anne got her hair cut too and wore English clothes, and while my parents were upset, it wasn't quite the ordeal it had been when I left.

Thanksgiving, 1984, Anne and Ben invited me to have dinner with them. They also invited a man who worked for Ben in his construction company to join us.

Ronnie was tall and lean, and had the longest eyelashes I'd ever seen on a man. We exchanged a lot of smoldering looks over the turkey and by the time we ended up at the sink after dinner doing the dishes together, I was already halfway smitten.

Later that evening we found ourselves alone together in the living room, Ben and Anne leaving us to it, I suppose. We chatted of this and that, and then Ronnie said, "I've just come back to the church."

"Oh?" I said, admiring the way his lashes framed his brown eyes.

"Yes," he said. "I had been attending church faithfully, but then I backslid and started doing drugs and, uh, was living with a girl for a while. But I've repented and now I'm back."

"That's great!" I said, along with some other inane things that make me blush now to recall.

He smiled at me, and I smiled back, and when he asked for my phone number later, you could have written lyrics to the beating of my heart.

Our first date Ronnie picked me up in a beat-up silver Chevelle, and we went to a fancy restaurant for dessert.

"I can't afford to buy a meal here," Ronnie said. "I blew a lot of money in my time away from the church. I hope this is okay."

I felt embarrassed to walk into a fancy restaurant just for dessert. I could tell the waiter wasn't exactly pleased, either, but Ronnie seemed unfazed and treated the whole thing as a romantic joke.

In the weeks that followed I walked around in a glorious fog. So! This was love! And if I felt a slight glimmer of unease now and then, what of it?

One of those times was when Ronnie told me how during his teenage years he had forged a check. He'd been caught, but there was something about the excitement in his eyes when he regaled me with that story that made me uncomfortable.

But, as the man said, love conquers all, and I pushed those disquieting thoughts into a timeout corner in my heart.

Eventually, Ronnie lured me away from my beloved Victory Chapel to attend his church. I felt uncomfortable there from the start, but I shoved my misgivings aside and tried to like the church for my boyfriend's sake.

Church services were held in a cavernous building with folding chairs instead of pews. There was a sophisticated worship band, and the pastor looked like a heavier, smugger version of Steve Carell. His sermons focused largely on "vision" and how we, as Christians, can count on being happy, healthy, and rich all our blessed days on the earth, if we're giving that all-important ten-percent tithe to the church.

Ronnie introduced me to his closest friends, four couples who were members of the powerful elite at that church.

Darrel and Eva were our age and the youngest members of the group. Eva was on the chubby side and obsessed with her weight, but then she slimmed down and became, if anything, more obsessed. Darrel was a tall, blond man with a diffident air, and he had some good qualities but they never seemed to have a chance to emerge in the face of Eva's relentless control.

Then there were Mack and Matty—Mack was quiet and had the look of an apologetic sheep, while Matty seemed to feel she had God's ear and loved to pass her special information from "Him" on to the rest of us. Especially to me, it seemed.

The oddest couple of all were Kevin and Mary. Kevin was very thin and looked like a bird with a lot on its mind, like a religious flamingo maybe. His wife, probably in an attempt to rebel against all that religion in the house, not to mention those skinny legs, went the opposite way and was a somewhat shallow woman with a plump face.

Finally, there was the duo who put on a happy, we're-so-perfect face in public, Clarence and Dora. I always suspected that something was amiss with the two of them, but that was not confirmed until one night when they threw a dinner party for all of us.

They lived in a large house in the suburbs, complete with big white pillars in the living room. Clarence and Dora greeted Ronnie and me at the door with big happy smiles, and we joined the other couples in the living room for pre-dinner chitchat.

The house was spotless, the banter empty, the company intimidating. No one in that group drank alcohol so I sipped fruit punch and realized, yet again, how uncomfortable I was with this group of people who had known each other, and Ronnie, long before I came on the scene. They all seemed to think they had a special dollop of God's favor on their lives, and while I was glad for them, I felt small because I lacked the religious elitism they all exuded.

I was relieved when we exited the sterile room with the pillars and went to the dining room, which was much nicer because it was adjacent to the kitchen and there were some delicious smells wafting toward us. Dora was a great cook and I was sure that my discomfort with the people would not diminish my pleasure in the food. At least that's what I thought then.

We were about halfway through dinner when Dora suddenly burst into tears and started babbling about her and Clarence's marriage and the problems they were having.

We all sort of froze over our ham loaf with pineapple sauce. I wanted to do something but felt I didn't know Dora well enough to offer my sympathy or indeed, that she would even welcome it. I wanted to kick her husband, who just sat there looking like he couldn't wait to plunge his fork back into his ham loaf and was about as helpful to his wife as a stuffed moose head above a fireplace mantel.

Then the moment passed and *everyone acted like it had never happened.* No one ever discussed it again and Clarence and Dora went back to being Mr. and Mrs. We're-So-Perfect.

We five couples continued to see each other at social functions and at church, and I almost convinced myself that I was happy.

Looking back I think Ronnie's friends breathed a collective sigh of relief that he had become my problem, and they could go on being happy, healthy, and rich, like the good Christians they surely were. But I remained determinedly oblivious to the undertones, and continued to struggle my way through the church and eventually even agreed to sing in the church band, which I considered a great honor because they really were good.

The piano player, an intrepid woman named Sandy and the leader of the band, asked me one night at practice if I'd consider singing a solo. I said no and she said Yes, yes you can, and finally one Sunday morning there I was, in front of several thousand people, belting out the words to a song. It felt good and completely ridiculous at the same time, but I enjoyed the compliments afterwards just the same.

Ronnie and I continued dating and one evening when we were sitting in his dingy apartment in Lancaster City, he said, "I need you to come to the doctor with me."

"Why?" I said, worried he might be terminally ill or something like that.

He just shook his head, so after work the following Monday, I obediently trailed along to the doctor's office, where I was informed that my boyfriend had an STD. The doctor had a technical term for it and he looked at me with what I felt was compassion, but I just sat there and didn't say anything because I didn't know what an STD was.

I admit it: I was, most certainly, a contender for the world's most innocent 23-year-old virgin. I had never had sex education at school, never had "the talk" with my parents, and while yes, I had spent the night with my Amish boyfriend Dave a few times, all we had done was kiss.

"I need you to take the pills too," the doctor said, handing me a bottle filled with evil-looking capsules.

I looked at Ronnie and he didn't meet my eyes, and to this day I am furious with him for allowing me to take those pills, the ultimate irony since we weren't even having sex. But I soldiered through and took the pills. Oh, I understood after the conversation with the doctor that my boyfriend had picked something up from the woman he had lived with before I met him, and I'm sure the doctor thought Ronnie and I were having sex, too. It was an understandable assumption. But why my boyfriend didn't set me straight, I don't know.

Regardless, the episode didn't dim my love. It helped that Ronnie romanced me a good deal, sending me roses, bringing little gifts, and finally, one Sunday afternoon in his seedy little place, he said casually, "Will you marry me?"

I said yes, yes I would.

He bought me a ring with a diamond so miniscule you almost needed a magnifying glass to see it, but I didn't care. It signified our romance and was an expression of his commitment to me and that was all that mattered.

It was by now December of 1985, and I had a wedding to plan! We chose the old standby, June, as the month we'd marry—June 6, 1986, to be exact. But then there was the problem of money. Ronnie never seemed to have any in spite of his construction job and I wasn't earning very much myself.

How on earth could we get married?

Chapter 19

I thought about my tiny savings account, the nest egg I had been able to cobble together from the ten percent I had been allowed to keep of my earnings when I lived at home. I had needed it the year after I left the Amish for an unexpected tax bill and when I called Dad and asked for it, his tone hurt me more than his words did, which were evil enough—"You made your bed, now you can lie on it."

True, perhaps, but that money had been *extremely* hard-earned. Long hours at market and working in the laundry at Bird-in-Hand Motel...I cried when Dad said no, not so much because he refused to give me my savings, which were still in his name, but rather because of how hardhearted he had sounded.

Would he succumb now? Ronnie had met my parents and they had been relatively polite, but I had no idea how they really felt about our relationship.

I paced the floor of my tiny kitchen and finally picked up the phone and dialed. My father picked up the phone on the third ring.

"Dad?" I said, wanting to be casual yet firm, but my voice came out squeaky and scared. I cleared my throat and tried again.

"Dad, may I please have my savings now? It's been five years since I left home and...and Ronnie and I are getting married and I need the money for our wedding."

I held my breath and waited.

To my great surprise Dad said, "Okay." That was it, just *okay*, and did I imagine it or was there a tiny bit of guilt in his voice? Had I still lived at home he'd have paid for my wedding, which could be expensive because the Amish serve full-course lunches and dinners to their hundreds of wedding guests.

The check came in the mail the following Saturday. I opened the envelope and looked at it for a while—that oblong piece of paper, all that was left of my past life. However, it was a laughable amount for even the most humble of wedding budgets. What to do?

An evening wedding was out of the question. Granted, we were part of a church whose members didn't usually dance or drink, but even so I could not afford full-out dinners. (Why my fiancé didn't pitch in is a whole other subject, but I loved him too much to care if he contributed or not.)

I drove to the Eden Resort Inn one cold January afternoon. The sky looked like it wanted to snow but was too sullen to do so, and the cold wind tore at my hair and made me wish I had a warmer coat than the ugly burgundy one I clutched to my neck and I wasn't wearing a scarf, as usual.

I liked the feel of the place immediately. There was a lightness about it, a brisk yes-I'm-not-the-Ritz-but-have-my-good-points humility that seemed to bode well for my scant bank account.

I had an appointment with the catering manager, and I am shocked that I didn't make a complete fool of myself given that I had no help whatsoever to plan my wedding. I had been a bridesmaid in a few weddings since I'd left home, and that was my sole exposure to English weddings. But even then I hadn't been involved in the planning, the wise brides realizing that I wasn't exactly a resource they could use given my Amish background.

The catering manager was a thin woman, one of those smiling types that inspire confidence and are not intimidating.

"I'd like to show you the courtyard," she said and I followed her back through the lobby and down a short hallway.

And then it happened, that *ah ha*! moment when a room and I fell in love, at once.

The room had skylights and the sun suddenly broke through the threatening clouds and shone through the glass, down on the plants and the water bubbling in a fountain in the corner. There was a lingering smell of good things to eat, like cinnamon buns hot out of the oven, omelets with cheese oozing out of the sides, and strong, hot coffee.

Then I thought—breakfast! Why not? Maybe the room inspired me because this was where they served Sunday brunch, but as I stood there I could see it—we could get married in this room, saving money on a church and all that, and then have breakfast in one of the smaller conference rooms.

All I can say is, that catering manager was a veritable genius, and extremely polite to boot. She didn't laugh me out of the place when I shared with her my ridiculous budget. I also saved additional money by not having a cake; who needed it at eleven o'clock in the morning?

So I had my venue and the food ordered. Next came flowers, and the photographer, and picking out my dress and the bridesmaids' dresses, and invitations, and preparing a guest list.

Would my Amish relatives come? I highly doubted it but I invited all my uncles and aunts on both sides and some of my cousins too. I also invited my beloved, cherished fifth and sixth grade teacher, Miss Hostetter. And, of course, Ronnie invited his family and friends, too.

I had three bridesmaids—my sister Anne, Ronnie's friend Eva, and his cousin's wife Sue. I chose rose-colored bridesmaids' gowns for them and shopped for my dress with a coworker.

I can only think that a special angel was assigned to me during that time, with a calculator in hand and a knack for all things matrimonial. Perhaps she had a few miracles in her sack of tricks too because my dress was *exactly* what I wanted and was drastically marked down. It had a fitted waist and a satiny feel to it, and my headpiece was a halo of white silk flowers with the veil flowing down my back.

I also bought Estee Lauder's "Beautiful" perfume as my special scent of the day, and when I hung my wedding dress in my small closet, and tucked the perfume in my dresser drawer, my heart was full.

Ronnie deigned to come to the hotel with me to check out the venue for our wedding, and as usual with us, we found things to laugh at together. He thought the cheese blintzes on the menu sounded funny and I laughed at the way he said it; he had a way of pronouncing things sometimes that sent me into gales of laughter.

Interspersed throughout the preparations was the heady thought of what my wedding night would hold, the secrets I would finally unlock, the lovemaking between me and the man I adored with all my heart. What would it be like? Would it hurt, that first time? Regardless, I couldn't wait and thoughts of *sex* added a good deal of spice to my life as I addressed envelopes and bought shoes and chose my wedding night negligee, blushing when the male sales clerk rang it up for me.

I kept my flower selection simple, and chose white lilies with rose-colored centers that would complement the color of the bridesmaids' dresses.

Music! I had no emotional connection with the traditional wedding march or whatever it was called, so what to do?

One night at church-band practice I thought: why not record my own song? Nothing I had written, I wasn't that brave, but how about a song I knew? Wouldn't it be special to walk up the aisle to a song I was singing?

I am sure the musicians were startled indeed when the quiet girl who sang backup for them suddenly spoke, and not only spoke but actually asked something of them. The lead guitarist, a man with a bored expression and a dismissive way of looking at me, asked me three times if what I meant was that I wanted to *sing* while they *played* and *recorded* it?

Yes, I insisted, that was exactly what I wanted, and after a few tries we got it on tape.

June 6, 1986, dawned bright and clear. It was one of those mornings that occurs now and then, when all of nature smiles.

My father had declined to walk me down the aisle so my brother Steve did the honors. He held out his elbow and I took it and floated toward the man standing at the front. As I looked up at him I knew he was the man I wanted to spend the rest of my life with, and had no doubt whatsoever that Ronnie would love me until, as the vows we'd soon say, death did us part.

Ronnie was looking at me as though I was the only person on earth for him and as the song I had recorded echoed out on the speakers, my voice sounding sweet and clear, I felt heaven lift me on winged feet toward him. Then he took my hands and looked deep into my eyes, and I felt transported to another place, a place full of romance and magic, devoid of earth's realities.

The pastor did his thing and we said the vows we had written and then we were husband and wife. I wonder if there are any more triumphant moments than when you hear the first peals of that music as you walk hand in hand back down that aisle as husband and wife?

The bridal party joined us in the receiving line and tears filled my eyes when I greeted my parents, who were on their best behavior that day, and the Fisher uncles and aunts, my relatives on my father's side who had endeared themselves so much to me by responding that they would attend…oh those dear, dear people, how I cherished them that day and will never, ever forget that they shared those splendid moments with me and Ronnie.

My mother's side, the Esh family, had not even bothered to RSVP with the exception of my Uncle Dave who was also no longer Amish so there he was, bless him.

And there was Miss Hostetter! My beloved teacher! No longer "miss" though, she was married now and attended along with her husband, but to me she would always be Miss Hostetter.

The breakfast was a smashing success. More than one person told me ours was the most beautiful wedding they had ever attended, and my bank account and I smirked a good deal about that.

I did not throw the garter or was it the flowers you threw? There were some traditions I could do without, and finally we were off to our honeymoon.

Chapter 20

ow a man can go from groom to monster in a few short hours is a puzzle I have yet to solve.

All that anticipation…all that planning…all that excitement…only to wake up the morning after our wedding night feeling traumatized, with a crucial part of my heart in a deep coma.

But denial is both friend and foe, isn't it?

It carried me through the rest of the honeymoon, in Colonial Williamsburg, Virginia, and then on to Virginia Beach where my new husband abandoned me one night. Just walked out of the hotel room and was gone for hours while I waited for him to return.

We missed our dinner reservations, and yet another part of my heart turned black with frost, the kind of frost that happens when spring has just provided its first warmth and buds sprout on hopeful stems, and then winter roars back with a vengeance.

Chapter 21

I felt better when we returned home. I loved our apartment, which felt blissful after my tiny, threadbare one. Our new home was actually a simple one-bedroom apartment with beige carpet and white walls, but I enjoyed it, especially the dining room that faced east and caught the morning sun.

We settled into a routine and I did my best to cope with my husband's atrocious bedroom etiquette, and tried to pretend I was happy.

And then, in May of 1987, almost a year after Ronnie and I married, my parents' world was rocked again when my sister Ruth Ann married a police detective from Maryland, a tall, handsome man she'd met while working at market for my uncle. She waited to get her hair cut until the morning of her wedding—brave woman!—and my mother had about seven conniption fits in the vestibule of Victory Chapel, where the wedding was held.

Ruth Ann looked gorgeous. Her lustrous thick, dark hair was cut in a sleek bob and her tiny waist was accentuated by the lovely white wedding dress she wore. My younger sister has always exuded a special kind of joyful effervescence, and that day, as the bride, she looked radiant in spite of Mom's disapproval.

Ronnie and I continued to attend his church and every Sunday my gut hurt and I tried harder and harder to convince myself that everything was fine, just fine.

Then we met Ed and Dorothy, another power couple at the church. They were evangelistic-minded and decided they needed a band to accompany them to their various events, and asked Ronnie and me to sing with them. I was flabbergasted. There I was, a relative nobody, and these almost-celebrities wanted *us*?

So we sang with their band, and then they started asking us if they could borrow our cars and even asked us to watch their children on many occasions, but somehow these did not feel like requests so much as royal commands. I finally stood up to Ed one Saturday afternoon when I was at their house in the suburbs taking care of their kids. He and Dorothy were about to leave for some spiritual weekend or other and he led me outside to their patio and showed me this extremely greasy, dirty gas grill, and asked me to clean it while they were gone.

Something in me snapped. I might watch his kids for free, and let him borrow my car, but I was *not* going to clean his damn grill for free too.

Ronnie became more and more withdrawn and started driving off by himself at night, often staying out for hours, and when I asked him where he was when he came back, he said he was "just driving around."

His late-night drives became more and more frequent, and then one night our neighbors invited us over. The husband was overweight and laughed a good deal, and his wife was small and laughed a good deal too. We spent an hour or so with them and when we came home Ronnie said to me, "They were high."

"What?" I said. I had zero experience with drugs and the couple had seemed normal enough to me. "How could you tell?"

He didn't say much, but something about his expression troubled me.

One morning it all came to a head.

Ronnie and I were supposed to sing in front of the church with Ed and Dorothy's band and it was a big deal for them because they were raising money to go on a missions trip overseas.

But Ronnie never came home. He had left the night before in his pickup truck and I paced the floor that Sunday morning, ready for church in a dark-blue blouse and off-white linen skirt, praying I'd hear his key turn in the lock.

Finally I could wait no longer and called Ed and Dorothy.

"Ronnie...I don't know where he is..." I said in a shaky voice.

"What do you mean you don't know where he is?" Ed snapped.

"Well, sometimes he...goes out by himself at night and...and this time he didn't come home."

"Do you realize how important this morning is? We were counting on you!" Ed said with extreme irritation in his voice. "Fine. Come by yourself."

No compassion. No thought for anything but his precious fundraiser.

I hung up the phone and waited another five minutes.

Finally I grabbed my car keys and headed to my gray Honda Civic. I unlocked it, slid in, and leaned my head against the steering wheel. How could I possibly put on a happy face and sing in front of several thousand people when I didn't even know where my husband was?

The church looked even more ostentatious to me than usual that morning—the lights harsher, the stage bigger, the people glitzier.

Ed and Dorothy barely spoke to me and the message could not have been clearer: *this is all your fault.*

I sang the songs in a paralyzed haze and left right after the worship service, not bothering to stay for the sermon.

When I came home there was a note from Ronnie telling me he had done cocaine with the neighbors. Just like that. *He'd done cocaine with the neighbors.*

My super-religious husband doing drugs? I had always imagined drugs as being an inner city thing, the criminal element, you know? But there in our sunny apartment, still in my church clothes, it seemed impossible, ridiculous almost.

The weeks that followed are still a blur to me. Ronnie emptied our checking and savings accounts and I immediately opened a new account in my name only and deposited my paychecks there so he would not have access to my money, and so I'd at least have funds to pay the bills and buy groceries.

When Ronnie cheated on me the first time I knew it the minute he walked up the stairs. It was six o'clock in the morning, which was not unusual—he often stayed out all night now—but that morning when he came into the bedroom I said, "You were with another woman, weren't you."

"Yes," he said, and undressed and went to bed.

I showered and went to work as usual, but I felt that someone had taken a sledgehammer to my heart.

The next time it happened, with a different woman, I knew again and this time he was in the kitchen when I asked him about it.

"Yeah, I was with someone else," he sneered, almost like it pleased him to hurt me.

"Ronnie, I have a right to…to know what's happening here…please, honey, tell me what's going on," I said between hysterical sobs.

"You have no rights," he spat.

Chapter 22

T herapy seemed like the next logical step so I called the church office and made an appointment with their in-house counselor. The following Tuesday afternoon after work, I clattered up the metal stairs outside the two-story office building on the church grounds and knocked on the door.

Ellis Archer, the therapist, opened the door and invited me in. He was tall and thin, yet had the muddy complexion of a man who ate cotton candy for breakfast, lunch, and dinner. Or maybe it was just the reflection of the brown polyester suit he wore. He gestured for me to sit down on the uncomfortable-looking sofa as he took the chair facing it. And then with a disinterested expression—he was probably counting the minutes till his next cotton candy fix—he asked me what the problem was.

I stuttered it out, feeling about as welcome there as a light bulb in an Amish house.

He listened and said, "Your husband probably slept with those other women because you aren't needy enough."

Come again?

Not needy enough? What does that mean, exactly?

(In hindsight, he was so correct—my Amishness, i.e. being too giving, probably did play a role in Ronnie's adultery. No one can live with all that sweetness and not crave a little sour now and then. However, that conversation was the equivalent of an emergency room doctor saying to the kid who has just smashed his motorcycle and is bleeding to death on the floor, "This is all your fault, you shouldn't have been driving a motorcycle in the first place.")

My whole body felt numb, and I can't remember much else of what he said because I was trying to recover from his accusation that Ronnie's behavior was my fault. At the end of the session he fired this soothing salvo straight from the cotton candy factory: "I'm sure your husband really does love you."

Revoke that guy's license, I beg you.

I dragged my way back down those metal stairs, holding on to the railing for support.

Since therapy had been such a disaster, in desperation I called the flamingo look-alike Kevin, who knew my husband better than anyone else in our group because Ronnie had lived with him and his wife for a while. Kevin then called a meeting without telling me he was going to do so. Present were Clarence, who had also been a close friend of Ronnie's before I met him, and Eva's husband Darrel, and some other men from our congregation.

Kevin told me what time to be there so there I was: just me and about eight men around a long table on a Sunday afternoon. There was a faintly unpleasant smell of garlic, like someone had forgotten to brush his teeth, and I felt like all the oxygen was being sucked out of my body while the conversation swirled around me, i.e., what they were going to do about Ronnie.

No one asked me what I wanted to do about the situation. I might as well not have been present while they discussed Ronnie's drug abuse and adultery, and I felt that they had decimated me, as a woman, to nothing.

After the discussion the eight of them pushed back their chairs with a collective air of satisfaction. I waited outside while they conferred, and then Kevin, who looked like a flamingo who has eaten a particularly delicious plump shrimp, strolled over to where I was sitting under a tree.

I stood up and he said, "After thinking about it and praying about it, we feel you should go back home to Ronnie. Imagine how wonderful he will feel when he realizes that all of us support him."

That was the moment when I began sleepwalking, emotionally and spiritually speaking.

I snapped out of my trance one Saturday morning, when I woke up to find Ronnie standing by the bed.

"Give me some money," he said.

I sat up and rubbed my eyes. "No," I said.

He grabbed me by the throat and started squeezing, and I thought, *this is it*...

Suddenly he released me and I fell against the headboard, gasping for air.

"You almost killed me," I said to him when I found my voice.

Soon after Ronnie's attempt on my life I drove to my parents' house before work one morning. They knew what he had done because one of my sisters had told them, and while I did not expect them to offer a solution, there was a part of me that hoped they would offer comfort even if in a nonverbal way.

As I sat with them at the kitchen table I wished I had not come. The atmosphere was hostile and my stomach hurt at the thought of discussing the strangling incident with the two people who had raised me, because by the looks on their faces there would be no comfort for me that morning...

"Just so you know, we do *not* believe in divorce," my mother said with a hard, cold look in her eyes. "It is your duty to stay with your husband."

My voice sounded very weak, like a small child's, and I said, "Mom, please, I don't want to talk about it."

She lectured on and on about what a sin it was to leave one's spouse until I could no longer hold back the tears and I said, "Mom, this is too painful for me to discuss, will you drop it please?"

Then Dad added his vote to hers—under no circumstances was I to leave my husband, until finally the words hurt my heart so much that I pushed back my chair and got up to leave. Dad thrust out his arm to block my path but I pushed past him and almost ran to my car. They stood there on the porch, the two people who were supposed to love me more than anyone else in the whole world, and as I reached for the car door something sort of exploded in my head and I shouted at them, "I can't believe you would expect me to stay with that asshole!"

It was the first time I had used that word, and as I drove home I was shaking so much I felt I wasn't fit to drive to work.

Then I called my father and told him I was sorry for shouting at him and my mother.

After work that day I called Mack and Matty, who had a big house and sometimes rented rooms to single women. I told them what had happened and that I needed a place to stay for a while.

Matty asked me to come over so we could talk about rent and such.

We sat at her dining room table in their stifling house, stifling not because it was too hot temperature-wise, but because it felt...I don't know, like there was very little air in it. I tried to concentrate on what Matty was saying, but I was in a state of shock and was having trouble focusing on her words.

Matty's skin had a yellowish cast and her brown eyes bored into mine as she said, "You realize you will have to pay rent."

"Of course," I said.

Then she listed, in great detail, all the other expenses I would incur for various things, like using the washer and dryer, until I wondered if they'd count how many times I flushed the toilet and charge me for each flush.

But, I felt, at least I'd be safe, so I moved a few things into one of their rentable bedrooms. And came to the conclusion that "safe" is a relative term.

One Saturday afternoon, a few months after I had moved in, Matty and I were sitting at her dining room table drinking coffee.

To surprise her I had cleaned the entire house that morning while she was out running errands. I cleaned all the bathrooms, vacuumed and dusted the living room and dining room, and scrubbed the kitchen floor until it shone, so I didn't feel quite as guilty about the tablespoon of Folgers I was consuming.

Matty fiddled with her coffee cup and looked like she had something on her mind.

"Is something wrong?" I said.

She looked spiteful for a moment—not a good look for her—but then she quickly arranged her expression to one of concern.

"I have something to say to you," she said.

"Well, what is it?"

"I can't tell you right now."

I was getting a very bad feeling in the pit of my stomach.

Matty toyed with her teaspoon, sipped a little of her coffee, and glanced at me with those sleazy-yet-religious eyes until I wanted to scream.

Finally she gave utterance. "Now that I've gotten to know you better," she said, "I can see why Ronnie is doing drugs."

She might as well have yanked a butcher knife out of the kitchen drawer and stabbed me in the stomach with it. It was like going to the emergency room for a heart transplant and leaving with a stab wound.

Later I would find the logic to deal with her crazy comment, i.e., if it were my fault that Ronnie was doing drugs, whose fault was it when he did drugs before he met me, his mother's? But to this day I still have trouble understanding why she did that to me. Was it because she had seen her husband looking at me admiringly? Was she jealous?

I moved out of their house and went back to Ronnie. Not a good move, not a smart move, but I felt that anything would be better than that airless house and Matty's hatred.

Chapter 23

M eanwhile I continued to go to church. Continued to try my best to believe that the members of that congregation were good people, and continued to take Kevin's advice to hang in there with my husband.

Then Ronnie forged my name on one of my checks and stole money from my account. By then I was in a desperate place financially. I was paying all the bills myself and he was using all his money, and now some of mine, on drugs.

Finally, after a long, horrible season of clinging to survival by my fingernails, Ronnie went to rehab. For about four weeks hope sang in my heart again. He was gaining weight, he was getting therapy, he was making progress. I visited him as often as I could and when he came home he looked like the man that I had walked down the aisle toward on our wedding day. I had felt like the luckiest, happiest woman in the world that day and I felt sure that we were now turning over a brand new leaf. And in spite of everything, I still loved him with all my heart.

Three weeks later I woke to the smell of sickly-sweet crack smoke.

Hope in tatters, I finally left him and moved to a seedy "garden apartment" and tried to get my life back together. I also left his awful church, and this time, I needed no one's permission.

I lived in terror that he'd find me and hurt me in some way, but I didn't hear a word from him. Then a few months later, I had just returned home from the gym one night when I heard the phone ringing.

"Hello?"

"Guess where I am."

Shaking a little with shock at the sound of his voice, I said, "I don't know, Ronnie, where are you?"

"In jail," he said, in the same tone one would use to announce that one was at a country club dinner.

The trembling in my body increased and I sat down. "Why?" I said.

"I robbed a bank."

The Lancaster County prison is an apologetic building with an air of yes-I'm-a-jail-but-I'd-rather-be-a-bowling-alley look about it.

I parked my car in the parking lot, wishing the sky wouldn't be quite as gloomy, quite as heartless. I drew my coat around my shoulders and trudged toward the entrance.

"Who are you here to see, honey?" The guard chewed her gum at me with a bored expression but her eyes were kind.

"Ronnie Patterson," I said in a wispy voice.

"Name?"

I gave it to her and she said, "Yup. You're on the list. Jewelry, keys, purse all stay here, hon."

I stripped off my wedding and engagement rings, earrings, and watch, and placed them in the box she provided.

The guards shepherded a group of us visitors through a narrow hallway and when the metal door clanged shut behind us I felt it, that stab of panic that signaled I was going to have to fight very hard to stay calm in this place.

Yet another hallway, yet another locked door, and then the group of us entered a communal visitors' room.

And then, there he was. My husband, in fluorescent orange.

He looked thin, almost as emaciated as when crack cocaine had wreaked its havoc on his already spare frame.

"Susie," he said.

I hugged him but could feel the holding back, the wall that he had erected a long time ago, and I backed away and sat down at a table in a corner of the room. Ronnie followed. We stared at each other and I noticed that he had yet another stye at the rim of his eye. He had perpetual problems with them and sometimes had more than one. A shame, considering how attractive his eyes usually were, but that large, angry-looking pimple distracted me. His teeth looked yellow, too, or maybe it was the reflection of all that orange. His lower teeth had never been pretty at any time—they were a crooked jumbled mess, and looked yellow and unkempt.

But he was still my husband, and I realized as I looked past the stye and the crooked lower teeth how much I still loved him. Tears I could not stop rolled down my cheeks. How had we come to this place? How had the man I had so adored, the church-going, romantic man I had pledged my eternal devotion to at the altar only a short time ago, ended up...*here?*

"Ronnie," I said as I wiped the tears away with my sweater sleeve. "How are you?"

"I'm okay. You look nice."

"Thank you."

I could not think of anything to say, anything that would express my disbelief at the circumstances without sounding accusatory, so I looked around at the other visitors and inmates, and almost smelled the bleak fumes of human failure. Tears rolled down my cheeks again, and when I looked at Ronnie his face looked hard, unfeeling. Any grief in my heart was not shared by him, clearly, and suddenly I couldn't wait to escape.

The guards announced that visiting time was up and ushered us back to the entrance where I retrieved my purse, keys, and jewelry.

I breathed cool night air into my lungs as I unlocked my car. I slid in and sat there with the keys in my hand. Was it worth staying in a marriage with a man who looked like the emotional equivalent of an icicle?

I started the car and drove slowly out of the parking lot. My limbs felt old, unresponsive. While the rest of the world seemed to be going about the normal business of life—eating dinner, watching TV—what was I doing driving out of a prison parking lot?

What was I going to do?

Divorce—I shuddered away from the word that seeped into my consciousness without permission.

No. *No!* No one in my family, no aunts, uncles, cousins, grandparents, great-grandparents, had *ever* divorced. We did not believe in it.

And wouldn't it be the height of cruel to file for divorce while my husband was incarcerated?

On the other hand, what kind of life was this for a thirty-year-old woman?

Chapter 24

I didn't know what to do about my marriage, but I made some other changes. I moved out of my horrid apartment and into a lovely house in Bird-in-Hand that my dad and my older brother Steve owned. It had beautiful hardwood floors and a big backyard, and while they charged me full rent, I could afford it because I usually shared it with one roommate and sometimes two because there were three spacious bedrooms.

It also felt like it was time for a new job; I had worked for my plumbing and heating CEO long enough. One night I read an ad for an executive assistant to the president and CEO of an insurance company and, even though I felt that it was over my head—it was a big, prestigious company—I applied anyway.

When they called me for an interview, I was stunned, but decided to go through with it. And so I found myself in a large conference room with a lot of Danish wood and two executives who were about as opposite in appearance as two people can get: the treasurer, Ethan, was a short, bald man with a pink complexion and an oily smile, while Albert, the CEO, was a tall man with a lot of gray hair, beautiful albeit cold gray eyes, and large teeth.

At first they asked me the typical interview questions but then the treasurer glanced at my resume and the application I had filled out, and asked the one question I dreaded most:

"Why didn't you go to high school?" he said.

I explained about my Amish background and why I only had a GED and was now attending college part-time.

They asked me some strange, rather personal questions about the Amish culture and the CEO guffawed a good deal while the treasurer smirked, and afterwards I was certain I had flunked the interview completely. (I also wondered what they would have thought had they known my husband was in prison!) When the human resources director, a scary blond woman who seemed joined at the hip with the CEO, called and said that they had been interviewing for seven months and were sure I was *it* and when could I start, I was shocked.

At first, I loved it. I felt so special when I swiped my security card at the employee entrance, and I loved answering the phone, "Executive Office, Susie speaking." And I felt amazing in my suits and high heels.

In short, I felt honored, and stunned, to be the executive assistant to those two men.

Albert and his stomach had an ongoing battle: sometimes Albert won, but on more occasions, the prize went to his stomach. He and his belly sauntered in every morning and tossed an arrogant good morning to me, and I was never quite sure what mood he'd be in. However, there was a side to him that I adored—he answered my questions and explained things to me, which of course, with my insatiable inquisitiveness, endeared him to me.

The firm was both a life and health insurance company, and it was at the beginning of the whole HMO/PPO thing. Albert patiently explained to me the differences, and while the subject was not exactly entertaining, I enjoyed those conversations at the round table in his corner office, which overlooked a prestigious section of Lancaster City.

Ethan was rather dreadful and his weapon of choice was shaming people. I typed memos for him that made me cringe on behalf of the recipient, because not only did he demean the employee, but he also copied the entire executive team as well.

One day I walked into the boardroom where Albert was pontificating to a group of managers. I handed him an urgent message from Ethan. He read it and then yelled at me in front of everyone, I guess because he didn't like the message. But the people in the room didn't know that, and I felt humiliated and angry.

So later that day—knees shaking and prepared to be fired on the spot—I went to Albert's office and told him how I felt about what he had done. He looked surprised at first and then complimented me for staying late to talk to him. Then he laughed, his big teeth showing, and said, "You're absolutely right, Susie, I shouldn't have yelled at you in front of everyone. But you know what? I'll do it again. I'll hit you over the head and I'll feel better. You bet, I'll do it again."

There were other instances like that, of course, but I think the one that hurt most was one night at a fancy corporate event in Hershey, Pennsylvania.

Mary Matalin and James Carville were invited to speak to Lancaster's elite at the Hotel Hershey. Our company was sponsoring the post-dinner reception and Albert put me in charge. I and four of my coworkers worked all day, arranging tables, filling balloons with helium, talking to the caterers, and making sure everything was absolutely perfect. The reception was a smashing success.

After it was over, I was carrying a stack of cocktail napkins emblazoned with the company logo across the room, my feet aching from the high-heels I'd been wearing for hours, when I saw Albert, he and his stomach resplendent in a tuxedo. He strolled toward me, a fat cigar in his mouth. He took the cigar out, looked me up and down, and said, "What have you there, Susie? Amish toilet paper?"

I learned a hard lesson that night: *Do what you did in the Amish culture: stay numb, expect nothing.*

It wasn't all bad, though. One of the things that made work life pleasant for me during my stint at the insurance company was my friendship with Yvonne, an Italian woman with lustrous eyes and long, dark hair. She wore her clothes with an air of great confidence and she and I became fast friends in a short period of time.

I was feeling better about my appearance, too—I had quit the awful hairdresser who had permed my hair and was now going to a downtown salon where a woman named Kelly expressed herself horrified that anyone had *ever* permed my hair. She highlighted it and cut it in a more flattering style.

Clothes shopping was also becoming easier. I discovered that I still liked dresses almost more than anything and while it wasn't always easy to find ones that were complementary to my hourglass figure, I found some lovely ones now and then, and interspersed those with the occasional business suit.

One day Yvonne and I walked the few blocks from the office to Central Market to pick up lunch. I loved it as much as I had as a child—the bustling atmosphere, the cheerful vendors, the colorful produce, the tempting breads and baked goods. After we made our selections we sat in the sun on benches in Lancaster's charming square, and Yvonne said, "We're going to rate men today."

My fork halted in its descent toward my salad. "What did you say?" I said.

"See that guy? On a scale of one to ten, what do you think?"

I felt absurd as I checked out the specimen she discreetly pointed out to me. My upbringing had not prepared me to look at men with a critical eye and I couldn't think of anything to say about the guy in the white shirt, khaki pants, and navy blazer.

"Well?" Yvonne said and we both giggled.

"It looks like he has good shoulders," I surprised myself by saying. "But I don't like his expression, he has a sour look on his face, so I'll give him a seven."

Yvonne clapped. "Bravo!" she said.

One night she took me barhopping. I had no experience with the bar scene and felt a little overwhelmed, frankly. Finally, after a long night, we found ourselves at the Conestoga on King Street, a place that was built in 1741 and my favorite of the bars we'd been to that night. However, it was stuffy and smoky and I felt crowded and in great need of space. As I looked around for a few inches I could call my own, Yvonne went to the bar to order drinks for us.

Lo and behold! Across the room were not only a few inches but several glorious feet of space. I steamed toward it in the manner of a woman who has been handed her personal manna in the wilderness and stood there drinking in, just soaking up, the fact that no one was jostling against my shoulders. After a few minutes, though, something felt off. You know how you feel when people are staring at you? I looked up to find a cluster of men looking at me with the oddest expressions on their faces. One guy in particular, a dude with a crew cut and a checkered shirt, looked puzzled, disgusted, and maybe even pissed off?

Yvonne and I had drawn a lot of attention that night from males of all sizes and descriptions and they had all shown approval, some of it verbal, some nonverbal, so I was surprised to elicit that kind of reaction. Then I turned around and realized to my great horror that I was standing in front of the dartboard!

Yvonne still teases me about that incident.

My next bar experience started out fine. One of my roommates invited me to join her and her friends at Quips Pub on New Holland Avenue. It was packed and loud, and I was standing there with a glass of Chardonnay in my hand, trying to look like I did this sort of thing all the time, when a strong-jawed man in a black leather jacket sidled up to me.

"Hi!" he said.

I smiled at him, delighted. "Hello."

He leaned toward me and said—or rather, practically shouted it, it was rockin' in that bar—"I'm Joe! What's your name!"

"Susie!"

"Hi Susie!"

"Hi Joe!"

He's from Philadelphia, he tells me.

Ah, Philadelphia, love Philly, I say all sophisticated-like.

Then: the dreaded topic.

"I have some cousins in Lancaster," Joe said, leaning in so close I could smell the Colgate on his breath. "Where did you go to high school?"

Suddenly, my cute outfit and sexy shoes mattered not at all, because they could not disguise what I was: an unsophisticated ex-Amish girl with very little education.

"I didn't go to high school. I was raised Amish," I said, looking down at the floor.

He reared back like I had struck him.

"You lie," he said, his smile gone.

I felt lightheaded from the cigarette smoke and the unaccustomed alcohol in my system, and the throbbing of the music and the squawking of the crowd beat a frenzied tempo in my head.

"It's true!" I protested. "I was!"

He backed away and put his hands up. "You're a liar," he said. "I'm not talking to you anymore."

I decided I wasn't cut out for the bar scene and wanted to go home, when a thin brunette staggered over to me with a pale-pink drink in her hand and said, "So, what do you do?"

"Do?"

"Yeah. What do you work?"

I opened my mouth to answer when she pointed at a guy across the room. "See him? I just told him I'm a dog catcher."

I giggled. "A dog catcher?"

"Yep." She slurped some of her drink. "And see that guy? I told him I'm a bug exshterminator."

I laughed some more while she stumbled off on heels never intended for thin drunk brunettes, and suddenly Joe's behavior made sense. He probably thought I had been messing with him on purpose.

Dog Catcher! Bug Exterminator! Amish!

Sorry, Joe...

The relationship I had built so carefully with my parents, that fragile, sacred bond, was severed almost to the point of no return during that time. My mother continued to lecture and nag me about the evils of divorce, and one day my father exhibited a cruelty that it still hurts to recall.

One of my roommates had begged for a kitten that she'd seen at a pet store and I relented and said fine, go ahead. She named him Hamlet and naturally grew tired of him after a week, and so that little ball of fur became mine. He was the sweetest little thing, all white with a butterscotch-colored mark on his face. He seemed to know how much I needed affection because he curled up to me at night and purred and purred, and my love-starved self, that inner child who had never had a stuffed animal or pet of her own, just soaked it all in.

I suppose I should have asked my father, who was my landlord, if pets were okay but it never occurred to me, and one day I came home to a note from Dad that said, "No pets! Not in the kitchen, attic, basement, garage! *Get rid of the cat.*"

Get rid of my cherished kitten? I called Dad and pleaded with him, but he had his cold-dad voice going on and said Nope, no way, and I said why don't we get together for breakfast Saturday to discuss it and he said okay.

So the following Saturday morning my brother Steve, Dad and I sat around the table at a local restaurant and before the coffee was even poured I said, "Dad, please. When I leave the house I promise I will have it professionally cleaned but please let me keep the kitten? Please?"

His expression could have chipped rock. "No," he said. "Get rid of it."

Tears filled my eyes and I stumbled toward the ladies room to try to compose myself when I heard my name.

"Susie!" a man at the counter said.

I glanced over and dabbed the tears out of my eyes.

"Eli!" I said. My boyfriend from my fourteen-year-old days, the nice guy with the sandy hair and kind eyes…wow. Talk about timing.

He hugged me and said, "You look fantastic."

It was the first time we'd seen each other since we'd both left the Amish. I'd heard he was married to a registered nurse now and had several children.

"Thank you."

"I heard about your husband," he said. "I'm sorry."

"Thank you," I said again and almost broke down right there in the restaurant.

"You deserve to be with a man who makes you smile, Susie," he said, and the comfort of those words is still with me to this day.

Thank you, Eli.

I went back to the table where my brother and father waited and realized I could not eat breakfast with them nor did I want to spend another second in their company because I needed to go home and have a good cry. So I went home and cuddled with Hamlet and wondered what I was going to do with him. I couldn't bear to randomly put him up for adoption. And then my roommate, the one who had brought him to the house in the first place, came to the rescue. She had friends who lived on a farm in upstate Pennsylvania who offered to take him, and one day she packed him up and drove away with my precious little companion.

My next roommate was a 58-year-old woman named Betty, who brought with her twelve cardboard boxes full of Santa Clauses of all types, some cute, some horrible, and a lot of other clutter that haunted me till the day she left, and indeed, the pair of oversized wooden mice she brought, one male, one female, still haunt me. The female especially had this condescending look about her and I tried not to catch her eye because it glared at me from under the wire-rimmed spectacles she wore.

Betty insisted on scattering her country décor about and I (gently) reminded her that the first floor was off-limits, decorating-wise, but she could do whatever she wanted in her bedroom. I take a rather spare approach to decorating; a few choice objects appeal to me more than a grand mess of bric-a-brac, but Betty ignored my requests and I'd come home from work and find my things swept away and replaced by wooden geese and dried flower arrangements, with the mice serving proudly as doorstops.

One day Betty informed me she wanted to bring her cat to the house. She'd gone through a divorce and the cat was with her ex, and she needed him (the feline, not the man).

"Oh no!" I said, thinking wooden mice were one thing, live cats another. "My father has a very strict No Pets policy."

She waved her plump hand in the air and swept my protests aside. "I'll go see him," she said, and asked for directions. My parents only lived a mile away and she drove off in her Pontiac with a determined look on her face.

She curveted back in thirty minutes later with a triumphant look on her face. "He said I could,'" she declared, and I felt my heart, the one that had bid my kitten a tearful goodbye, crumble.

I turned away so she could not see the hurt expression on my face.

Chapter 25

W ork continued to be a mixed bag. Yvonne and I had lots of fun, of course, but she worked in a different department, and I was alone in the executive office with the big boys. One day Albert asked me to "use my judgment" to find a frame for the watercolor he'd had commissioned from a local artist, a painting that showed the Lancaster City skyline at sunrise, and the colors were beautiful.

"If I don't like the frame you pick out, I'll fire you," Albert said, and I wasn't sure if he was kidding or not. I couldn't always tell.

"But what do you *like*?" I said.

"Use your own judgment," he said again with a twisted smile.

Let's just say I've never taken a project more seriously. The framer, a fantastic guy with a downtown shop, spent at least an hour with me poring over different types of frames and mattes.

"I like the oak one best," I said. "It's warm and elegant at the same time."

He nodded his approval. "Yes, and I'd go with a soft white matte," he said. "With all those colors, you want something simple so the painting stands out more."

"I agree," I said, and when I came back to the office Albert asked what I had chosen. I shook my head and said, "Wait and see."

A week later we had the great unveiling. My knees were shaking as I carried the painting into the conference room where it would hang, and Albert followed me in. I placed it on the table and carefully removed the brown paper.

My boss picked it up and studied it.

Long silence.

"I like it," he said, and walked out of the room.

I took a couple of deep breaths, patted the oak frame, and hoped I wouldn't be asked to pass any more of those kinds of tests.

However, Ethan, the treasurer, was in his own way worse than Albert. He found the chink in everyone's armor and zoomed in for the kill. Mine, of course, was my Amish background and he took every opportunity to taunt me about it.

I gleaned strength from the new church I was now attending, whose pastor was a man with dark hair, blue eyes, and a fantastic fashion sense. He preached great sermons and was compassionate about what I was going through, what with a husband in prison and parents who could not exactly be called supportive.

One Sunday after church, he asked me what I was going to do.

"I don't know," I said. "Ronnie is getting out of prison soon and I don't want him back. I'm scared of him."

He looked at me with kindness in his eyes and said quietly, "If you choose to divorce him, we'll support you one hundred percent."

Ronnie's exit from prison ended up being a non-issue for me. He moved to a place closer to where his family lived, about twenty miles away, and soon found a job and seemed to be okay. However, when he did not show me any kindness or offer to reimburse me for the money he had stolen from me, hope gasped its last breath. I found an attorney and even though I cried while I did it, I filed for divorce.

Ronnie refused to sign the papers.

My attorney charged me for every piece of correspondence he sent to Ronnie and since I was the only one paying for the fees—Ronnie had no attorney—I was starting to get angry.

Months dragged by and finally one day I called him. "Ronnie, what we had is over. Would you please do this one favor for me and sign the papers so I can move on with my life?"

"If you had been the Christian wife you should have been, none of that would have happened," he said.

Angry red stars popped in my brain. This man had cheated on me, stolen from me, verbally abused me, almost strangled me, and last but certainly not least, was atrocious and abusive in bed.

"You bastard!" I said. "Fine. Don't sign the papers! I look forward to our day in court when I can tell the judge exactly what happened here."

He signed the papers the next day.

The day the divorce was final I threw a party.

Chapter 26

T he following summer one of my coworkers asked if I wanted to go to Dewey Beach in Delaware with her and her two friends over the Fourth of July. I didn't know the woman well and had never met her friends, but I hadn't been to the beach in ages and it would be a nice change.

Well! Let's just say that the two friends were the bossiest women it has ever been my misfortune to come across. My coworker and I didn't have a *prayer* of getting our vote in as to where to eat and so forth, and since one of the bossy women was driving we couldn't do much about it. It was not quite the carefree time I had hoped for.

So on the last day of that fateful four-day weekend, I soaked in the sun as well as the peace. The other three women had staggered off the beach with their various accoutrements and I was alone at last. I stretched out on the blanket, novel in hand, drink at elbow, breathing in air that felt, finally, like salty, tangy, bossy-woman-free oxygen.

Even my swimsuit felt happy. Black with white polka dots, it couldn't compete with the itsy bitsy teeny weeny polka dot bikini of song lore but it had its place and felt just right, did my two-piece that day.

I became aware of eyes on me, the way one does. It puzzled me because it was around five-o'clock, that lovely hour on the beach when most human mammals have gone in search of showers and grub.

Then I saw him. He had dark curly hair and he buried his face in a magazine the second our eyes met. I dismissed it and went back to my book.

125

"Excuse me."

I looked up and there he was, holding a tissue to his chin.

"Sorry. Cut myself shaving."

I laughed. As an introduction it tickled me and I love being entertained, especially by men as humble as this one seemed to be.

"I'm Craig," he said. "I'm sorry to interrupt you, but would you be interested in going on a walk with me?"

"Sure."

So we walked along the ocean, and as I dug my toes in the wet sand and watched the waves do their eternal thing, I listened as Craig told me about places he'd traveled to and things he'd done, and I answered his questions, too. When we returned to my towel he asked for my phone number, and wrote it down on a page he ripped out of the magazine he'd been reading.

The following months were some of the sweetest of my life. On our first date Craig drove from his condo in Reston, Virginia to my house in Bird-in-Hand on a Sunday morning and we had brunch, and then went to an Amish schoolyard and ran through the grass barefoot and rode high on the swings, laughing like children. When he kissed me briefly before he left, the touch of his lips stayed with me for hours and I could not wait to see him again.

We spent a lot of weekends together after that and Craig always found the best things to do. We drank strawberry daiquiris in the sun in St. Michael's, Maryland. We went to the Torpedo Art Gallery in Alexandria, Virginia, and ate the most delicious New England clam chowder I've ever had at the Fish Market in Old Town. We went to Maryland's Assateague Island and picnicked on wine and grapes and sandwiches on the beach.

Craig also took me to see a show at the Kennedy Center in Washington, DC. I felt like royalty as we walked into the beautiful lobby with its red carpet and sparkling chandeliers. And while the show was spectacular, the best part for me was the man sitting next to me.

In short, Craig healed my heart. And while he may not have been a churchgoer, or prayed in public, or professed to be anything religious at all, he took the burned-out shell of a woman that I had been and almost made me whole again.

Our relationship gradually ended as summers tend to do, but I treasure those memories of our time together and will always be grateful to Craig for loving me at a time when I needed it most.

The following Christmas I felt an odd urging to call Ronnie and wish him a Merry Christmas. I had not spoken to him since that last terrible conversation and, indeed, had healed to the point where I almost never thought about him anymore. The feeling to call him grew stronger so finally I got his phone number from Information and dialed it.

The phone rang while I hoped no one would answer. Someone did.

"Ronnie, it's me. Susie. I was just calling to wish you a Merry Christmas."

There was a shocked silence and then he said, "Oh. Hello."

"How are you?" I said, and he sounded stable, if not wildly happy, perhaps, and I was glad for him.

Another long silence ensued and finally I said, "Ronnie, I want you to know that I've let go of everything that happened and I hope you can…forgive yourself and have a happy life."

There was a long pause, and then Ronnie said, so quietly I had to strain to hear, "Susie, not a day goes by that I don't regret losing you."

It wasn't an apology—not that I had been expecting one—but it was good to hear nonetheless.

Merry Christmas to me.

Chapter 27

A s fate would have it, Dewey Beach yielded up yet another surprise the following summer. He sat at a corner of the bar smoking one bitter cigarette after another and it was clear he held that party beach crowd in utter contempt. If Craig had been a smooth, buttery, merlot, this guy was a shot of hard-brewed moonshine, whiskey that is guaranteed to take some of the skin off your throat as it goes down.

Morton was not handsome, really, except he had interesting hazel eyes and thick brown hair cut by a barber who did not believe in soft edges.

He attracted me somehow, maybe because he was so different. He didn't flirt with me at all but rather complained about the crowd, in between sipping Coca Cola and puffing on his cigarettes. He said he played the piano and I said I sang and the first glimmer I had that he might be interested in me was when he suggested that we get together sometime so I could hear him play and maybe sing with him. He wrote my number down on a crumpled paper napkin and yes, I was intrigued.

We spoke on the following Wednesday and made plans for the weekend. He lived in the Washington DC area, and when he showed up at my house in Pennsylvania on that rainy Saturday night, he looked grim and forbidding. He shoved a bouquet of straggly-looking flowers into my hand and on the way to dinner, swore violently at the other drivers and mocked Lancaster County. I felt his big-city snobbishness keenly, almost as much as if he had said my dress was ugly.

I enjoyed our dinner conversation though, and he said he worked for the government and had a master's degree in political science. However, when the bill came, he said grumpily, "Well! It's a good thing I brought my credit card."

I was surprised by his comment and a little hurt because he had asked me to choose the location. I had picked out a moderately-priced restaurant, nothing fancy, and his comment made me feel my company was not very special to him. However, we continued dating, and sometimes I drove to Washington DC and sometimes he drove to Pennsylvania. Morton had this strident walk, an almost cross way of stalking around that had me practically running to keep up, but I found his whole grouchy demeanor to be so different it was enticing, or maybe subconsciously I was choosing someone who was as far a departure from my charming ex-husband as it got.

He took me to Buffalo, New York, and introduced me to his parents our first Thanksgiving together. I was nervous, of course, as most are in that situation, but I was especially so because Morton's father was a brilliant guy, a retired professor who had taught at Harvard and Berkeley, and most recently at the University of Buffalo. I was terrified his folks would not consider me worthy of their son because of my Amish background. But they welcomed me with open arms, and while I found Morton's mother's manner odd after she had had a few at dinner, when she wasn't drinking she was lovely to me.

I loved breakfast time in that house in Buffalo. We sat in the sunny dining room and passed sections of the *Wall Street Journal* back and forth, while classical music played on the stereo. They introduced me to bagels and fresh lox, which I greatly enjoyed, and the WSJ is still my favorite newspaper.

Sometimes Morton showed a tender side that I loved, a vulnerability that came through especially when he played the piano, which he did beautifully. And when he finally worked up the courage to tell me one day that he was in Alcoholics Anonymous and had joined a number of years back because he was afraid he was following in his mother's footsteps, he admitted that he was scared I would break up with him because he knew about my ex-husband's former drug addiction.

After some troubled thoughts, I decided it wasn't a deal-breaker, and carried on.

How to describe the weeks that followed? I was somewhat happy with Morton, but my relationship with Mom and Dad was frayed almost to the breaking point. Now that they were over the whole shunning thing, they had begun treating me like their personal taxi service, like the Saturday night my mother called and said she had guests for dinner, and would I run to the store and I said sure, and when I drove in the driveway I saw three cars parked there, so their guests obviously were not Amish. My mother ran out and said, "Here, I'll take that," and grabbed the item out of my hand. I could see she didn't want me to come inside because she was ashamed of her non-Amish daughter.

My job was getting to me, too. I had worked for Albert and Ethan for over three years by that time and while I didn't realize it, slowly, slowly, rage was seeping its way up through my internal system and getting ready to surface. One day I followed the wise advice given to every young professional at one time or another: *Don't burn your bridges.*

I didn't burn mine but rather blew them to smithereens.

Chapter 28

"Y ou're a pig," I said to Ethan one afternoon in July of 1996.

His oily smile turned to a shocked frown and I left his office, grabbed my purse, and instead of waiting for the elevator, ran down four flights of stairs and out the door to the parking garage. I drove home in a state of nerves, almost too dazed to drive, and when Albert called me a few hours later to fire me it was almost an anticlimax.

But rage, my new best friend, was not yet finished.

The next morning I packed up my car and drove to my parents' house. I found Dad in his office and blew in with what I am sure was not a meek air.

"Dad," I said, "I want to talk to you."

He looked up from his paperwork and frowned. "What is it?" he said.

"I'm leaving town today, and I want to…"

His face turned ugly. "What do you mean, you're leaving town?" he said, and barraged me with words, words that cut, the same words I'd heard ever since I'd left the Amish church.

"Dad!" I cried. "Please stop. I want to talk to you."

He yammered on. I warned him one more time and when he still did not let me speak I kicked his left ankle and spun around to go to the house to look for my mother. Dad followed me out and I could tell that he was in a state of cold fury. He beat me to the house and yelled for my mother, who came out to the porch wiping her hands on her apron.

"Susie!" she said. "What's going on?"

"I have some things to say to both of you," I said, and had only gotten out a few words when they began talking at once, the same stuff I had heard over, and over, and over again.

I held up my hand and said, "I am an *adult*. I am thirty-five years old. I have never asked you to understand or even support my choices and I am sorry I hurt you, but all I am asking for is some respect, and I need to share how *I* feel for once in my life. *Please.*"

They stood there, looking smug in the knowledge that they were right and I was wrong, and both began speaking at once until finally I could stand it no longer.

"If the two of you do not give me this one chance, as your daughter, to tell you how I feel, you may never see me again," I said. "My heart has been hurt too many times and I don't think I can take it anymore."

Again, they both opened their mouths at the same time and the words poured out, how ashamed they were of me, how wrong I was to leave the Amish in the first place, how it was all my fault my marriage had ended...

I took one final look at the faces of the two people I still loved, so very much, for what I knew might be the last time. As I walked to my car, shaking but resolute, I thought, how can they justify their condemnation of me? How? If they'd be strict Amish, it would still be hurtful, but more understandable. But the two of them? They had been bending and even breaking the rules for as long as I could remember. So why couldn't they give me a break?

Goodbye house, goodbye parents, goodbye Lancaster County...

I drove west on Route 340, past the red brick house I'd rented from my dad where I'd laughed with roommates, and entertained dates, and cuddled with Hamlet the kitten...past Bird-in-Hand Motel, where I'd folded sheets and towels...past

133

the Farmers Market where I'd dipped ice cream for tourists...past the Old Village Store where I'd bought candy as a child with my cousin Barbie...

A few miles later I turned right onto Route 30 and headed south to my new life.

Part III

Chapter 29

I was waiting for Morton when he arrived home from work that evening, I and my packed-to-the-gills car. After he'd expressed his surprise, he unlocked the door to his basement apartment, and listened while I told him what had happened. He wiped away my tears, and then went to his closet and pushed aside some clothes and said, "Here, I'll make room for yours."

I could not have survived those first weeks without him. He not only gave me a place to live until I could find an apartment of my own, but also helped me search the want ads for jobs I could apply to, and I soon realized, as I pored over the newspaper day after day and made countless phone calls, how different looking for jobs in the Washington DC metropolitan area was from looking for one in Lancaster County. But finally one morning there I was, at hectic Union Station, with two appointments scheduled: the first with a placement agency, the second with a company that did something obscure that was connected to the political scene in the District of Columbia.

I wasn't really hungry but needed to eat before my interview, so I ordered a banana muffin and coffee, and when the muffin came it looked like it had swollen to twice the size the baker had originally intended. I picked at it and felt the energy of the place around me, the clacking of the trains as they entered the station, the weary way the wheels turned, as though life held no future meaning for them either.

The cavernous station seemed oddly devoid of smells. With all those people milling about, you'd think one would smell perfume and sweat and that indefinable something humans emit when they're scared or in love or whatever but no, I didn't smell anything but emptiness and maybe it was because the ceilings were so high and the space so vast, but I felt like I was the only human in a sea of mechanical people who had all been programmed for their day except me.

What had I done? And what had I been thinking, telling my sleazy boss he was a pig? There I was, in the nation's capital, with no job, no references, no friends except Morton, and, I forced myself to admit it: no family at all because I was sure not only my parents but also my siblings were convinced I had lost it for real this time. I had only talked to one of my sisters, and she'd sounded cold on the phone and said it as clearly as if she'd voiced the words out loud—*you're crazy and we want nothing to do with you.*

And who could blame them? *I had kicked my father in the ankle.* Who does that? Who? Sure, it was the pent-up rage of years speaking, but did I really have to alienate everyone at once?

What if I couldn't find a job in this city? Who would hire a unsophisticated ex-Amish woman with only a smattering of college courses to her name? Sure, I'd supported the president and CEO of an insurance company for almost four years and before that the president and CEO of a plumbing and heating company for three, but would that hold any water in this hard-bitten town?

This felt like the real leaving, the end of everything familiar, even more than the day I left home and the Amish church. At least then I had had some of my siblings' support, but now all that was gone.

I also realized that there were aspects of my job at the insurance company I would miss—the lovely executive office, with its Ficus trees and skylights, and I'd even miss Albert booming his sarcastic good morning, and Ethan sauntering in, a newspaper tucked under his arm.

And I'd miss Lancaster City, that unassuming yet intelligent and artsy place with its attractive square and cheerful Central Market. I'd miss the quiet bustle of a city confident in who it was without shouting about it.

But this place? I had loved Washington DC as a child, we'd come here on a field trip when I was in the eighth grade and I had enjoyed the sense of history and the monuments and the feeling of important things happening. I'd liked it when I visited Morton and he'd shown me around, but experiencing it as a tourist was very different from how I felt now, with nowhere else to go and no income. I felt the underlying power of the city, the sinister edge, the danger of getting caught in its jaws and being chewed up and spit out with no memory of who you once were.

Chapter 30

Finally, after what felt like hundreds of interviews and hundreds of lame responses to that awful why-did-you-leave-your-last-job question, I landed a job as executive assistant to the president and CEO of a nonprofit organization in Alexandria, Virginia. My old boss at the plumbing and heating place came through with a glowing reference (for which I dearly thank him), and finally I was employed again.

My new boss had white hair and watery blue eyes that liked to scan me head to toe—he did this first thing when he met me, actually—and took his time about it. But otherwise he seemed harmless enough, until one day when I sent him an email asking if I could have a day off to take care of things like dentist appointments, etc. It was my first request for a day off and, having learned the hard way from my last boss not to appear in person in front of The King unless you had to, I emailed him.

No response.

I emailed him twice more and finally, my dentist appointment fast approaching, I did the unthinkable and asked him in person if it would be okay to take a day off.

He frowned at me and said, "I didn't know anything about this."

"I emailed you three times," I said.

He leaned forward in his fancy office chair and turned a bright shade of red. A vein throbbed at the side of his neck and he shouted, "Are you calling me a liar?"

I took a few steps back and said quietly, "No. No, I'm not."

I cancelled my dentist appointment.

After that incident I realized that if I kept my mouth shut and stayed alert I'd probably be okay. But from then on if I wanted a day off I announced it instead of asking for permission.

I liked where our office was located. I enjoyed strolling down the cobblestone streets of Old Town where George Washington himself had walked, and sometimes I hiked all the way to the riverfront at lunchtime and watched the sailboats glide across the Potomac River. But not even the beauty and comfort of Old Town could buffer the horror of the quarterly board meetings.

Hotshot board members flew in from various parts of the United States and it was my job to reserve hotel rooms, provide for catering during the meetings, find the executives some fancy restaurant to dine in after the first day of board meetings, and also attend the meetings and take minutes. As I sat there with them around a big conference table, there were times I was afraid I'd go mad with boredom. And some of them could be extremely demanding, and while I respect the rights of all humans to choose whether or not they will Eat Meat, during those harried couple of days I wanted to kick the high-maintenance vegetarians.

One of these was an executive from our office, a tall, gaunt woman with skin the color of bleached sand. I dutifully jotted down her (very detailed) instructions and then, the day of the event, pointed her out to the waiters and said, "See that woman in the blue suit? She gets the pasta primavera with the broccoli and red peppers."

Oh, how I suffered during those board meetings. To this day I despise the term "taking minutes" because a) it makes no sense and b) what it really means in lay terms is that you have to take a bunch of hot air and condense it down to intelligent matter.

I hate sitting still for long periods of time anyway, but sitting in a conference room from morning to night with a bunch of egotistical humans spouting off what they considered to be Lovely Thoughts was almost more than I could take. It brought back memories of when I was a child in church, terrified that I'd get up and scream just to break the monotony.

So I found ways to amuse myself. One of those ways was to decide what animals those board members looked like. My favorite was a woman with tightly permed white hair who had a narrow face and very skinny ankles. Need I tell you that she could have walked into any pet store and been sold as a poodle, no questions asked?

Then there was the man who looked so much like a brown bear I could hardly believe it. He had that same inquisitive where's-the-honey look in his eyes I imagine bears have. He also had that slightly edgy expression that warned if the restaurant I chose for dinner did not please him, growls would be heard and heavy paws would be felt at the backs of necks, or more specifically, at the back of my neck.

Regardless, I entertained myself so much with the animal game that sometimes it was all I could do not to laugh out loud.

Other than those meetings, work wasn't terrible—I knew how to sidestep my boss's temper tantrums for the most part and realized he was really more child than adult. It amazed me sometimes that he had a PhD because his writing skills were atrocious and I had to do a major overhaul on all his correspondence before it was ready to send out.

And while I missed my family terribly—that first Christmas alone with Morton was almost as sad as that Christmas at the Nettle farm had been—there was something rather horribly beautiful about the anonymity of a big city. Washington DC and I still didn't like each other very much, but she hid me well and I didn't have to feel much. I could disappear in the throngs of people going to and from work every day and I could forget, almost, the fields I missed so much and that I had ever worn a cape and apron.

I told no one about my Amish background. All I said was that I was from Pennsylvania, and was thankful people were too self-centered or lacking in curiosity to delve deeper.

But the gods couldn't quite let me forget completely, so one Saturday afternoon I was cleaning the bathtub when I got a call from a woman with whom I had worked at the Mennonite resort. How she got my number, I don't know, but after I had expressed my surprise at hearing from her she said in that rather malicious tone I remembered, "I heard you were in the DC area now and that your family isn't speaking to you and that...well...you might have some...problems."

It hurt me deeply, and my budding confidence staggered to the ground, like a newborn colt that is kicked down and trampled on before it has a chance to walk.

Chapter 31

I finally moved out of Morton's cluttered apartment into a place of my own. It had French doors that opened onto a small balcony facing tall fir trees. Trees! Nature, at last! It was a gift I did not take for granted, and while there were thousands of people living in apartments around me, at least in that tiny space I could pretend I was alone because I could see sky and the occasional squirrel dashing up a tree.

I was glad to put some space between Morton and me. He was becoming increasingly nasty, arriving home from work and taking whatever stress he had encountered that day out on me. It was also bliss to put things in their proper place rather than finding bills in the silverware drawer and piles of unfolded laundry on the dining room table. I hung up the pictures I had brought with me from home, and for a while I was happy, until the lease on Morton's apartment was up and he moved in with me and brought all his clutter with him.

And one day to my great surprise he proposed to me right there in the apartment, just like Ronnie had. No fanfare, no big romantic plans, just "Will you marry me" and then he brought out a jewelry box he had bought for me and in one of the drawers was a modest diamond.

I still didn't have any close friends and my family was gone, and so I accepted his proposal in the panicked fashion of a shipwrecked soul whose survival depends on accepting the rope that is tossed to her.

When I found out several months later that I was pregnant, terrified doesn't even begin to describe how I felt. I had gone from a virgin on her wedding day to this—living with my boyfriend, pregnant, and while at least I had a ring on my finger, I felt guiltier than I had ever felt in my life.

The thought of being a mother was completely overwhelming. Growing up I probably wasn't like other Amish girls in that I didn't think about babies or what my future would hold. Rather, I walked around feeling like my heart and my future were in a deep freeze. I felt like a freak then and, now that I was pregnant, I still felt like one.

The only contact I had made with my family was a brief visit with my sister Ruth Ann who lived with her husband and two children on Maryland's Eastern Shore. It was a difficult encounter and I didn't stay long. She was the only member of the family I told that I was getting married and asked her to please tell the others.

With the help of Morton's parents, my fiancé and I cobbled together plans for a wedding on July 6, 1997 on Cranberry Island, Maine, where his parents had a vacation home. And while I knew in my heart of hearts I was not in love with the man I was marrying, he represented something even more important to me at the time—security.

Morton's two brothers did not attend the ceremony but his parents did, and his father was a gift that day. He bustled about and was not only the best man but also the usher, and he seated the 80 or so guests, friends from the island they'd known for years who seemed delighted to be part of the ceremony and brought lovely gifts, pottery and such, from the island's gift shop.

After the reception at the local community center, Morton and I honeymooned our way down the New England coast. I enjoyed some of the picturesque fishing villages and charming inns we visited, and while it was not, perhaps, the

honeymoon of my dreams, at least it wasn't as traumatic as my
first one had been and with that I was content.

Chapter 32

I n August of 1997 we moved to a townhouse in Lake Ridge, Virginia, a suburb thirty miles south of Washington DC. I was ecstatic because now, instead of a few fir trees, I had a whole group of trees to look at that were nestled at the bank of the Occoquan River. The view soothed my soul and did much to help me get through some of my husband's mood swings.

I longed for my sisters, who all had children and could have offered me comfort and advice, but even though I shared with them the news that I was pregnant, none of them visited or called me so I slogged on alone. It was the oddest thing, being pregnant, like someone or something had taken over my body and I never knew what would happen next. There were magical moments, like the first time I heard the heartbeat, which brought tears to my eyes, and that first sonogram? How to describe that moment?

However, there were aspects of pregnancy I didn't enjoy much, like the clothes shopping. I wanted to ask the designers: if I don't want to wear a dress with a rounded collar sporting an appliquéd daisy when I'm not carrying a child, why would I want to start now?

I enjoyed the last trimester the most. The first one, all I wanted to do was make like a cat and sleep all day on a sunny (wide) windowsill; the second, I had to deal with those furtive "is she just getting fat or...is she pregnant?" glances; and finally, the third, well—I was boldly large, and when the baby kicked it made me laugh.

I knew I was carrying a boy which stunned me because originally I had thought I was carrying a girl, but gradually he and I bonded and I loved to sit on the sofa in the middle of the night and put my hand on my belly and pray for him. Those were holy moments, moments I would not trade for anything in the world

Morton and I were attending a church by then in Springfield, Virginia, and while I liked the pastor and his wife, I was still wary of church people after my experience at Ronnie's church. So I kept myself carefully guarded and did not attempt to befriend any of the women there.

I was shocked and touched when eight of them threw me a baby shower one Sunday after church. Those lovely women gave me some wonderful baby gifts that were both practical and adorable, and I hope they will be greatly rewarded for their kindness and generosity to the quiet woman with the lonely eyes.

Joshua was born on December 29, 1997, and when I look back at those first three months after we brought him home, I don't know whether to laugh or cry.

Morton went back to work immediately and neither my mother nor my sisters came to help, so I was left to cope by myself. I had thought that because I had five younger siblings, taking care of an infant would come naturally, but no! Oh, indeed no. My body was still reeling from the ordeal of childbirth and I had a lot of discomfort to deal with for a while, and breastfeeding? Oh, my gosh. When my milk first came in I looked up at the ceiling because I thought it was leaking. Not kidding.

Breastfeeding was so much more difficult than I thought it would be. There was something abjectly terrifying about knowing that I was *it* as far as sustaining my child's life was concerned and the first several days I was afraid he was going to starve because he didn't seem to be drinking very much and he looked so small and thin in that big crib.

While there were moments of incredible sweetness—like the morning I said something to Josh as he cooed in his infant seat on the table while I ate breakfast, and he laughed just at the sound of my voice, my heart melted!—the hardest thing for me about being a mother was the lack of time to be alone with my thoughts and of course, dealing with the ever-present guilt that I was a terrible mother for even thinking that way. But somehow, we struggled through and then, when he was three months old, it was time to go back to work. I felt sick at heart when I dropped my baby off at Barbara's, the babysitter I am convinced was a direct answer to prayer because she had that just-right combination of crisp authority mixed with a nurturing spirit. Even so, I will never forget how difficult it was to drop my precious bundle off at her house that cold March morning.

However, caring for an infant certainly put my job in perspective—it seemed ridiculously easy in comparison and even my boss seemed less of a challenge.

The year flew by and Josh's first Christmas was approaching. I ached to see my family and to introduce them to my child, and it felt like it was the right time to make peace with them all. I called my mother and she sounded subdued but glad she would be meeting her grandson.

The day dawned bright and clear, and my shoulders ached with tension as I loaded the gifts I had bought into the trunk of the car. I gave Josh his blanket and a stuffed animal to keep him company, and smiled at how adorable he looked in his car seat, with his mischievous eyes and rosy cheeks. I thought (hoped) that my parents would find him irresistible in spite of fate having dealt him such an unfortunate mother.

Five minutes down the road Morton announced he had to use the bathroom, so we stopped at the gym so he could go. He got back in the car and I felt quiet as we covered the miles north to Pennsylvania, and since my husband was in one of his surly moods, conversation seemed pointless anyway. Josh, thankfully, was fast asleep in his car seat.

We had been on the road for several hours when I said, "Can we stop please? I haven't had coffee yet, and I'd love a cup."

Morton complained, but turned off at the next exit, only to find that there were no restaurants immediately within sight and that he had to drive several miles before finding a McDonalds. He became so verbally nasty that I was afraid it would wake Joshua, but I knew from long practice that engaging in conversation when Morton was in that mindset would make me the target of even scarier rage, so I remained silent.

When we turned into my parents' driveway, I felt emotionally spent before we even walked in the front door. And then my son, who was usually so full of cheer and bonhomie, shrieked at the top of his lungs when my mother tried to hold him, and he pulled hard on Dad's beard when the unfortunate man came within range of Josh's determined fingers. Not a good start, one could say, but somehow it broke the ice. My siblings, though somewhat subdued, seemed happy to see us and my sisters especially exclaimed over Joshua, and he soon warmed up to them.

I couldn't believe how good it was to see them! My brothers and sisters are my anchor in life, and somehow, in my heart of hearts, I knew it was going to be okay with all of us. And my nieces and nephews…how I had missed them! I hugged them all, and there was a part of me that wanted to fling myself on the floor and weep that, at last, I was reunited with my family.

As I watched Morton charm them, I stifled the hurt that clearly, he could turn his social skills off and on at will. However, I was grateful that he was making an effort, and my siblings peppered him with questions about the political scene in Washington, D.C., and about his job as an analyst.

I am almost ashamed to admit how much I enjoyed the meal that day. Amish women, my friend, can *cook,* and one of my favorite Amish dishes is called "rühsht." It's a combination of stuffing and chicken or turkey and then baked (the secret is *lots* of butter) and they serve it for lunch at weddings. I've never made it, and don't want to—it's magic, and to learn now would be like having a unicorn as a pet. Regardless, I stuffed my face because I hadn't had rühsht in years, and also enjoyed the other fabulous dishes only my mother knows how to make.

(She has a special gift with seasonings, that woman. I howled in fury—well not quite, but you get the point—when my local Safeway advertised that they had "Amish potato salad" at their deli. I asked for a taste and let me tell you—no offense to Safeway, they do their best, but please! Amish potato salad? I think not. Darling, it takes a knowledgeable hand with the vinegar and sugar and years in a cape and apron to pull that off.)

We exchanged gifts, and snacked again at the end of the day, and then time to go. As I strapped my sleepy child into his car seat, I gave thanks that the bridge, that tenuous bond between my world and my family's, had been rebuilt. And I hoped that this time, it was built to last.

Chapter 33

A few years passed, precious and sometimes exhausting years of caring for a small child and working fulltime, and then one day my boss at the nonprofit announced he was retiring and it was time, again, to look for a new job.

After my interview with Scott, a partner at a large accounting firm in Washington DC, I wrote in my journal later that day, "He's a snake."

Giving snakes a bad name is what I did. Snakes slither, yes. They (occasionally) release venom and they (sometimes) behave in ways that scare us humans out of whatever wits we have left on this sorry planet. *However.* They are honest about it. They are snakes and act in a way that is expected of them.

I wasn't going to accept the position when Scott offered it to me, but when he left me a pleading voicemail practically begging me to work for him, and when a gigantic basket from Dean and DeLuca showed up at my doorstep filled with all kinds of goodies like wine, olive oil, chocolate, crackers, and gourmet cheeses...well, I capitulated and said I would.

However, my intuition had not failed me. That man was, in short, evil. One day we were coming back from a meeting in Chicago. As he tapped away on his laptop he said to me, "My day is not complete unless I write a nasty email to someone."

He was the most high-maintenance traveler I've ever met, before or since. He would only fly first class, which was fine, but there were only certain seats in first that were acceptable to his royal ass. I had to print out a copy of the first class cabin layout and then he'd pick which seat he wanted, and if it wasn't available? God help us all!

He traveled to New York City a lot and I always ordered limo service to meet him at the airport but if the car was even a few minutes late, he'd call me and ask, in that deadly way he had, *"Where the hell is my driver?"* I wanted to say, just once! that I had no control over traffic in NYC but refrained, with some difficulty.

There were many horrible events, too many and too tiresome to list. After a year and a half I finally got a new job, and when I handed the HR department my resignation letter the groans were so loud I felt rather cheered. I had heard that before I came Scott had gone through assistants like tissues, and that was confirmed when the HR director said to me, "Susie, we're sorry to see you leave, but I want you to know that no one can believe that you've lasted this long, and that you still have a smile on your face."

During my exit interview I said that while I had learned a lot from my boss, I felt psychologically damaged as a result of working for him. The next day I got a call from the company's corporate HR attorney.

"Susie," she said, "Why didn't you come to me? We hate to see you leave, and I could have transferred you to another department. I can't stand this guy and have a file an inch thick on him."

I wanted to ask her where the hell she had been when I needed her and besides, I hadn't even known of her existence. And why did they keep Scott on if he was so bad?

When I stepped into the lobby of the Willard Hotel on the first day of my new job, it sang to me. She—for this hotel was surely a she, an old belle who wore just the right amount of red lipstick and just the right clothes to accentuate her spectacular features—hugged me to her genteel bosom and said,

"You and I, honey, are going to have some *very* good times together."

(I am glad, now, that she did not tell me I would leave in dishonor and disgrace.)

The interview with the general manager, a Frenchman named Francois, had left me feeling rather breathless. I had had no prior experience with the quiet yet forceful charm of men like this, men who, generation after generation, knew just how to bow that oh-so-subtle bow that American men had kicked off the Mayflower along with their other ties to Old Europe. Everything he did was like watching art in motion. The way he wore his reading glasses, the way he glanced over them with large brown eyes set in a face with a strong jaw line and high cheekbones, and even the way he said my name, in that charming French accent of his, sounded romantic. His suit was designed to make him look like a man who is doing his clothes a favor by allowing them access to such a fine body. His hair was curly and, though gray, did not age him in the least. In fact, the only feature that defied all this perfection was his teeth. They were yellow and maybe even a little seedy.

When we had discussed wages, Francois had won that battle, hands down. The amount was less than I was worth and I knew it, and he probably knew it too. But he declared that out of compassion (!) he could not allow his executive assistant to earn more than some of the other important people in the hotel, and who was I to argue with that?

Money aside, I was going from a corporate mausoleum to a magnificent hotel full of life, activity, color. Except, perhaps, for the bevy of black and white pandas that greeted me my first day on the job.

I have always loved panda bears, but when one is glared at by a panda mug with cold eyes and an expression that reminded me of my judgmental Aunt Anna Mary, well, it's a bit much. In addition to the mug, there was a panda screensaver, panda poster, panda pillow, stuffed pandas numbering about twenty-six, panda mouse pad, panda necklace, panda figurine, and panda pens all belonging to my coworker Carrie, who sat at the desk across from me.

Carrie liked to chat, and one day she told me that a few months ago my new boss had kidnapped one of her stuffed pandas, and then sent her a ransom note and she'd cried—cried!—until she'd recovered her stuffed darling from where it had been shoved into the cushions of one of the sofas in the lobby.

I tried hard not to laugh when she told me that story, and after some months had passed and Francois and I were on excellent terms, I suggested to Carrie that we get back at him in the form of yet another bear which I found poetic and Carrie said she found it poetic, too.

When Josh was a baby someone had given him a stuffed brown bear that lay in front of the gas fireplace in our basement. That bear was so real-looking that even though I knew it was there, it still often startled me when I walked into the room.

I stuffed it into a large shopping bag and one day when Francois was at lunch, Carrie and I giggled together as we tucked it half in, half out of the kneehole of his desk. When that elegant Frenchman came back from lunch and caught sight of that bear, lying with great insouciance on his office floor, he screamed and jumped about a foot.

Then Carrie and her pandas departed and a slender woman with a great smile named Christina took her place. After we broke the ice, which took about six minutes tops, we laughed together (and occasionally raged, if the occasion called for it), and sometimes we crossed the street to our favorite deli, where she always ordered a grilled cheese sandwich and I a tuna salad on rye.

She loved hearing my "Josh stories" and then her parents, a lovely couple with kind hearts, offered us the use of their condominium in Florida the week between Christmas and New Year's. Josh and I went by ourselves and we were thrilled, just thrilled! The condo was fabulous, and on Josh's birthday we drove to Sarasota to have dinner with two of my brothers, who were staying at the house my parents own there (*shhh, it has electricity, don't tell the bishops!*).

One day Francois called me into his office.

"I ordered twelve shirts," he said.

Sure enough, he was surrounded by a sea of twelve white shirts, all supposedly custom-made to fit him.

"They are what is considered to be an athletic cut," he said as he closed the door, shrugged off his suit jacket and began unbuttoning his shirt.

"Wait!" I wanted to scream out. "No! No! No!"

But I stayed frozen in place while he peeled off his shirt and donned custom shirt number one.

I wanted to shout with laughter. It was extremely tight, and my boss was in good shape but that shirt looked *ridiculous* on him. What to say?

He frowned at himself in the mirror. "Too tight, you think?" he said.

"Maybe just a trifle," I replied.

"They're all going back!" he said with a muttered curse (in French). Then he picked up the phone and began a feud with the tailor that would last many months to come.

One day my boss asked me to have lunch with him in the employee cafeteria. Terror set in because before I met him I didn't realize what a big deal it was to hold your knife and fork properly. He had told me a story a few weeks prior of a couple he and his wife had dined with who had a teenage son who apparently *didn't do the right thing with the silverware.* My boss had been repelled, absolutely repulsed, by the sight.

As we rode the elevator down to the cafeteria I am sure my boss had no idea what was going on inside my head at that moment. He was probably thinking, "*Par bleu!* What should I put in my beautiful body today?" and I was thinking, "How the heck am I not going to make a fool of myself with the cutlery?"

And just so you know—this is yet another thing I treasure about my Amish background. A fork, my friends, is a utensil. You pick it up, you stab a piece of chicken or shoofly pie with it, you finish, done, everything well and good. No one is watching to see if the fork is at that precise place under the index finger. (Actually, an Amish bishop once raised the question whether forks should be used at all. One's feast, he felt, could be handled very well with just a spoon and knife, and the fork could be seen as worldly. The rest of the bishops in that council meeting apparently thought that was taking things just a Little Too Far so the fork stayed, but still.)

My boss and I chose our food from the small buffet and sat across the table from each other. He had a beautiful plate of greens and some fish and a few fries.

I had the same.

He picked up his fork.

I picked up mine.

He picked up his knife.

So did I.

And do you know, I believe in that one terrifying lunch I got it, without his ever knowing that he was teaching my uncultured self a thing. And I'd like to add—much has been said about the French, not all of it positive, but I'd like to toss into the mix that there is no one like the French the world over, I am convinced, who handle their forks and knives as artistically, as beautifully, as respectfully, as the French.

156

Chopsticks were yet another hurdle, and one of my coworkers laughed so hard at my efforts over a sushi lunch one day that I was determined I was going to learn, no matter what. Before that, I had always given up and attacked my sushi with a fork and knife, to the dismay of various waiters who had to be asked a second and sometimes third time when I asked for metal instead of wood. Now the time had come to learn and I knew it.

Oh, I had tried. That same coworker had shown me how to pick up the chopsticks, how to lovingly grasp that delicate piece of sushi, how to dip it into that soy sauce/wasabi mix, and then yum! eat it.

My sushi roll fell apart, the rice sort of collapsed into the soy sauce and the chopsticks laughed so hard I thought they'd crack. But then suddenly one day *voila*! I had it and felt really smug about my chopstick expertise until the day I went to lunch with a man who wore a beautiful business suit and looked like he had just stepped out of GQ. When we both broke out our chopsticks and he rubbed his together in a snappish way, first I thought *why?* and then Oh, forget it, no matter how hard I try I'll never be as good as I should be at this stuff. (I found out later it was to ensure there are no splinters in the wood. Oh, my God. Will it ever end?)

Then one of my coworkers in the food and beverage department of the hotel invited me to a wine tasting at one of the embassies in DC and I felt awed as we walked into the spectacular interior. It was all dark wood and marble and soft lights, and I was even more intimidated when I saw the crowd gather around the various tables where bottles of wine nestled in gracious splendor, waiting to be tasted by erudite palettes. I caught snatches of words like "a good nose...austere...complex...monolithic..." and by the time I reached the last table I felt horribly out of my element.

But that last bottle of wine took pity on me. It was a lovely bottle that had a pretty label in shades of pale pink and spring green, and it spoke to me. I held out my glass and a beautiful Latino woman poured me some white wine. I swirled it, and sniffed elegantly with my (Amish) nose.

"Ah!" I said to her. "This would be a perfect wine on a summer day, at a picnic, with brie and fresh bread and grapes…"

She nodded and smiled at me. *"Perfeccione!"* she said and we two, and the wine, were in complete accord.

Regardless, that experience taught me that my palette was about as un-erudite as it gets, so I signed up for a wine class thinking I'd learn something about vintages and so forth. I didn't feel like going, wanting to get out of DC after a long work day, but instead trudged up the street to a local hotel and descended to the conference room where round tables were set with eight wineglasses at each setting. (Those glasses almost did me in. Let's just say there were more goblets in the room than people, and leave it at that.)

I got through the whites, and left before the lecture on the reds even began. I have the utmost respect for people who know their wines—I've met some brilliant sommeliers who delighted me with their knowledge—but for now, I think I'll stumble happily along and drink *vino* when I have the opportunity and pray I never embarrass myself too much.

My great equalizer is champagne—I have yet to drink a champagne I don't like. I bought a bottle on sale at Wal-Mart last Christmas for about three bucks and I think I enjoyed it (almost) as much as the bottle of Dom Pérignon given to me by a man I met at the Willard Hotel who was *beautiful.* Cinderella's prince. The tall, dark, and handsome kind of which fairytales are made.

When he rose from the sofa in the Willard's lobby I wanted to stop and stare, as one does at a spectacular piece of art. This was not a man one should ever take in at a single glance. No, he required better than that, and if his expression showed that he was aware of the impact he was having on me, I didn't begrudge him that knowledge.

However, I had worked all day and you know how it is—some mornings when you walk out the door you feel anywhere from good to full-out fabulous, by lunchtime the sheen has worn down some, and by about three o'clock in the afternoon the fluorescent lights and hours in front of a computer screen have taken their toll and you feel more like a greasy slob than a hottie.

Rob and I had exchanged emails, quite a few actually, and spoken on the phone often prior to his visit to the hotel because he was hosting a dinner for some prestigious food and beverage directors and he needed a liaison at the hotel to introduce him to our chef and help with the menu. Somehow he ended up with me.

He was introducing a new vintage of Dom Pérignon to the food and beverage directors and was also hosting a party to celebrate that spectacular champagne. It was a big deal because while they were planning to introduce it to various cities, Washington, D.C. was the first.

"Hello, Susie," Rob said, and kissed me on the cheek.

"Hello," I said back, and kissed him on the cheek, too. He smelled good, as of course he would.

"Did you check in?" I asked as he gathered his suitcase and followed me to the elevator.

"Yes," he said as he opened the door of his suite and gestured for me to go in. "Thank you for upgrading me. This is spectacular."

"You're welcome," I said and went to shake his hand goodbye but he hugged me instead and paused just a beat.

"How would you like to come to the Dom Pérignon party tonight?" he said.

"Oh! Me? Are you sure?"

"Of course I'm sure. I'll have to be there early, but here's an invitation and the address." He flashed me a smile and my knees wobbled.

I walked back to my desk in a rosy glow. I was stunned to be invited to the party. He had told me about it during one of our phone conversations, and it sounded like it would be one of the most elite events of its kind all year: select politicians, socialites, wealthy entrepreneurs, and business tycoons would attend—and now me.

I called Morton and asked if he could watch Josh, and then made an appointment at Allous, the beauty salon next door to the Willard, before rushing home for a quick shower and hopping into my black cocktail dress. I drove back into the city and asked the owner of Allous to do something special with my hair. He blew the fine strands out to something resembling glamorous, and I hailed a taxi and was on my way.

That party shall remain in my mind as one of the most original, breathtaking events I have ever attended.

I got out of the taxicab and walked up a long flight of white marble steps. A waiter in a tuxedo handed me a flute of the most delicious champagne I have ever tasted—it was the essence of summer, and strawberries, and passion, in one beautiful glass.

Feeling rather giddy after just a few sips, I walked into the room, which had been decorated sparsely, yet every single element was perfect. There were people everywhere, some well-dressed and some who just thought they were, but it didn't matter because they all had the ultimate accessory: a glass of Dom in their hands.

Rob greeted me, looking impeccable in a dark suit, white shirt, and sexy tie, and introduced me to three of his female coworkers, who were all very kind to me, given my non-celebrity status.

And then the inevitable happened—one of the wealthy bachelors attached himself to me, not because he wanted to flirt with me but because he wanted to pour his heart out about a recent breakup and he had just seen his ex at the movies with another man and...he had a chin that looked somewhat given to wobbling and I was really afraid he was going to start crying, not that there's anything wrong with shedding a few tears, I do it occasionally myself, but please! At a Dom Pérignon party!

I tried to shake him off and was feeling less and less compassionate toward this well-dressed leech and more and more impatient. Finally, all I could think of to console him was to feed him some green grapes from my plate, and of course, that was when I looked up and caught Rob's disapproving eye on me.

Finally after about three glasses of champagne and a final glance around the elegant room, I decided it was time to leave. I shook off the leech and found Rob close to the entrance. He took my hand and for a few breathtaking moments I felt desire there, but maybe it was just my imagination, and the champagne, talking. I thanked him for a glorious evening and walked back down the steps with my head held high.

Damn! Sometimes it feels good to color outside the lines, socially speaking, doesn't it?

Rob and I continued to stay in touch and I'm ashamed to say I developed quite a crush on him. However, I blame him, too. I had received another job offer and was considering leaving the Willard. One day Rob came into the lobby, unannounced, all the way from Los Angeles, and when the concierge called and said he was asking for me, I fluffed my hair, applied fresh lip gloss, and waltzed my way down to the lobby.

He didn't even say hello, he just grabbed me around the waist and kissed me, and I'm not talking about a quick peck— I'm talking about a full-out kiss in the lobby of that grand belle of a hotel. I think it's one of the few times in my life that I understood the meaning of the word *swoon*, because darling, when he released me I nearly did. Swoon.

We didn't say much, and after a few minutes I went back to my desk with my cheeks burning and my heart racing. I didn't accept the job offer after all, and Rob and I went to happy hour one night some months later when he was in town.

It was a disaster. He was distant and cold, and my crush on him died on the vine that night.

But hey, it was good while it lasted and I still think fondly of him. I enjoyed the bottle of Dom he gave me one New Year's Eve I spent alone. I hope he won't be too mad when he finds out I downed it with a few slices of leftover pizza.

Another memorable occasion at the Willard was the day I met former President Clinton. I was already feeling pretty full of myself because I had met Tom Cruise's eyes the day before, not because he was trying to or anything but rather because I was standing in the Willard's Peacock Alley, the famous promenade between the front and back lobbies that had felt the footsteps of President Lincoln, Mark Twain, and many other renowned personages. Suddenly the double doors to the Willard Room, the hotel's restaurant, snapped open and there he stood! Tom Cruise.

His eyes, as I said, met mine for one startled instant and then he turned to his right and headed to the back lobby area.

I have always prided myself on not being a celebrity worshiper like so many in this crass world of ours. Oh, yes, I've said to myself more than once, they're *just people* no better than I am, but all that commonsense thinking fell by the wayside and I was swept toward Mr. Cruise with the crowd of people who followed after him. I felt rather dizzy and not in control of my ability to choose—I wanted to see more of him! I did! I did!

He disappeared into the elevators with his entourage and I walked back down the stairs, a humbler woman for the experience.

The next day it was my job to be the employee liaison present while they filmed the movie *Minority Report* and it was one of those times when I asked myself the question, how did I get here? In Washington DC, in a room that held Steven Spielberg, Tom Cruise, and former President Clinton? A fabulous way to spend a couple of work hours, but then it was time to go back to reality and my desk so I quickly checked emails and phone messages and was heading to the front lobby to deliver some letters to Guest Relations when I realized that the Secret Service agents stationed in Peacock Alley were standing at attention, so I sort of melted against the wall, not wanting to get into their bad graces.

Then the double French doors opened, with President Clinton at the fore and an entourage behind. At first he turned left to head to the lobby, but then he spotted me, standing between the two Secret Service agents. He turned right and walked over to me and shook my hand. Of course, like an idiot, I was scrambling to think should I address him as Mr. President even though he was former when he said, "Hello, how are you?"

All I said, in what was probably the worst faux pax in the history of this country, "Fine! How are you?"

He didn't seem to mind, and off he went and I stood there for an extra few minutes feeling rather snookered.

But even more exciting than meeting President Clinton was the day one of my former Weavertown Mennonite School classmates came to the Willard and had lunch with me. How to describe that moment for a woman who has never had a high school reunion and has been shunned by all her teenage friends? I don't know how Mahlon Stoltzfus found out I worked at the Willard, but when I met him at the concierge desk and he hugged me, I was happier than I can explain.

Mahlon had always been athletic and handsome and still was. He bought me lunch, and I'd like to say to him—*Thank you, dear friend of my childhood, you will never know what that meant to me.*

Chapter 34

Eventually, Francois was transferred to another property overseas and I inherited another French boss. He was the opposite of the other one physically—where Francois had been tall, strong-jawed, and attractive, Pierre was small, thin, and rather pale and weedy in appearance. And yet, he had that suave thing going on that so many of the French seem to have, that ability to wear just the right clothes with just the right air.

The first time we spoke he ran down the list of things he expected and, like the good listener I aspire to be, I repeated back some of what he said, i.e., so what I'm hearing you say is so and so and so and so.

Then the trouble between us began. I said, "And now I'd like to tell you what is important to me." That man looked at me with the disdain of a farmer who hears the manure he's mucking out from the cow stable give utterance and request one or two things, like respect.

I said, "It is important to me that we keep the lines of communication open and if there is something you'd like done differently, please tell me. I realize this is a high-stress job, but as your executive assistant I expect to be treated with courtesy and obviously I will also communicate with you if I am uncomfortable about something."

Oh, my gosh. The look on that man's face!

He introduced me to his guillotine mentality the very first week. He had invited all his managers to a meeting in one of the conference rooms, and I attended as well so I could take notes for him. There were round tables scattered about and it was rather touching to see the eager yet apprehensive look on my coworkers' faces because in the hotel business, like most companies I suppose, changes usually occur so that the new boss can put his or her stamp on the place.

My new boss steamed up to the microphone and "Please! Give me your ideas! I am open to anything you want to say, any thought on how we can improve the Willard Hotel! Do not be afraid…"

So the employees spoke their opinions, and since I'd worked at the place for years and knew many of the people in that room, and how hard they worked and how loyal they were—the Willard, sweet old belle that she was, inspired that—I thought many of their ideas very good indeed. But when my new boss and I reached the executive office, he took off his (impeccable) suit jacket, hung it up on a hanger, flicked a speck of dust off his right shirt sleeve, and said, "I want to fire…" He spewed a list of names—people I knew were hard workers and made valuable contributions to the hotel, and then added, "I didn't like what they had to say."

To say I reeled where I stood is an understatement. I was also disgusted, and something in French that I'm sure would describe my emotion perfectly, oh yes maybe it's how the guy felt who had the unhappy job of collecting the heads when they fell off the blade of the guillotine. After I caught my breath I said, "Pierre! This is America! You can't fire people just because you don't like their ideas."

He looked at me with complete disinterest, turned his back and walked to his desk, where he opened his top desk drawer and said with a peevish expression, "Can you order me *gold* paper clips?"

Oh, those were hard days. I had ordered some high-end office supplies for Pierre because when he embarked on our fine shores the Frenchman was angry that his stapler didn't match his scissors. And the gold paper clips? Do you have any idea how hard it is to find those in this country? We, as a group, seem to accept that *silver!* is the popular choice and my search for gold took me hours and hours and ran into days, actually, but finally one day I handed him several boxes of *gold* paper clips.

Also, I wrote a lot of letters for him; however, I was not allowed to use a single contraction. For example:

Dear Ambassador _____*,*

We are indeed honored that you are gracing us with your presence and hope that ~~you'll~~ *you will enjoy your stay. Please* ~~don't~~ *do not hesitate to ask if I may assist you in any way.*

Kind regards,

Amazing how many times we use the humble apostrophe. It took me quite a few panicky moments of realizing OMG I did it again and said isn't instead of is not, etc.

Pierre was quite fond of celebrities and anyone in power, but sometimes that backfired on him. He insisted not only on greeting them but also saying goodbye, and that annoyed some of our resident CEO-types, because the last thing they wanted was to be halted in the lobby by a weedy Frenchman first thing in the morning.

It made Guest Relations crazy, too, and they often complained to me that he insisted they call the rooms of these moguls and find out just when they'd be in the lobby checking out. Frankly, I'd feel the same way if I were those guests—when in a hotel I like my peace and quiet. That's one of the beautiful things about hotels—peace and quiet—and even if I were some schmuckity-schmuck, I'd say Please! I'll check out when I'm ready, and don't need a bon voyage.

One day I got a call from a major corporation's travel service. "Susie," the guy said, "this is Joe. Our CEO doesn't want to come back to the Willard again because last time he was so harassed by your general manager that unless you can assure me it won't happen again, he's going to stay at the Four Seasons. He's always loved the Willard and doesn't want to switch…is there anything you can do?"

I pondered for a second or two. I loved the Willard, too, and hell yes, I was scared, but my loyalty was to the place, not the man who, I thought, should learn what American corporate types really wanted. I would have been glad to explain it to him had he been willing to listen.

"Leave it to me, Joe," I said.

This particular CEO traveled under an alias and was always accompanied by several bodyguards, and it was a comfort that my boss wouldn't see the guy's real name on our guest list.

I hurried down Peacock Alley toward the lobby.

"Good morning!" I said to the Guest Relations manager, a tired-looking woman with stiff blond hair and a nervous smile, but then, many of us sported nervous smiles during that time.

"Belinda," I said, "The _____ CEO is coming to the hotel on Thursday and does *not* want to be greeted by our boss, nor does he wish to be bid adieu by him. He wants to be left *completely alone.*"

She gasped. "But Susie! If Pierre finds out! I'll lose my job! He greets and says goodbye to *all* the CEOs and celebrities if he can."

I smiled at her and hoped it convinced her. "Blame me if anything goes wrong," I said. "But I promised the company I'd handle it, and we're going to lose a major piece of business if Pierre bugs that poor man just one more time."

So we laid our plans, and when the guy showed up with his bodyguards, everyone left him alone. That beleaguered CEO had what I hope was the deepest, sweetest night of sleep in his life at our fine hotel. He must have, because we kept the business. And my boss never found out what I had done.

December rolled around, and along with it, the dreaded mailing of the holiday card. I am sure assistants everywhere will shudder with me in collective horror at the thought of this hideous task and I won't belabor it here—it sucks, and we'll leave it at that. However, my boss had about a thousand people he wanted cards sent to and a large majority of them were international; the guy had contacts from all over the world, and the addresses were a *mess*. He'd brought them with him from France, and I cleaned them up the best I could but in some cases there were email addresses where mailing addresses should be, that sort of thing. I didn't have time to prepare all those labels so our sales and marketing department came to the rescue and offered to give the addresses to a service they used for some of the mass mailings they did.

I breathed a sigh of relief when Pierre agreed that they could help, and while I knew I'd still have to stuff the envelopes and do all the rest of it, at least I wouldn't have to create the labels myself.

When they came back, I pasted the labels on the envelopes and noted there were still some with incomplete addresses, so I put those aside to show my boss so he could advise me—and I'd like to explain now why so many people pant to become U.S. citizens. It has puzzled many of us Americans but honey, it is for the beauty, the pristine wonderfulness of our *zip codes* and our *telephone numbers*. The former, five digits, and our telephone numbers are always 3 digits-3 digits-4 digits. Always, my friend, always.

Other countries' telephone numbers are, frankly, a mess. Sometimes it's something like 7756 43406 11 and then sometimes you blink because you see one that's a crisp 556 7893 or something like that so you never really *know* if you have the right amount of digits. And zip codes? Please! Don't get me started!

So, anyway, I needed my boss's help because there were a lot of incomplete addresses and I had no idea how I could locate the information I needed.

I handed him the list and waited while he glanced over it. Then he looked at me, and his glasses did too, and they both thought I was scum, just scum, for not instantly! figuring it all out.

"This was your first project, Susie," he said. "And you failed. I am very disappointed in you."

He helped with some but not all, and the following Sunday I came in and worked all day, hours I was not paid for, fixing those damn labels.

But that was nothing compared to what my boss did shortly thereafter.

He was on a three-week vacation in Paris and I had a parent-teacher conference scheduled at 5:00 p.m. on a Tuesday during my boss's absence. I emailed him about it and also told the manager on duty that I would need to leave the office early that day so I could make it to my son's school in time.

When my boss returned, he called me into his office and closed the door. With a sour expression on his face he said, "Just because you're a mother doesn't mean you can leave the office whenever you want to."

Ever feel like the earth is shaking under your feet and that all the roots of your hair are screaming in fury?

I looked right back at him and said, "Pierre, I hope you're not expecting an apology because I'd do the same thing again. My son's education is a priority for me."

I turned and walked out of his office and fled to the ladies room where I shook for a while, in anger and in a trembling dread that I'd be fired.

Oh, yes—I felt the blade of the guillotine nick my neck that day.

Chapter 35

I loved so many things about the Willard, but most especially the variety of nationalities of the people with whom I worked.

One day at lunch in the cafeteria a woman from Iceland described her country with such fond affection and such careful detail that I instantly put it on my (long!) list of places I wanted to visit.

Then there was my Russian friend, a waiter who recorded some classical music for me and labeled it simply, "For you." He stopped me in the hallway one day and said, "Susie, you are like the moon, beautiful and sweet." I still consider it one of the best compliments I have ever received.

Another cherished coworker was the Filipino man who emptied my wastepaper basket every morning. He took such pride in his work and was always dressed beautifully in a neat vest, white shirt, and black pants. We always smiled at each other and, without words, communicated, "You are a treasure on the earth."

It hurts me, even now, to tell you what happened to my two dear friends and a number of others as well.

I came in one morning to find that they had been fired after twenty years of loyal service. I don't think it is putting it too strongly to say it felt like something evil had entered the place and massacred the most precious part of it; the light died out of that old belle's eyes and she and I mourned together and still do.

Everyone was talking about it. I was told the Russian waiter had eaten some leftover food, food that would have been thrown away after a banquet. He had worked a double shift and the cafeteria was closed, and he was hungry.

The Filipino? He had eaten half a cheeseburger that he had gotten at the employee cafeteria, and then wrapped the other half in a napkin and taken it out with him and was caught on the way out and fired.

The story was that the powers that be didn't want to pay those dear people who had served so faithfully all those years the benefits due them as long-term employees and so my boss conspired with Human Resources to get rid of them.

I don't know how I made it through that day, but when I woke up the next morning it was with the knowledge that I could not stand by and do nothing. Even at the cost of losing my job I couldn't, so I made an appointment with the president of the controlling company of the hotel, the man whose family owned the majority of the Willard's shares, and we met for coffee at a Caribou a few blocks from the Willard.

While we stood in line to order, he opened the conversation by telling me he didn't think much of Pierre, and felt he was just using the Willard to "climb the company ladder." And so I felt more comfortable pouring out my story over coffee at a table by the window.

"Those people did not deserve to be fired," I said, and tried hard not to let the tears that were in my heart reach my eyes. "Please, can't you do something?"

Short story is that he and his father, who was the chairman of the company, did nothing, and I heard through the grapevine that wind of our conversation reached the ears of the vice president of the hotel's managing company, the corporation that employed all of us. This vice president was a sleazy man with white hair and a greasy smile, and since my boss was his hire I fought back the bile of fear every day for a while.

Then came the furniture disaster. My boss ordered some furniture for the lobby and Peacock Alley, furniture he had imported from France to the tune of three quarters of a million dollars, and it was a joke. And I mean that literally—people laughed when they saw it because in the hotel's magnificent lobby it looked like dollhouse furniture. It was too small, with short, stick-like legs on the tables, sofas and chairs, and even our clients commented on it.

My boss liked to spend money and wasn't the excellent budgeter the previous general manager had been. Before we knew it, even though business was booming, we were in a budget crisis. Guess how he fixed it? There were twelve of us administrative assistants in the hotel. We were all told we were forced to take off one day a week indefinitely, which of course is a twenty percent cut in pay. In my case, I was the only one in the executive office doing that job so I squeezed five days of work into four, and that was that.

One morning I lay on my closet floor crying because I simply did not have enough in my bank account to cover my bills and I knew, much as I loved the Willard and the people I worked with, I had to look for a new job, not only because I needed the money but also because I could no longer bear to work for a man who treated people like my boss did.

I found a new job, and couldn't believe how sad I felt when I turned in my resignation. I wrote a letter to the CEO of the managing company explaining why I was leaving, and gave my boss and HR two weeks notice.

I was looking forward to spending those last precious days with the many wonderful friends I had made there, people like my friend Katie, and Meredith, women I had bonded with and whom I had finally told about my Amish background, and after their initial shock, they'd handled it perfectly, teasing me once in a while but never in a cruel way.

174

Three days after I turned in my resignation, I was greeted by our grim-faced human resources director, a woman who took evil in the workplace to a whole new level. This was a woman who had no business calling herself a human resources director because there wasn't an ounce of human compassion in her, at least in my experience. Not only did she seem to derive pleasure from conspiring with Pierre to fire people who didn't deserve it, she also made it clear that she could not have cared less what any of us employees faced in our personal lives, no matter how traumatic the event.

You may have watched the news coverage about the terrible tragedy that took the lives of some Amish schoolchildren in Lancaster County in the fall of 2006? When a gunman opened fire on those little girls? I have tears in my eyes as I write this, because one of the little girls, Naomi Rose Ebersol, was related to me on the Fisher side. On the day of her funeral I was crying so hard at my desk that I could not even think about finishing my workday.

My boss was out, so I emailed the human resources director explaining the situation and how I felt, and she didn't write back, nor did she ever offer any condolences. So in my opinion she should be banned from *ever* bearing the title of anything with "human" in it.

She ushered me into Pierre's office and they both looked at me with accusing eyes.

"You need to leave, now," my boss said.

"Why?" I said.

"We know about the letter you wrote to Corporate."

I said a few things, just a very few, and what had begun as a glorious job, my best ever, ended in disgrace and humiliation.

I gathered up my purse and few personal items and as I walked out the back entrance I bid my sweet belle, the grandest of the grand hotels in the United States of America, a tearful, heartbroken goodbye.

Chapter 36

I t is very hard for me to write about the period of time when Morton and I separated and eventually divorced.

The deterioration of our marriage began much earlier, but it all came to a boil when I was employed by Denny, one of the partners from the accounting firm where I had worked, who had started his own consulting company.

The office was in Fairfax County, Virginia, and I was thrilled because I had an office of my own. There were only four of us employees at that time, one of whom was Celine, the chief financial officer, who was a tall woman with unusual turquoise eyes. She often came in late, and one day when I was there by myself and the boss was out, she stopped by my office.

"Hi, Celine," I said as I looked up from the Excel spreadsheet I was working on. The sheen of the new office space had long since passed and I was numb with the agony of staring at numbers on a computer screen. I was now doing billable client work and wallowing in spreadsheets all day wasn't my thing, at all. I needed some contact with the outside world to make work tolerable.

Some weeks earlier Denny had given me some of Celine's work to fix. She had tried a new system and made a mess of things he said, and while I appreciated his faith in me, I felt a frisson of fear that he was asking me, the executive assistant, to fix our CFO's work. However, he was the boss and I did what he asked.

"Who do you think you are?" Celine hissed.

It was one of the times when silence seemed the better part of valor. The correct answer would have been Susie E.

Fisher, the middle initial standing for Esh which is my mother's maiden name, but somehow I felt the question was rhetorical so I kept my mouth shut.

She stepped closer to my desk and her face took on that blotchy shade of red not recommended if high blood pressure runs in the family.

"You are an idiot," she screamed. "You don't know even know how to use Excel."

Of all the things I've been accused of in my life, this was maybe the most deserved. I know the basics but ask me to do one of those cool formulas and I'm lost.

"I know!" I said. "You're so much better at Excel than I am!"

She looked like an engine that has gone into neutral unexpectedly but she thrust it back into drive and tried another tactic.

"And you're sleeping with Denny!" she shouted. "He wanted me before *you* came along!"

I ache for my Amish life at these times, I really do. I'll bet none of my former Amish friends have ever been accused of sleeping with their bosses because a) they don't have bosses since most of them work at home, taking care of their kids and cooking and cleaning and b) they have the good sense to stay away from these types.

It was true that our unmarried boss had made a quiet pass at me at lunch one day. I elegantly refused and he equally elegantly accepted my refusal. All nonverbal, all gracious. No lawsuits, no fuss, just a girl not wanting a boy who signed her paycheck and that was that.

"Celine, no, I am not sleeping with Denny."

And then she said something that convinced me she needed professional help, and fast.

"And you are not my mother!"

178

Whoa! Of all the things I've been accused of this was most unlikely because she was older than me by a few years, and I could gladly agree that I had not, indeed, given birth to her nutty self. Thank God for that!

"Celine, I think you need to leave my office."

She pushed her way closer to my desk, where I was shaking internally in spite of my calm front, and for a terrified moment I thought she was going to hit me. There was a crackling sound in the air after she finally stalked off and it was the sound of my job going up in smoke. It would be my word against hers, and she was the CFO while I was only the jack of all trades in the office, the one who had called Verizon and gotten the phone lines installed and purchased china and gotten our 401(k) set up and did payroll and watered the plants and typed letters and answered phones and lately, done billable client work.

The next day I shared with Denny what happened and fully expected to be let go on the spot, but I underestimated the good heart of that man. He waited until Celine was out and then asked me to join him while he called his attorney on the speaker phone in his office. I shared with her what had happened and that I did not feel safe alone in the office with Celine. The attorney advised my boss that under no circumstances was he to leave the two of us alone together, and a week later Denny fired Celine, CFO or not.

He hired a few more people, one a brilliant Yale grad with a finance degree, and a few weeks later over dinner I said to Morton, "I don't think Denny needs me anymore. I'm so bored and would love to focus on writing for a while…how would you feel if I'd take a few months off from work before I look for a new job?"

I was bored not because I didn't have enough to do but because Excel was weaving its insidious, numbing energy into my brain and I felt myself growing weaker and weaker, creatively speaking, every day. I was afraid eventually I'd forget I had a right side of the brain, it was becoming so dusty with misuse.

I was shocked when Morton, a man who was fond of his creature comforts and the income I brought in, said, "Okay. I think we can make it for a while without your income."

I sealed the death of my marriage with that decision but didn't know it at the time, and I turned in my two-week notice the following Monday.

Denny gifted me with a bottle of champagne and a beautiful scarf, and another chapter of my life ended.

Chapter 37

A t first it was bliss. I attended a four-day creative writing seminar taught by a bearded, mustachioed man with a rather pompous air, but I drank in his jeweled words like a hummingbird sipping on the finest flower in creation. For the first time since I was fourteen years old, not counting maternity leave and my jobless period after I fled Lancaster County, I had no boss and no occupation other than focusing on my creative side.

We were in the perfect setting for the occasion—a cabin surrounded by trees, and I loved hearing the birds chirping as I sat in the woods, tablet on my lap and pen in my hand, working on one of the many challenging assignments we were tasked with during the four days.

There were five of us in the class and I felt intimidated by the talent and artistry the other four women displayed. When it was my time to read my work, I felt very small and shivery inside, but they were so encouraging, I soon got over that. However, when I spent individual time with the instructor to show him a portion of a novel I had written, I felt almost nauseated with fear because he was very hard on all of us.

I sat silently as he scanned the pages, and while he didn't shake my hand and say "This is wonderful," he didn't spit on my manuscript either.

One of the best gifts that came out of that seminar was a friendship with a woman named Aileen who loved high fashion and was one of the bubbliest, most positive people I've ever met. Somehow she managed that without being annoying, which I think is quite a feat. She and I are still friends, and it is thanks to her that I can pronounce the Dolce in Dolce and Gabanna. I also credit her for sending me some fabulous shoe websites, where I found footwear that kept Little Susie very happy indeed.

In short, the class was a lovely interlude but all that was shattered only a few weeks later when Morton came home in an ugly mood one day and said, "What! You've only been looking for a job *half* the day?"

"But Morton," I stammered. "I thought you said it was okay for me to write for a while."

The tone of his voice wasn't that surprising; he had a habit of lashing out now and then when it suited him. But the subject of my looking for work was a surprise since we'd agreed to a two-month break for me.

He stormed out of the room and then he began making crazy purchases we didn't need, like a set of expensive kitchen knives. The stress of his rage drained my creative productivity so I gave up trying to write and began looking for a job in earnest.

By Christmas I was feeling desperate, and then Morton raised the topic of whether we were good together and maybe we should think about separation. I tail-spun into full-out panic. I was aware that our marriage was far from perfect, but I had no income and a four-year-old son to support. What if Morton left me? What would I do?

Christmas that year was a sad affair. I gave Morton a Macy's gift certificate which seemed impersonal but it was all I could afford. And since we had had always had separate accounts I had no access to his money, but it was important to me to acknowledge our relationship somehow.

A few weeks after Christmas I needed the stepladder that we kept in the storage room of the basement. I hated that area because Morton was a hoarder and the room was so full there was hardly room to walk. I shoved aside some of the items, still looking for the stepladder, when suddenly I gasped. There was a new microwave, salt and pepper shakers, dishes, and other things one needed to start up a new place.

I stood frozen for a few seconds next to the water heater, my heart pounding. When had he done this? How long had my husband been planning to leave me?

When Morton came home from work I asked him what it meant.

He shrugged and said, "I used the gift certificate you gave me toward that stuff. I don't think this is working out, Susie."

The following week I made an appointment with a therapist, and so did Morton. I was dealing with intense guilt because while I had loved Morton once, I knew when I married him that I was using him to provide me and the child I was carrying with the security I craved. So how could I be angry with him for wanting out of our marriage?

It wasn't the first indication I had that there were problems, of course, but I tried to make do with what we had, until a trip to St. Lucia when Josh was two years old cracked my wall of denial, cracks I did not want to see but once they were there I could not ignore them.

Morton's parents came to Virginia to babysit Josh, and it was supposed to be a romantic vacation for us.

I love the ocean at any time but that first night on the island was especially beautiful, with a warm breeze and a full moon, and I wanted to take a walk on the beach. However, Morton wanted to watch a hockey game and I waited while he raged at the TV and the universe in general because he couldn't get ESPN. I remained silent until he was absolutely certain, after calling the front desk and fiddling with the remote for the hundredth time, that hockey was not an option and then I timidly asked if he wanted to join me outside. He grouched about it but came along, and we made our silent way out to the beach.

"It's a lovely night," I said as the waves did that loyal thing they always do, that reassuring, timeless splash against the shore that always seems to restore my faith in God as creator, helper, friend.

"Yes it is," my husband said. "But I'd rather be watching hockey."

Points for honesty, but it hurt just the same.

The next day along with about twenty other tourists we took a catamaran ride to another island. Morton was nitpicky and borderline nasty to me all the way there and I shut down and was very quiet, feeling unspeakably sad that in the midst of all that beauty my heart was so heavy.

We toured a coffee plantation, which I found charming, and on the way back, we were provided with snorkeling equipment and told to go for it. I had not snorkeled before but Morton had, and he was impatient with me as I struggled to figure out how to use the equipment. Once in the water I panicked and felt like I couldn't breathe, and finally I gave up, told Morton to enjoy himself, and scrambled back on the boat.

Not two minutes later I was joined by an athletic, good-looking guy who looked like he was happy to get out of the water too. I felt subdued and not at my gregarious best, but I told him my name when he asked—he was a Canadian named Kelly—and responded to his amiable attempt to make conversation as best I could.

Then he said, "I realize I have absolutely no business saying this, but I couldn't help but notice how your husband was treating you today."

I was so shocked I looked him full in the eyes for the first time and his blue eyes gazed sympathetically back into mine.

"You deserve better than that," he said quietly. "Life is too short to accept that kind of treatment from anyone, let alone from the man who should love you the most."

I stayed silent, digesting his words. Then Morton came back on the boat but I didn't move over to sit with him, and Kelly and I chatted all the way back to St. Lucia about casual subjects.

Morton scolded me later for conversing with "that man"—goodness knows how he would have behaved had he known what the guy had said to me while Morton was flapping his way around the Caribbean—but I hardly noticed because Kelly's words kept tapping away in my head, unwanted truths that might eventually lead me down a path I did not want to go.

There were other episodes, times when I had endured Morton's outbursts because to fight them scared me too much. They were never related to an argument we were having; rather, he struck at me verbally out of the blue and often I'd sit at my desk at work feeling like I had a black eye. After really vicious assaults, I felt like I had bruises all over my body.

But who would understand? On the surface my husband was great—he had a steady job, was well-educated, and never cheated on me to my knowledge. And always, after he was nasty, he'd be extra nice for a week or two to the point where I wondered if I had imagined his bad behavior. But then the cycle would start all over again.

One morning I told a woman I worked with how I felt after a particularly nasty conversation with him. She looked at me with a blank expression and said, "You have everything."

Case closed, and point made: if you can't see where a verbal fist struck, the bruises aren't real.

Josh, my son, yanked me out of my semi-denial one afternoon when I was putting towels in a new portable linen closet we had bought.

"Look, Josh!" I said. "We're giving our towels a new home!"

He studied me as I folded a thick white towel and placed it on the bottom shelf.

"Well," he said in the pragmatic tone he had even at four years old, "Why don't we give Dad a new home, so he can be angry at someone else."

I can't say I got a lot out of my therapy sessions but it helped to talk out what was going on. Eventually Morton's therapist wanted to meet with me, so one cold December night I sat next to my husband in a stuffy office with low light and a man with a trimmed beard who wore the expression adopted by many of his profession, i.e., I'm here for you. Speak, my children, speak.

The words tumbled out of my mouth before I could stop them. "I feel like a battered wife," I said, and when the therapist asked me why, I explained how sometimes, when Morton was at his angriest and lashed out at me verbally, I felt that even though you couldn't see the bruises, they were there nonetheless.

When we returned to the house, Morton raged at me as I cowered on the sofa.

"I've never laid a hand on you!" he shouted. "What do you mean, battered wife!"

"I...I don't know," I said. "I wasn't planning to say that."

The following weeks were some of the most hellish of my life. My sister gave me a James Dobson pamphlet to read on divorce and I sobbed my way through it until it felt like all the tears had been wrenched from my body by an unseen force, a force that defined the world in good and evil with no gray.

Yes, I knew it did incalculable damage to children when their parents divorced. Yes, I knew it was better for couples to stay together, if they could.

Where was God in the midst of all this mess? I was already divorced once, and the thought of going through it again was so agonizing I couldn't even pray about it, but rather sent up a silent wail of agonized entreaty to the heavenly father.

Chapter 38

"Hi, Mom," I said as I sliced six ragged pieces of cheese pizza and put them on a plate for dinner.

For frozen, this doesn't look half bad, I thought as I tossed some baby carrots into a bowl, poured two glasses of ice water, put it all on a tray, and walked upstairs with the lot, the phone attached to my ear.

Josh lay sprawled on my bed with the remote in his hand.

"Go ahead and start, honey," I said as I placed the tray on the nightstand. "Grandma Fisher is on the phone."

"I don't want to talk to her!" he mouthed silently.

I sighed, and nodded. Josh and my mother had never hit it off. He doesn't understand my parents, and as soon as he was old enough to talk, he demanded one day after a family event, "Mommy, why do they wear those funny things on their heads?"

He hated the smell of propane gas in my parents' house, he didn't like the exuberant, overwhelming way my mother sometimes greeted him, and he didn't get my father at all. He also had some issues with how they treated me—he'd seen me in tears after lectures from them, and while I accepted the occasional painful conversation as the price to pay for a relationship with them, Josh's loyalty was to me, not them.

"I'm sorry, Mom," I said to my mother on the phone. "I'm going to have to cut this a bit short because we were about to eat dinner."

I left Josh happily watching TV and munching on pizza and headed downstairs.

"I heard you and Morton were having problems," Mom said.

I sat down on the carpeted stairs. Apparently she hadn't heard we were already separated. Thank God for small favors.

"Yes," I said and closed my eyes, waiting for the firing squad.

"Susie!" she said. "Make him good cooked meals! Mashed potatoes and meatloaf! Men need that, you know! And get together with other couples, that's really important!"

Two for two. Don't know about you, but after a long day at work and a grim commute, I don't usually cook a big meal, too. Weekends yes, but mashed potatoes during the week ain't happenin'.

And getting together with other couples? She was so right, that was a healthy part of a good relationship, and Morton and I had not done well in that area. I didn't like the way he treated me in front of other people and I had never really gotten to know his friends, not that he had all that many. I guess when you're unhappy as a couple you lose the heart to do much socially. At least that's how it was for me.

"Mom," I blurted out. "We're separated."

The squawking that ensued trashed any strength I had left, so I said goodbye to her as soon as I politely could and watched TV with Josh, seeing but not really hearing.

My mother's opinion wasn't the only thing I was worried about. I was also terrified I was going to lose the house. Northern Virginia was in its boom real estate period at that time and Morton wanted his half of the equity as if we'd have sold the house. A lender had approved a certain amount for a mortgage in my name only, but I still needed a huge chunk to give Morton what he was asking.

In my heart of hearts I felt that it would be unspeakably cruel to uproot Josh from his familiar surroundings on top of all the other changes he was experiencing. He seemed to be doing okay, but who really knew what was going on inside that precious heart? Regardless, I was determined that if there was any way I could swing it, I would hold on to that property for his sake.

I had never asked my parents for help, financially or otherwise, since I left home. The risk was too great and I'd known what I was doing when I left the Amish—I had cut myself off from their approval and therefore their support. But I had no one else to turn to, so finally my inner mother bear trounced my reluctance to turn to my parents, and one morning, literally shaking all over, I called my father.

"Dad," I said after I'd greeted him and we'd chatted a while. "I was wondering if I can borrow some money from you. You know Morton moved out and I'd really, really like to keep the house for Josh's sake. I've been approved for a mortgage but not enough to pay Morton his share...I know I've not been the daughter you wanted but if there's any way you can help...I would pay you the full amount back, plus whatever the current interest rate is, of course."

That call was one of the hardest things I've ever done in my life. I waited, still shaking, and then Dad cleared his throat and said, "Actually, I have almost that exact amount sitting in an account that I was wondering what to do with just this morning. I'll have to talk to Katie...see what she says..."

"Why don't you and Mom come down this weekend and you can look at the house, make sure it's a good investment for me, and then we can talk about it?"

"Okay," he said, and that week while I prepared for their visit every particle of my body was on high alert, as if the slightest sound, slightest breeze, would set off a four-alarm fire.

Finally late Saturday morning they rolled in with my brother Steve, who drove them down in his car. I served them the chocolate chip cookies I'd just baked and coffee, and then Dad inspected the house head to toe.

"Looks good," he said as he checked the baseboards in the living room and opened the kitchen cabinet doors. Not Manie L. Fisher quality to be sure, but they did fine for my beloved townhouse.

I prepared a light lunch, chicken salad on croissants, a green salad with toasted slivered almonds and dried cranberries and a light vinaigrette dressing, and key lime pie for dessert.

In the afternoon my father changed the batteries on my smoke detectors and a ray of hope dawned. Would he help? It seemed Dad was enjoying the first bit of practical parenting he'd done since I'd left home, and I melted as I watched him expertly snap the plastic cover back on the kitchen alarm.

I cooked dinner, salmon in lemon dill sauce, wild rice, and steamed asparagus, with coffee ice cream for dessert.

They loved it, just raved over it, which made me feel good but I was still nervous as I settled them into my bedroom for the night and showed them where the fresh towels and washcloths were.

I tossed and turned on the sofa and finally got up early the next morning to brew coffee. When my mother came downstairs she looked irate.

"I couldn't find a single Bible in your room last night!" she said.

I spilled some coffee grounds and shuddered at the thought of my mother rummaging around in my private space.

"Mom," I said. "I have a Bible. One Bible. It's down here, in the living room."

"Well, I didn't know what to read!" she said.

191

After breakfast Dad said, "Susie, can you run me to the store? I need to pick up some things."

"Sure," I said, and as I drove down the road I felt the tension build in the car; it was the ugly energy of a man who has unaccustomed control over his daughter and knows it.

He did his shopping and finally when we were almost back at the house I couldn't stand it anymore.

"Dad," I said, "Did you decide? Are you going to loan me the money?"

His face turned ugly and he stared straight ahead. "It's not our doing that you're in this place," he said.

Crack! Baseball bat to the heart. *It's not our doing that you're in this place. You got it right, Daddy, it's not. I did this to myself. I'm English, I'm getting a divorce, again, and yes— you're Amish, and perfect.*

I don't know how I got through the next half hour while my parents packed their suitcases and prepared to leave. I said goodbye to them, and then ran to my bedroom and flung myself face down on the carpet and sobbed.

Josh found me there and patted my shoulder. "It's going to be okay, Mom," he said.

Chapter 39

J osh was right—it was okay, if okay meant stretching myself rather to the limit financially. Someone counseled me to look into a second mortgage and my bank approved it, so finally I had my house.

Mortgaged to the hilt, yes, but it was in my name. Mine! Every window, every door, every wall, was mine, and I was going to make the best of it. I paid Morton his share and had some left over to paint and such.

First order of business—rip the floral border off the living room and dining room walls and the hyper picnic-on-crack border off the kitchen walls. I'd had to live with those borders for two long, exhausting years. Morton had called me at work one day and said, "Mind if I paint the first floor today?"

"Mind?" I said, like any wife would. "Of course I don't mind!"

We decided on yellow for the kitchen and foyer, and blue for the living room and dining room. I imagined something in a pale lemon yellow and an eggshell blue—yellow and blue are harder to screw up than most colors—and I said Sure, sure, I trust you Morton, go ahead and pick the colors yourself.

When I came home that night that yellow struck me over the head with a sun-scorched fist. I have never, before or since, seen a yellow that *mean.* It had an F-you quality, and I could not *imagine* creating a good meal in that kitchen.

I really didn't think there was a shade of blue I didn't like. I love blue usually, anything from pale blue to deep midnight. But that blue? In attitude, it was similar to the living room I'd hated as a child—that cold, sunless room with the

193

starved pillows and dishes imprisoned behind glass in a china cabinet. Because it grabbed you and handcuffed you, that blue, and then it fed you to the rodents to eat.

And then later without telling me, Morton added those borders.

Needless to say, it was time for change.

I called a local painter and he was a gift, that man. He took my requests in stride and rejoiced over them. Actually said his painters would love the change from painting beige walls all the time.

When one of my friends heard I was painting she told me that she and her husband always! painted a small patch of color on the wall first. Then they looked at it in the daylight and at night, and then, after a few days of patch-gazing, they'd decide: yes or no. If no, they'd start all over again. This particular friend bossed me mercilessly and I have since fired her as a pal because she was annoying as hell, but at the time she felt it was her duty to guide Susie E. Fisher in the way that she should go and practically *insisted* I do it her way.

Of course, I didn't—those paint swatches and I had a ball. I picked out all my colors in one fell swoop. Josh had earlier decided he wanted his room painted red and black and I said, "Red and black? Are you sure?"

My confident-in-his-choices child said firmly yes, red and black.

So for his room I chose red with an orange undertone for three of the walls and black for the other, with the same motif in his bathroom.

For the kitchen I chose a lovely spring green, with one matching wall in the dining room. The rest of the first floor— and this was the color I was most unsure of, I knew it could go either way—was a deep, deep rose.

The small spare room was the most sedate of the lot, a calming blue. The basement was sort of a "Finding Nemo" motif, with the wall at the gas fireplace a lovely, pale burnt orange and the rest of it light turquoise blue.

I loved it, just loved it, and then I went a tad crazy, ordering things to decorate with. Nothing high end, I didn't have the money, but I ordered stuff on eBay, that sort of thing, and one of my favorite finds was a gigantic stuffed mother leopard with a cub, which still sits on the built-in shelf in my bedroom. Every time I looked at it I was reminded that God is my mother and my father and he watches over me with, I hope, the same fierce protective love that is on the face of that mama leopard.

My next task was to clean up all the mess my husband had left in his office space in the basement. He was a hoarder, and had saved almost every scrap of paper, every piece of junk, since we'd moved in and there were piles and piles which I knew probably also contained things that mattered to him so I drew a deep breath and dived in.

My heart lurched with hurt when I saw, mixed in with all the junk, some of the gifts I had given him, things that I had picked out with great care now reduced to rubble.

It took me two days. Days of hard work dragging bag after bag of trash up the hill to the curb and boxing up valuables.

It brought back ugly memories of when I had sifted through Ronnie's trash after he'd gone to prison. I'd gone to the place we'd rented together and cleaned, and sorted, and boxed up his good stuff too and then I called my ex-father-in-law, a rough-around-the-edges kind of guy with a crew cut and a loud laugh, and asked him if he'd please pick everything up and take it home and keep it until his son got out of jail.

Mr. Patterson owned a hammer mill that he used to grind up feed for the local farmers and he and I had always gotten along well He drove into my driveway in his pickup truck and packed the boxes in his trunk, hugged me hard and then crawled back in his truck and was gone, forever. Afterwards I threw myself onto my bed and cried for a while.

I would also miss my second father-in-law, Morton's father the professor, and while he could not have been more different from Ronnie's dad, I'd shared a bond with him, too.

That's the bitch about divorce or indeed about any breakup, isn't it? Why isn't there a way to walk away from the bad and keep the good? The trauma of leaving behind a relationship is severe, extremely so, and added to that is losing others we love, not just the one with whom we're breaking up.

I drove to Morton's the following Saturday afternoon and snapped open my trunk which was filled with his good stuff. He didn't have the grace to look sheepish but did thank me, and finally, with his things gone, the house and I celebrated.

Free at last.

Those were good days, excited about having the deed to my own home, interspersed by some fragile moments of loneliness.

If you're divorced or separated or if you've broken up with a live-in boyfriend or girlfriend, you know what I'm talking about when I say that there were times when I'd wake up in the middle of the night, with my child in the bedroom across the hall, feeling so isolated, so frightened by all the responsibilities I carried alone, so delicate in that king-sized bed, that my very bones felt brittle and breakable.

I know this sounds crazy but I think the lowest moment of that year was the night Josh wanted me to make him a paper airplane.

I'm hopeless at that sort of thing, and I tried and tried and he wanted me to do it so badly but I just couldn't, and was tempted to call Morton who only lived ten minutes away. Finally my son gave up with a frustrated look on his face, and I gathered up all the crumpled up pieces of paper and threw them in the waste can and cried for a while.

The other low moment was one day when I bought my child a workstation for his collection of plastic rescue heroes. I was crazy for attempting to put it together, because not only have I betrayed my Amish maternal genes by not being able to cook up vast meals for dozens of people unless I have help, I also betrayed my paternal genes by being completely hopeless at anything having to do with carpentry or painting or whatever.

The good folks at Home Depot overestimated my talents quite a lot, I'm afraid. I like going to Home Deport or Lowe's, it makes me feel so ultra-feminine to walk amongst all those slabs of wood and power drills and hammers and all, but once I get home with the stuff I've bought I look at it, and it looks at me, and we both shrug our shoulders and realize that's probably going to be the extent of our relationship.

(There's only one man at Home Depot I did not adore on sight. I was looking for a hand trimmer, shears I guess they're called, to trim the tiny yard outside my townhouse. I cannot even begin to tell you how much I *despise* those weed-whacker things. The sound they make is like a dentist's drill gone postal, and what is *with* that string thing you have to arrange? I don't get it, and the one time I tried to use one I shaved a bald spot on my yard and it still hasn't forgiven me. So I decided to go back to my Amish roots and do it the sane, calm way, but I couldn't find what I needed so I hailed a man who looked like he was dreaming about martinis on a balcony in St. Thomas. I told him what I wanted and he went all Vanna White on me, showing me one weed-whacker after the next, arranging them lovingly for my inspection. No, I insisted, I want *shears* but he kept showing me one green monstrosity after another until finally in desperation I said, "I used to be Amish and I WANT SHEARS!" He dropped the Vanna act and reached way, way back on the shelf and found me some damn oversized scissors, and handed them to me with an I-wash-my-hands-of-you air.)

However, usually I love the Home Depot guys, they're the salt of the earth, so when I needed to hang curtains one fine Saturday afternoon, I drove to my local Home Depot where a kindly gentleman named Sam assured me it was easy to use a power drill. He patted my shoulder and said, "You can do it!" and something in me said No, no I can't even though I'm the daughter of a cabinetmaker and should know how, I don't, and never will.

Only so much agony should be shared in one story, and I'm reaching my limit so suffice it to say that after numerous attempts and a lot of swearing (quietly, my kid was in the house), Josh found me at nine o'clock at night standing on the windowsill sobbing.

To this day I don't know how I managed it. I made a lot of holes in the wall, I know that, but for the past seven years those curtains have stayed put, somehow!

But back to Josh's rescue station—it had a set of instructions written by a sadistic dude wearing a vest scattered with marijuana ash because no one in his right mind could've done it, of that I am sure. There were all these plastic pieces and lots of Exhibit A type things and arrows pointing to this and that and my brain instantly, as usual, said Oh no, honey, I don't think so.

My first grade teacher, Mrs. Leatherman, said to me one day, "Susie, you don't like following directions, do you?" and I looked at her with my big brown eyes quite startled.

"*Moi?*" I should have said in French just to be a smartass, but little Amish girls a) don't know how to speak French and b) aren't smartasses, ever.

198

But it surprised me a good deal. I mean, I thought I was being a model first grader, simply model, and how she picked up on that tidbit about me is really puzzling.

But it's true—I don't. Directions make me want to weep and maybe even gnash my teeth. Am I the only person who buys a new cell phone, glances at the Fat Booklet of Instructions, and says Hell, I just want to make a phone call?

So I suffered a good deal over that rescue station, and several times I was face down on the living room floor bawling and doing some (quiet yet violent) swearing into the carpet fibers. Josh kept patting me on the shoulder and saying, "You can do it, Mom!"

And damn if I didn't. Four long, weary hours later, we had ourselves a rescue hero station. The helicopter pilot might have been confused because the plastic landing strip was on backwards and a few other things were ever so slightly askew, but boy, was I proud, and Josh was happy, which is what it was all about, anyway.

Chapter 40

O ne day Josh came home from school and said that he was invited to participate in a support group for children of divorced parents and did I want to sign the form.

"How was it?" I asked him after the first session.

"Awful. Just a bunch of kids sitting around playing games and talking about how miserable their lives are."

"Do you feel your life is miserable?" I said while I held my breath.

"No," he said, "I don't," and ran off to play.

One day I broached the subject of therapy with my son. I wanted to make sure that Josh had every resource available to help him deal with the choices his parents had made.

"Would it help you to talk to someone else, Josh, an outside party, about…things?" I said.

"What things?"

"The divorce, how you felt about it…"

"Mom," he said. "All that would happen is some woman would hit me in the eye and when I'd say Ouch, that hurt, she'd hand me a tissue and say Go ahead, honey, cry, get it all out."

I laughed. "Josh, I'm serious, it might be a good thing, really."

"Absolutely no way. Mom! I'm fine. Really."

One day my mother told me about this adorable grandson of some English people she and Dad knew. "He's such a good Christian!" she said. "They say that every night he kneels beside his bed and prays."

I could just picture this annoying paragon clasping his hands in prayer and lisping, "Now I lay me down to sleep…"

Josh has never been that kind of child. The first prayer I remember my son praying was one night when he was about three years old. I suggested that he say a few words to God before bedtime. Josh said briskly, "God, tell everyone in heaven to have strawberry shortcake for dessert tonight. Amen."

Then there was the night I was driving him to his guitar lesson with this fantastic Berklee-trained rocker/musician, Gregg Smith. Josh enjoys his lessons with Gregg, but that night I was drained from getting up early to write and working all day, and it was cold and dark out, and all I wanted to do was turn around and go home and crawl under the covers.

"Josh," I said, "would you pray for me please? I'm so tired."

Josh sat quietly for several seconds then he said, "God, please give my mother a holy cup of coffee."

It seemed that my heart waited a split-second to beat so it could absorb the sweetness and creativity of that prayer.

Those people can have their Now-I-Lay-Me-Down-to-Sleep kid. I wouldn't trade my child for all the angelic cherubs in the world.

My mother over-estimated my cherubic qualities when she called me one morning not too long after my divorce was final and said, "Can you help Sally get ready for church?"

I clutched the portable phone in my hand so I wouldn't throw it. Sally is my youngest sister, and my mother's only Amish daughter. Sally and I are very close in spite of the differences in our lives, but drive three hours just to clean her house? When I work full-time, am a single mom, and barely have time to clean my own house?

"Mom," I said. "I care about Sally, you know I do, and I wish I could help. But are you really asking me to drive all that way just to clean? My plate is already really full…"

I took a deep breath and felt that stab of hurt I always feel when it seems that my mother doesn't recognize me as a person except when she needs something from me.

"You need to stop thinking about yourself and start thinking about the Lord and others," my mother snapped.

My brain felt like it wanted to explode inside my head. Think about the Lord and others? When all it seemed I had time for was to pay the bills, take out the garbage, keep my bosses happy at work, do laundry, oh yes and lest I forget, spend what we so adorably label *quality time* with my child?

Then my mother quoted the Bible at me and I quoted it right back, which I shouldn't have done, and hung up feeling awful.

I waded around in fury and misery for a couple of days, and then I emailed my sister Anne. "We have to have some standards here, right?" I wrote. "Sally aside, does it even make sense to clean for the very church that shunned us? Does it?"

She wrote back and said she agreed, we shouldn't, and Mom was way out of line for asking me to drive all that way just to clean Sally's house. But then compassion got the best of me and sure enough, the Saturday before church was to be at Sally's house, I drove to Lancaster to help her.

Bon Jovi was a great comfort because I listened to "It's my Life" as I drove past the peaceful farms. (There's something so soul-balancing for me about listening to loud rock music when I'm in Lancaster County. As I roar by barns and horses and buggies, the mix of Amish and English blends together inside me and I feel whole.)

I turned into Sally's driveway and got out of the car and stretched, and paused to admire her garden. She had planted sunflowers—my favorite flower—and they grew tall and proud in a row at the front. They looked so cheerful that I wanted to hug each of those tall stalks, silly as that sounds.

There were also tomato plants, and corn, and string beans...

And to the left, her yard and flowers looked lavish and beautiful, and birdfeeders were scattered here and there.

Then, there she was—my sweet sister, rushing down the sidewalk toward me, her pretty face alight with welcome. She was wearing a blue dress and black "bibshatz," the casual apron Amish women wear on weekdays rather than the cape and apron they wear on formal occasions.

I hugged Sally and followed her to the farmhouse. Her kitchen felt uncomfortably warm in the August heat and I realized how accustomed I had become to air conditioning, even though I only use it when absolutely necessary because I prefer open windows and fresh air. But it is nice to have AC when you need it, and today was definitely one of those days.

I hugged my nieces and nephews and wandered to my favorite spot in Sally's house, which is the view from her kitchen window. A sense of homecoming and calm seeped into my soul as I looked at the quiet green pasture where cows grazed.

And then: time to work. I brought wash in from the line that smelled like fresh air and sunshine. After I finished folding laundry I asked Sally for a bucket so I could wash the floor.

"Are you sure you want to do this?" Sally asked as she filled a red plastic pail with soap and water. "Your clothes look so nice..."

"Of course I'm sure." I hugged her and washed the floor the right way, which is to say, on your hands and knees. The better to get the corners, as my mother would say.

After that I stepped outside with my niece Rebecca, who wanted to show me where church would be the next day. Since it was summer it would be in the barn instead of the house, and as Rebecca, who has blond hair and brown eyes and will surely be a beauty one day, showed me where the benches were set up neatly in rows, where the men would sit on one side and the women on the other, nostalgia flooded me as I smelled the hay on the other side of the barn. It was one of the good smells of my childhood, one of my favorites actually, and I breathed it in with gusto.

Then one of Sally's Amish neighbors stopped by to help. She had a placid expression and the most naturally rosy cheeks I've ever seen—step aside, Estée Lauder!—and dark hair. She brought snitz pies for the after-church luncheon and then offered to pick string beans in the garden but her baby, whose face looked so much like John Cusack's at his most neurotic it was uncanny, shrieked her disapproval and I asked if I could hold her. Mama agreed, although I thought she looked at me funny when she handed her wailing baby girl over to me, sort of a scared-of-English-germs look. But she handed her child over anyway, and the baby calmed down as I walked up and down the garden with her so she could see her mother picking beans.

On the way home I stopped in to see my parents, and my mother greeted me like our fight had never happened.

Happy, as always, that peace had been restored—amazing what washing a floor can do for my relationship with my mother—I started the car and was driving west on Rt. 340 toward home when I felt this strange unfinished feeling, a nagging sense of something left undone. I pulled into the Turkey Hill Minute Market and bought a container of iced tea. As I drank it—gosh, those folks make delicious iced tea—I thought, how about visiting my teenage enemy, Naomi? She lived close to my cousin Barbie...how would it feel to go see them and talk about what had happened when we were all sixteen?

I drove south on Rt. 896, through glorious countryside, and when I turned into Barbie's driveway my shoulders felt tense and I took a deep breath as I knocked on the door.

"Susie!" my cousin said. She was barefoot and wearing a green dress and an apron that looked like it had a tomato juice stain on it. "Come in!"

I hugged her and stepped into the kitchen, and saw that she had been canning tomato sauce. "I'm sorry, Barbie, this isn't a good time for you..."

"It's okay!" she said. "It's so good to see you."

We chatted a bit and then I said, "How would you feel about walking over to Naomi's house? I'd like to..."

Like to what? Fix that abandoned sixteen-year-old? What had I been thinking?

"I'd like to talk about what happened when we were teenagers," I said quietly, and Barbie nodded, almost as though she had been expecting and maybe even hoping for that conversation.

As we walked together to Naomi's house I brushed away a fly and inhaled the quiet beauty of the farmland.

Naomi opened the door in answer to our knock and took a full step back when she saw me standing there beside Barbie.

"Susie!" she said. "What...what are you doing here?" She looked older and wearier, but her eyes were as haughty as ever.

"Can we come in?" Barbie said.

"Yes...of course." Naomi opened the door and I followed Barbie inside.

We sat down at Naomi's oblong kitchen table and I discreetly studied my surroundings. The house felt oddly depressed and dark, unlike Barbie's cheerful rather disheveled one, and there was almost a brooding quality in the air.

"I wanted to share how I felt about what happened when we were sixteen," I said.

Silence fell in the kitchen. Barbie looked sad, and Naomi looked down at her hands and said, "Yes, that was very hard for me. There were times when I cried because I just didn't know what to do."

Really, bitch? I thought. *You're making this about you?*

Barbie said, "Susie, I am very sorry for the way we treated you. It's been bothering me for a long time and I hope you can forgive us."

"Of course," I said, and after a few more minutes of stilted conversation we walked outside together.

"Susie, how do you stay so *thin*?" Naomi said.

Well, that helped. By some standards, i.e. Hollywood's, I'd be considered curvy rather than ultra-skinny, but by Amish standards I suppose I might appear svelte. However, the question seemed rhetorical so I thanked Naomi and when she went back home, Barbie and I walked back to my car in companionable silence.

"Wait!" she said after I had started the car. "I want to get you some tomato sauce."

She ran inside, covering strings flapping in the breeze, and came back out clutching a can of homemade sauce.

"Thank you, Barbie," I said, as tears welled up in my eyes. I opened the car door and hugged her, and drove away, feeling more at peace than I had in a long time.

Chapter 41

A few years passed and Josh started asking for a dog. I felt a cat would be less work; my plate was full enough already, so on the way to the pet store that Sunday afternoon, Josh declared in a Biblical manner: "His name will be Zack."

Zack was a tiny, sweet ball of black fur with white paws and some white around the neck and face. He also had beautiful gold-green eyes. A few nights after we got home I woke up and felt a presence, so to speak. I switched on the light and there was Zack under the nightstand, looking up at me with an oh-please-may-I-curl-up-with-you look on his face and ever since, at some point during the night, he usually curls up against my shoulder and purrs for a while.

We took Zack to the vet for his shots. The doc looked at him, examined his paws, and said, "This is going to be a very large cat."

I looked doubtfully at the tiny kitten huddled on the examining table.

Large? Really?

But damn if he wasn't right—Zack is hefty, and beautiful, and adores me. However, he and Josh only tolerated each other, so Josh again began begging for a dog.

I bought Josh a book, one of those inclusive things that lists all the breeds and explains what care they will require, and our first step was a visit to the animal shelter. I wanted to take them all home, those sad-eyed dogs, but instinctively I knew that none of them was right for a child, they were all full-grown, and when we walked out my heart was breaking.

We found our puppy at a pet store. I realize that can be an iffy proposition and I had no intention of getting our dog there, but Josh begged to at least stop in and look. Sure enough, behind one of the windows of those cages was a three-month-old Golden Retriever. She had the cutest face you've ever seen and was chewing vigorously on a cow hoof.

"Mom!" Josh said. "Can I play with her?"

So the guy brought her out into a fenced-off area and my son and that dog rollicked around for a while and then Josh looked up at me with that expression, the one guaranteed to melt my heart. "Mommy," he said. "I'll do anything just please, please can we get this dog? She's the one, can we? Please?"

"We need to sleep on it, and think about it," I said, and talked to the pet store people about what she'd need, etc, and they showed me the paperwork which seemed to be in order. She was from a line of Goldens from England, and the next day she was ours.

And again, my son proclaimed her name.

"Angel!" he said.

"Not Fluffy, or Goldie, or Hester?" I said doubtfully. She seemed a bit mischievous frankly to bear such a good-girl name, but Nope! Josh insisted: Angel it was, and still is, although I reserved the right to call her Sadie when I found her chewing one of my shoes. I paid a neighbor to walk her at noon but still, she was a challenge to train, and chewed everything from the windowsills to the corners of the coffee table to the occasional shoe I was crazy enough to leave within her reach. I got up with her at night and walked her in the early hours of the morning. Josh did his part, too, but there were times I thought I was going to lose my mind over that dog.

What can I say? Angel is a sweetheart, and adds so much love to our household.

One day when we were leaving the dog park a handsome man came down the path with a Golden Retriever in tow. She looked so much like Angel it was uncanny, but the resemblance was purely superficial—his dog was one of those obedient hounds that sicken the hearts of owners like me who, yes, took her dog to training classes and taught her how to *sit* but somehow the dog gets it that I'm not so much ruthless dictator as dreamer. She and I will be walking sedately on the dog path close to my house and I'm concocting sentences in my head and suddenly she'll spot a dog and/or human and boom! off we go and I'm trying to pretend that I love being dragged about by a large dog, all the while crying, *Sit Angel, sit!*

"But there's a person I simply must greet," she says, and who the hell am I to stop her because frankly I almost can't.

There are only a very few dogs in my neighborhood she's not crazy about.

One is the most elegant dog you've ever seen called, what else, Elizabeth. She wears a purple collar that matches her owner's purple Crocs and the two of them stroll smartly down the path while Angel and I make our boisterous way past them. Angel sniffs and whispers to me, "Really, Mom, is that bitch *human?*"

The other is a pair of small white fluffy dogs that shriek like demented fiends when they see us approaching.

"Sheesh!" Angel says, and if you are a dog owner you know just what I mean by the way your dog looks at you after an interaction with other dogs. "Insane, what?"

In spite of my occasional impatience with her, Angel loves me anyway, and sometimes at night I wake up to find Zack curled up against my shoulder on one side and Angel on the other. Sometimes they rest peacefully at their respective posts but other times…

"You are a thug dressed like a cat," Angel said to Zack one morning.

Zack waved a paw in my direction. "Well, at least one of us is tough. She's too nice for her own good."

"I'm prettier than you are."

"You're a slobbering hound."

"You're a fat feline who doesn't know the meaning of the word I've Had Enough."

"That's three words."

"Says who?"

I laughed and shooed them off the bed so they could continue fighting somewhere other than across my body.

Sweet, sweet pets.

Yes, they shed and occasionally snipe at each other, but they consider it their sacred duty to look after me, and above all, see to it that I am loved.

Chapter 42

osh and I celebrated Christmas of 2008 with my family in a beautiful cabin in Pennsylvania. My Amish brother Lee and his wife Liz were unpacking the groceries they had brought when Josh and I arrived. Lee is a few years younger than my sister Ruth Ann, and I consider him to be the calming element in the family. He's one of those people who always has interesting things to say and is constantly reading something, whether it's history or biographies or fiction…and his wife Liz is always welcoming to me and my non-Amish siblings, and for that, I treasure her.

Then my youngest brother, Merv, arrived, exuding that youngest-child carefree spirit he's always had. He's all grown up, though, and is an entrepreneur, and sells gorgeous furniture. Neither he nor my oldest brother Steve ever joined the Amish church so they sort of slipped out, so to speak, and their departure from the plain way of life seems to be a non-issue for my parents.

There was snow on the mountain, creating just the right effect for our get-together, and later that night, after everyone had arrived, I basked in the warm camaraderie my siblings and I always generate when we're together, a feeling I never take for granted because I lost it for a while after my move to DC, and it continues to be one of the things for which I am most thankful.

A ping pong table was set up in the basement and a fierce competition had sprung up. I was inching my way up to the finals—what with seven siblings plus spouses and children, we had a lot of fun on our way to finding the reigning champion—when I ran upstairs to get a glass of water and heard my cell phone ringing.

"Hello?" I said, out of breath because I had just beaten my brother Steve, a very sweet victory because he had almost always beaten me when we played at home as kids.

"Susie. It's Morton. I'm in the hospital."

My heart rate sped up in alarm. "Are you okay? What's going on?" I said.

"It's my pancreas. I have to stay for some tests but I'm probably going to be here for a few more days."

"Do you need us to come home?"

"No. No. Absolutely not. I just wanted you to know."

I sat down on the sofa and heard the sharp ping of the ball as someone slammed it across the net downstairs.

The smell of the sugar cookies I had baked earlier still clung to the air and it filled me with sadness for my ex-husband who lay in a hospital while we celebrated the holidays.

Josh and I went to visit Morton as soon as we came home and he looked pale and disheveled in a faded blue hospital gown.

"What caused this, Morton?" I said after we had greeted him and asked how he was feeling.

"I don't know. Diet, I guess." He didn't meet my eyes and I had a bad feeling in my gut as we said our goodbyes.

The next day I Googled his illness and sure enough, the article said that most of the time it was caused by alcohol abuse.

My ex-husband ended up in the hospital four more times until the doctor told him if he drinks *at all* it could kill him because his pancreas was in such bad shape.

It was a terrible time, and one night Morton hit a new low. He had told Josh he would attend his violin recital, and if this has happened to you as a parent, you'll know what I mean when I say that I have seldom been more heartbroken than when

I saw Josh scan the room looking for Morton the entire time during the recital.

The next morning Morton called me crying. I admitted how disappointed Josh had been and then I said, "Morton, as one of my favorite verses says, God's mercies are new every morning..." I was crying as I said it and then so was my ex.

"Susie...I'm so sorry..." Morton said.

"I know, and I'm sorry too. Josh will get over this but please, get help, okay?"

Not too long afterwards Morton went to rehab and our relationship is now civil, which is all I ask. However, I thought I would always feel guilty about invading his life, i.e. showing up at his door and giving him almost no choice but to take me in when I moved to the DC area.

Until one night, during the writing of this book, when I chucked off my goody-two-shoes and let 'er rip.

My ex had taken Josh to his guitar lesson and I had to pick him (my child) up. It was not good timing because I was at that stage in the creative process where I wanted to scream at anyone who interrupted me, sort of like when I was giving birth and Morton touched my arm—every mother will know what I mean when I say that I wanted to scream at the top of my lungs *Do not touch me!*

Josh's music teacher had moved to a lovely yet remote spot and my ex had given me directions. I don't have a GPS yet, so I get lost on the occasion but this time, it wasn't my fault because, while Morton is usually an excellent navigator and has helped me on more than one occasion when I've needed it, this time, his directions *sucked.* They were, in fact, wrong, which in hindsight was a gift, because in between calling him, I sobbed and screamed and shouted out my pain, words I could never say before because of my incessant need to take care of everybody else but myself.

Joshua finally gave me the correct directions and when I pulled up to where he was standing on a cedar deck, guitar case at his side, I said through the window, "Josh! I am a wreck, darling, a wreck."

He heaved his guitar case into the trunk, buckled his seatbelt and said, "Why?"

"Because...oh honey, when I'm at this stage of the writing process everything irritates me, everything, and then I was mad because I had the wrong directions..."

Irritates is putting it mildly. The problem with my writing is that I do it in my head first, which is fine if, as I said, I encounter no humans or animals or maybe even furniture during that time. After I write in my head for a while, I put everything down on paper and then on the computer. Time-consuming, yes, but the only thing that works for me.

In a perfect world, when I'm in creative mode, I'd have a dog walker, a nanny, a chef, a housekeeper, a gardener, a driver, a cleaning service, and a PR person to soothe and reassure the people I offended because a) I didn't notice them or b) noticed, and hated them.

"Also," I said to Josh, "I can't stand Morton."

I rarely say stuff like this, I've made it a point to be as positive as I can about my ex for Josh's sake, but I could tell that my verbal brakes were shot and I was gonna say what I was gonna say.

"Why?" Josh said.

"He gave me the X#%^& wrong directions and I just didn't need that tonight."

Yes, I said That Word, it slipped out, and Josh said Mom, language! and I said I know, I know, but when I'm in this place it's my favorite word and I just can't help it!

"I'm sorry, Josh," I said. "I know how sad it makes you feel inside when your parents don't get along."

My son turned and looked at me with his unusual gray-green eyes. His expression said *Oh please, I'm not four years old anymore* mixed with *I'm here for you, Mom.*

"I see I'm going to have to keep a very close eye on you tonight," he said. "Don't get an I-Hate-Morton tattoo, you know you'd regret it."

Pleasure zipped through me at the thought of a tattoo like that, but as I braked at a red light I said meekly, "You're probably right."

"Also, don't do drugs, and don't jump."

"Okay," I said, even more meekly.

"I think we should go out to dinner."

"Why?" I groaned. "I've been sobbing and I look a mess."

"You could use a drink," he said kindly.

"Where do you want to go?"

He mentioned a local Italian restaurant located, fortunately, minutes from our house.

"But it has low ceilings," I said in the vein of a woman who would complain about the gold in a palace being too bright. But I turned into the strip mall where it was located anyway, and after the hostess had seated us Josh said, "See, this isn't so bad, right? You needed a small, windowless place to cry in."

"Well, maybe…"

"Did I nail where you were, emotionally speaking?" he said and I nodded yes.

Chapter 43

W hen the cop pulled me over on the Beltway that Friday afternoon, I wanted to scream.

"Do you know how fast you were going?" he said, and why they ask that question is beyond me because clearly *they* know and at that point what does it matter how the hell fast I was going because even if I guess it right on the nose, I don't think the cop is exactly going to pat me on the shoulder and say Very good! 73! No ticket!

So I handed him my license and registration in a marked manner, i.e., fine, ticket me but don't insult me with your questions, and then he said, "So what's your hurry?"

"My mother is in the hospital."

His pen halted mid-stride and he looked a little more human when he said, "Okay. But I don't think it will help anyone if you get into an accident on your way there."

I drove off still trembling a little, cops always have that effect on me, and plunged back into get-out-of-town-early-on-a-Friday DC traffic. Here's the thing—73 miles per hour is quite normal for I-95. Regardless, I had to at least keep it within ten so I drove a sedate 65 m.p.h. the rest of the way until I reached Route 83 in Pennsylvania where, bless their hearts, the speed limit is 65, and took it up to 75.

My dad had sounded so scared when he had called me earlier. Mom had had two valves in her heart replaced a few years earlier, and now they'd done a procedure to try to correct her erratic heartbeat. Her heart was beating too fast and it was, quite literally, wearing her out.

Mom calls me very occasionally but Dad almost never, so when I answered my cell phone at work earlier that day and heard his voice, I was surprised and a little alarmed.

"Susie," he said in that quiet way of his, "Mom had her procedure done this morning and I think everything is fine but we had a little scare. There is no reason at all for you to come home but I just wanted you to know."

Had he shouted, "Please get up here now, I need you," the message could not have been clearer. There was a tone in his voice I'd never heard before, that of a frightened man who needs the support of his daughter, no matter how excommunicated she might be.

So there I was, covering the miles as fast as I dared and finally turned into the visitors' parking lot at Lancaster General Hospital, feeling sweaty and exhausted after three-plus hours in my car on an August afternoon.

The newly renovated lobby of the Lancaster General looked more like a Ritz Carlton than a hospital, and I hardly recognized the place where I had come as a twelve-year-old for appendicitis and a few years earlier with a broken collarbone after falling on the ice one morning.

I asked the receptionist where my mother was and in that friendly way Lancastrians seem to have, she gave me my mom's room number and directed me to the elevator. I punched the up button, hoping my white cotton dress wouldn't cause Mom's heart any further stress. It was long, definitely inches below the knee, but there was a hint of cleavage. At least I didn't have slacks on—that would have been a no-no.

My heart did a little unsteady beating of its own when I saw her lying there, looking too weak to care what I had on.

"Mom!" I said, and rushed to kiss her cheek.

"Hi Susie," she said as I removed a Bible from the chair beside her bed and sat down.

"So what happened this morning? How are you?"

"Hesslich!" she said, and a little color came into her cheeks. (*Hesslich* is an Amish swear word and means "ugly" in German.)

"I called and called for the nurses this morning..." She complained for a while and I was relieved to hear it. My mother casts aside all semblance of Amish sweetness when in a hospital bed, as we found out when she had her heart surgery, and if she was grumbling it meant she had at least a little strength left to fight the good fight.

She had one of my father's blue work kerchiefs tied neatly over her hair and her starched organdy prayer covering lay on the nightstand. It was strange to see her in a pale color, i.e. the bleached-out blue favored by hospitals, rather than her usual blacks, dark blues, greens, and purples.

"Would you read a Psalm to me?" she said as the afternoon wore on. There wasn't much to say, it seemed, and it felt odd, it just the being the two of us—usually there were other siblings or my father around, but today I was the only one in attendance and I wished there was something I could say to cheer her up, create a bridge between us.

I picked up the Bible. "The Lord is my shepherd, I shall not want," I began and she closed her eyes as I continued, "He leadeth me beside still waters, he restoreth my soul," and suddenly I found I had to struggle through tears to continue.

Mom and I both love the Psalms, and I am sure when David the shepherd penned those words all those years ago, he never realized that one day a daughter in desperate need of providing comfort would find it in those beautiful words.

"Yea, though I walk through the valley of the shadow of death, I will fear no evil, thy rod and thy staff they comfort me. Surely goodness and mercy shall follow me all the days of my life and I will dwell in the house of the Lord forever."

I looked over at Mom and saw she had fallen asleep. I tucked the Bible under her prayer covering and pulled out a paperback from my purse, a dog-eared Agatha Christie I had planned to read on my lunch break that day.

Then the silence was broken when a hearty voice boomed, "Is this Katie's room?" She sounded like one of those cheerful types that do so much to blight the souls of those they think they're comforting. She was wearing brown polyester pants and an equally inspired top, and was followed by a couple of satellite females, not as bright or as hearty but doing pretty well as lesser stars.

My mother's eyes snapped open and she seemed much happier to see them than I was. I had been enjoying the peaceful time with her, the echoes of Psalm 23 still soothing me after my harried drive from DC to Lancaster.

What has always hurt my sisters Anne and Ruth and me is that Mom has a lot of friends like this, churchgoing women who, like the one in the brown pants, wear "normal" clothing and cut their hair. So according to my mother it was apparently okay in God's eyes for them to dress like that, but not us because we were raised Amish and as such were supposed to stay that way.

The three visitors waxed on about all things spiritual while I stood at the window feeling useless, and then one of the satellites pulled out a book from her bag and I bit my lip to keep from laughing.

"Stories from Hell" was the title and I couldn't help but think, was it really the book to give a heart patient? But Mom thought it just fine—she seemed to enjoy that sort of thing a little more than is healthy, in my opinion—and the three women continued talking in a very spiritual vein.

Suddenly the leader said, "Katie, what do you think of my hair?"

It was a rich brown color, very abundant, and was pulled back in a bun at the nape of her neck. She wore no makeup and no jewelry and so when Mom said she thought it looked nice I was surprised when the lady said, "It's a wig. My hair was getting thin at the top so I thought, why not?"

Then the nonentity in the room—yes, that would be me—just had to open her mouth and say, "Oh! How wonderful! One day you can be a brunette, the next day a redhead, and the next a platinum blond."

Three shocked pairs of eyes—oh wait, make that four, my mother's joined the fray—scanned my stupid self head to toe.

I subsided meekly back into silence and when the women left my mother sighed and said, "They are such nice women. So Christian," and I wanted to open my mouth again and ask her why God found them so fabulous—what with their slacks, and cut hair, and in one case wig—wig!—if I was such a germ in the Heavenly Father's universe. At least I had the grace to be wearing a dress in my Amish mother's presence, even if I hadn't realized when I got dressed that morning that I'd be seeing her that day.

But I held my peace, and then Dad walked in looking elegant as usual but a bit rattled, and very glad indeed to see me. He allowed me to hug him and even (sort of) hugged me back. I told him I was going out for a little while, I was badly in need of air—hospitals and I appreciate each other but agree that the less seen the better—so I walked out onto Duke Street and down to Market Fare, a restaurant I had occasionally frequented when I worked in Lancaster City.

I ordered a glass of Pinot Grigio and an appetizer and to my horror, tears ran down my face so I grabbed my sunglasses and wore them while I ate. The doctors had told my father earlier that Mom's heart was fragile and it could go either way—

she could have some years of quality life or...and the "or" was suddenly hitting me hard.

What would I do without Mom in my life, the mother who had star-gazed with me while we hung wash on the line early in the morning, the mother who had laughed and said in Pennsylvania Dutch, "Everything will work out!" when we missed the Lancaster bus to Bird-in-Hand...the mother who had made sure I had new dresses every year for the school Christmas program...

The restaurant was quiet at that time of the day; it was after three o'clock by now, and I called an ex-boyfriend, one of a select few I knew I could count on to provide me with manly comfort, and told him how worried I was about Mom.

He soothed me while I talked and knew just what to say, bless the man, and when I hung up I felt better. The glass of wine eased some of the stress caused by being stopped by a cop and dealing with wig-wearing women carrying books about hell.

On the way back to the hospital I picked up a couple of PayDay candy bars for Dad, I knew he loved them, and a *USA Today* newspaper, and by the time I reached the hospital was ready for the next go 'round of daughterly comforting.

Dad left around six o'clock and Mom ate her hospital supper with appreciation, I was glad to see. An hour passed. Nothing to do. Finally I said to Mom in the tentative tone of voice a husband might use when asking his wife if she'd like to lunch at Hooter's, "Mom, how about if we watch a movie?"

"A movie!" she cried in horror.

"Yes," I said firmly. "A movie."

I picked up the remote and looked at the selections, most of which would have been fine for an average American ten-year-old, but by my mother's standards would surely be classified as Tales from the Pit.

I clicked through one movie choice after another. *No. No. No. No. No. No.* And then...*Hmm.*

It was a movie I'd not yet seen—*August Rush*—and I prayed Dear God please let this movie not be the disaster it could be if I make the wrong choice.

"How about this?" I said as my mom stared at the TV screen with accusing eyes, just waiting for the unbridled sex and violence she was sure it would provide.

Only a few minutes had gone by when my mother gasped, "She's not wearing any clothes!" as she watched Keri Russell play the violin.

"Relax, Mom," I said. "It's not that kind of movie."

To my great relief and I'm sure my mother's, the next shot showed a head-to-toe Keri and this time you could see that her strapless gown came down to her ankles.

Mom fiddled with the newspaper and pretended to read the Bible, but I saw her sneak glances at the TV, and finally she gave in and watched full-out. She asked countless questions about plot points which I patiently tried to answer, but after a while I became engrossed too and fought irritation when she said things like, "Now who is that man again?" and so on.

Dad came in around the middle of the movie and bless his heart, sat quietly watching, and when the credits rolled Mom cried, "Wait! What happened then? Did they all get together or not!" and I had a hard time explaining how Hollywood likes to do the whole ambiguous thing at the end of some movies.

(*Whew!* I'd like to personally thank the director of *August Rush* for that fine movie. I'm sure she never dreamed she could engage a recalcitrant Amish woman into watching it almost against her will, and if that's not a sign of genius I'm not sure what is.)

Dad asked if I could drive him home, and we walked in peaceful silence to the parking garage. It was one of those summer nights I love, the air soft and warm, and a few blocks down Duke Street Dad said, "Have you ever been to the symphony?"

I smiled at the memory that question evoked. My friend Mike, a man I had dated briefly when I still lived in Pennsylvania, took me to my first symphony in Philadelphia…it was one of those romantic, sweet dates I will never forget.

"Yes," I said, "A number of times. But my favorite was the Philadelphia Orchestra. The music was so beautiful it brought tears to my eyes."

"Katie and I saw the symphony in Boston," Dad said quietly.

I glanced over at him in the darkness. *How hard was it for this man to be Amish?* I wondered. Yes, I had a lot of my mother in me, but I had inherited Dad's love of travel and thirst for adventure, and maybe his appreciation of the arts too?

I loved my father very much at that moment.

"Did you enjoy it?" I asked.

"Yes," he said, and there was a wealth of feeling in that small word.

I am grateful my parents have so many non-Amish friends, people they've met while traveling or through my father's business, and those kind folks often invite my parents to visit them when and if they can. It expands Mom and Dad's horizons and is probably the only reason my father, and maybe my mother too, have survived in the Amish culture.

The next day my older sister Anne came to the hospital to visit Mom and I was very happy to see her. Anne has a no-nonsense air about her in these situations that I sometimes lack and I greeted her with glad cries of welcome. Dad was there too, so she and I slipped down to the cafeteria.

"Do you remember last time we were here," I said to Anne as we sipped coffee, "when that nurse asked Mom all those questions prior to her heart operation and how she answered when the nurse asked her if she'd ever smoked?"

"Yes," Anne said and we both laughed.

That had been Mom's prep day for the operation. Anne, Dad and I were in a tiny room with Mom while a nurse asked her in crisp tones about her health history. About fifteen questions in, the nurse stood poised, pen in hand, at yet another check box and said to Mom, "Have you ever smoked?"

Mom hesitated. "Well," she said with a guilty look on her face, "one of my brothers offered me a cigarette behind the barn one time and I wish now I wouldn't have taken a few puffs but…"

The nurse looked up, startled out of box-checking mode.

"Mom," I said gently, "I'm sure she wants to know if you've ever had a smoking *habit*."

Anne and I had tried not to look at each other because we were both trying not to laugh. The nurse cleared her throat, smartly checked the box, and moved on to the next question.

"How's Mom doing with her heart medications?" I asked Anne, who lives close to our parents and checks in on the situation now and then.

She sighed. "Not great, I'm afraid. She takes half a pill when she's supposed to take one, that sort of thing, and she's always on some natural remedy or other which would be fine normally, but I don't know how some of the stuff she takes reacts to the meds the docs have her on."

"Ugh!" I said. "What are we going to do with her?"

We finished our coffee and headed back upstairs, where we were informed that the next step was for Mom to have her lungs tapped because they were concerned about fluid buildup. Anne said she needed to use the restroom and would find us later, so I waited next to Mom after they had wheeled her out to the hallway. There were tubes and things everywhere and I was afraid to touch anything, so I stood next to her hospital bed and tried to be as unobtrusive as possible.

"Let's *go,* Susie!" Mom said.

"Mom, we have to wait for an attendant. I can't just take off with you."

"Oh, come on," my mother said, and I realized not for the first time just where I've inherited my impatience.

"Mom! I really can't. There are too many tubes and things and I have no idea where we're going, anyway."

She seethed quite a bit and, by the time an attendant came, had an extremely rebellious look on her face. The woman took Mom down to the basement level while I followed in her wake, and then we waited, yet again, until finally a bright-eyed woman with auburn hair entered the room. She did some tests and then turned her back and tapped some information into the computer.

Anne and I exchanged glances over Mom's head.

"Mom," I said, "please promise me that when we leave the hospital you will do *exactly* what the doctors tell you to do. Not half a pill when they say a whole pill, okay? Join a motorcycle gang if you must, get a tattoo, whatever—there are other ways to express your rebellion—but *not* with your medications."

I saw the redhead's shoulders shake as she continued typing and Anne smothered a laugh. My mother raised her eyebrows and her facial expression was a sight to behold. It was, basically, the most rebellious, I'll-do-what-I-want expression I've ever seen.

And she wonders where I get it!

The technician turned and informed us of the good news that there wasn't enough fluid to do the lung tap after all. She wheeled Mom back out to the hallway to wait and Anne and I followed. By then the redhead's curiosity was a tangible thing and she hesitated a moment but walked away, only to return a few moments later, her hair bright under the harsh fluorescent lights.

"Who *are* you?" she said to Anne and me.

"We're Katie's daughters," we said together and I laughed and said, "Were you thinking maybe we were some random women off the street who just decided to hang out with this Amish woman for a while?"

"Noo..." but she looked like she had about a thousand more questions she'd like to ask before she hurried away to take care of the next patient who, one can only hope, was a little more obedient, a little more patient, than one Katie née Esh Fisher.

Chapter 44

M om's health improved rapidly after that procedure, and I was thrilled when she was well enough to attend the Fisher reunion soon after that.

I *adore* my father's side of the family. There is something special about the Fisher clan—an elegance and intelligence mixed with a sparkling sense of humor. However, even though some of my siblings were attending as well, I still felt nervous as I drove into the driveway of the couple who was hosting the reunion, and my hands felt sweaty as I approached the circle of Amish women sitting on lawn chairs on the grass. Most of them were dressed completely in black—black dresses, capes, aprons, shoes, and stockings—with the white organdy prayer covering the only relief.

I shook hands with each woman, in Amish tradition, and one of them said to me, "So, Susie, where do you work?" When I told her the name of the firm she said, "What do they do?" And when I said "Executive search" it sounded downright freakish in that bucolic setting.

One conversation left me a little misty-eyed. A woman I didn't recognize—I think she was a distant cousin—smiled at me when I shook her hand. "I combed your hair when you were a little girl," she said, and some faint, distant memory emerged of when I was a child of about six years old and a teenage girl combing my hair before a wedding. I'd felt so honored, and I'm sure she has no idea how much it meant to me that she recalled that memory and shared it with me. To those of us who've left the Amish, every conversation with those we've left behind is precious, every smile a gift, and I never take it for granted.

227

The next woman, the wife of one of my cousins, took a different tack.

"Do you have any children?" she said and I thought I detected a slightly malicious gleam in her eyes.

"Yes. One, a son," I said, and waited…and then it came.

"How about your husband, is he here today?" she said, and I could tell by the look on her face she knew I was no longer married but wanted to hear me say it. I gave her the pleasure. Heck, why not. Any woman forced to wear black on a hot summer day deserves whatever entertainment she can find.

"I haven't had much luck with husbands!" I said brightly. "I had two, and lost them both."

"Ooh," she said, and drew it out a bit.

I smiled at her and moved on, glad I could provide her with that juicy tidbit of gossip and yeah, sure, it hurt me a little, too. I never like it when people find pleasure in my pain but it happens, doesn't it.

And then: Barbie! My beloved childhood friend! No shaking of hands with her. I took both her hands in mine, pulled her to her feet and enveloped her in a giant hug, and we grinned at each other. Her eyes, framed by those long, curly eyelashes, still sparkled with humor and we settled in for a cozy chat.

One of her sons is close to Josh's age so we talked about motherhood and reminisced about childhood for a while, too, those fun Sunday afternoons spent playing in the barn while her brother Ben serenaded us with "In 1814 we took a little trip…"

"You know what?" Barbie said.

"What?" I said, all agog. Oh yes, I recognized that tone, the one that said good times were about to be had.

"Wouldn't it be fun to go back someday, to where we both used to live?"

"Yes!" I cried with enthusiasm. "Why not tonight, after the reunion?"

"Hmm!" Barbie said. "I'll have to ask my husband…"

Ah yes. Those pesky husbands. Since only one of us had to deal with that issue—not that I'd be asking mine for permission, if I had one—we stepped into the barn where long tables had been set up for each family to eat the packed lunch they'd brought.

I spotted Barbie's husband dozing into his beard on a lawn chair near the middle of the barn. I was closer to him than she was, and she called out to him, "Sam, is it okay if Susie and I get together later?"

He looked at me rather doubtfully, and who can blame him? I knew the dude well and we'd never seen eye to eye, so to speak.

I couldn't resist. I leaned close to his ear and tried not to notice how repulsive his beard was. "You don't have a choice," I said.

He blinked. I doubt any female had ever informed him he didn't have a choice about anything and in his shock said Fine, go ahead.

I winked at Barbie and moved to where my family was starting to gather around our designated table. I greeted my brother Junior, who is one of those guys whom everyone seems to like. He is intelligent and well-read, and just a good guy, all around. However, in spite of how much I admire him, I still seethe a good bit that even though he left the Amish church just like I did, and is excommunicated, he gets the star treatment from Mom and Dad. One day I asked Mom why they treated him so much better than me and she said, "He respects us." Talk about twisting the knife in an already raw wound!

I sat down between Junior and my sister Sally, who was garbed in black like most of the other Amish women, and then Mom and Dad trekked over to the table with "that look" on their faces.

They pointed at a couple of folding chairs away from the table and then Dad said to me—not to Junior, just to me— "Susie, you can sit here," and Mom nodded her head in agreement.

Something inside me snapped. "No," I said quietly. "I'm staying right here."

They capitulated immediately. Reminded me of the time I had thrown that ugly shoe across the kitchen, when their usually sweet daughter expressed "that side" of herself, the one that says You can't make me like something or do something that doesn't make sense.

So we siblings ate at the table, and Mom and Dad sat in the folding chairs. Sally compromised somewhere in the middle and pushed her chair back a few inches from the table to observe the shunning rules, in case anyone was watching.

I am sure my Amish cousins have no idea how much I enjoyed that afternoon, reminiscing of times we'd had as children and teenagers. They still all have each other while I'm alone in the big city so to speak and I soaked in the moments, knowing it would be a long while before I'd see most of them again.

Then my father addressed the gathering, and I was so proud of him. He did a fabulous job and the group enjoyed the tales of my grandmother Susanna, that fiery woman who dropped the occasional swear word and wasn't afraid of anyone or anything, from the sound of it. Later I said to Dad, "Do I look anything like Susanna?"

I'd always felt she was a kindred spirit but since she had died when I was a child and the Amish aren't supposed to take photographs, I had no idea what she had looked like as a younger woman.

My father has never paid me a compliment on my appearance but that day he came as close as it gets. He studied me for a moment and said, "Yes, I believe you do. She was an attractive woman."

Barbie and I convened with her younger sister Sadie and my sister Ruth Ann, who had also been close friends as children, and later that night, the four of us ended up in a buggy, Sadie at the reins. When she finally drew the horse to a wild stop at the Bird-in-Hand Farmers Market, I breathed a quiet sigh of relief. It had been a long time since I'd ridden in a buggy and while I trusted Sadie to keep control of the horse, I was still a little nervous. Crawling out of the buggy in red patent-leather stilettos with 4" heels wasn't easy. I was wearing a dress and that part was fine, since I had lots of practice crawling out of buggies in a skirt, but the shoes and I agreed they were not exactly appropriate footwear for the odd buggy ride.

We crossed the street and browsed around the Old Village Store where we'd bought candy as children. If you are ever in Bird-in-Hand, please stop in—it has the most eclectic mix of stuff you'll ever see, from hardware to delightful old books to giant wooden spoons for stirring vats of lemonade.

After we'd explored the store to our hearts' content, we walked to Barbie and Sadie's old home place, the small farm where we'd had so much fun as kids. A young Amish couple lived there now along with their passel of children. The woman who opened the door looked rather flushed and said she was making corn on the cob but Come in, come in. She could not have been more gracious as we roamed around the rooms and reminisced.

Back at the market, the horse patiently waited for us to crawl back in the buggy and drive the short distance to Mom and Dad's house. Barbie and Sadie exclaimed over our old rooms and other things that triggered happy memories, and then Mom insisted that we all stay for supper.

I was touched when she whispered to me, "I know how much you like chicken corn soup so I'm making that for you." We sat outside around the picnic table and Mom and Dad sat at the table with Ruth Ann and me and ate with us. Barbie and Sadie scraped their chairs back to observe the shunning rules but were close enough to join in the conversation.

After eating, we helped Mom with the dishes and then flew back to Sadie's house—that horse had had just about enough of four giggling females—and afterwards, when Ruth Ann and I got into her car and waved our goodbyes, we agreed it had been a day we would never forget.

Chapter 45

A fter a visit to Lancaster County, work seems more foreign than ever and yet somehow familiar too. If the color of Amish is black (opaque, blocks out danger but also sunlight); then the color of the corporate world is beige (without personality, smacks down individuality). These two entities' negative traits often feel the same to me—don't think, don't feel, don't create. Just work and shut up.

I can't describe the office I'm in now, except to say that it is a gray and beige mausoleum. Why in the name of all that matters is there so much horror in our corporate décor?

And the art! Our office is close to the White House and sits smack dab at the core of the powerful DC scene known simply as K Street. On one of the walls of our big fancy conference room is a doughnut covered in green slime. Not a real doughnut, of course, but a larger-than-life-sized painting of one. I despair when I look at it. A pretty price it fetched I am sure, but why? why? would anyone consider that art?

That room brings out all my worst behavior, with the Halloween party last fall as a prime example. The party planner, who takes a czar-like approach to these things, commanded us all via email to **come in costume.**

I rebelled. No, I said. Yes, she said. She had bought butterfly wings for all of us administrative professionals, as we're called these days, but I marched into the conference room without my wings. The best that could be said for me was that I had slapped on some glittery eye shadow and called it a costume.

"Go get your wings, Susie!" the czarist barked.

I seethed, but I did it. I was the angriest butterfly in the history of the world, but then I tossed down a few peanut M&Ms and put my best smile on, and tried to forget I had the damn wings strapped to my back.

Then the managing director walked in wearing a business suit and a smile. No costume. I sidled up to him and said, "What did you come as, scary businessman?"

He looked at me with the expression I've become so familiar with at work, i.e.—"Huh? What?"

It entertains me, if it doesn't them, but it also scares me because I'm never really sure what's going to come out of my mouth.

Gary, another senior client partner who brings out the worst in me, is a man I've labeled amphibian. I always think he'd be so much happier if he had a lily pad to sit on rather than an office chair. One December he took me and some coworkers to his club for lunch. I had been there before and wasn't a big fan; it felt stuffy and pompous to me, but still, I enjoyed the break from the office. And imagine my surprise when we sat down and the tadpole ordered a round of tequila shots! My, these amphibians do live!

I happened to be sitting next to him and over salmon (mediocre) and wine (great) he regaled us with stories of the executive search business.

However, the happiest prize was yet to come: he and I were the last ones to get up after lunch and I was collecting my purse and preparing to follow my coworkers out when I saw Taddy dipping his fingers in his water glass.

"What are you doing?" I said.

"Washing my fingers."

"No one does that!" I said, which goes to show one should never start a business lunch with a shot of tequila unless one is prepared to state the obvious.

Which I am always happy to do, and the non-obvious as well.

However, my favorite story, and I consider it legend, about our resident frog-to-be happened at a partners' conference in Florida. Allegedly he had had quite a few drinks at happy hour and as he staggered back to his room someone jostled his elbow.

"F**k you!" our finger-washer said.

Guess who the jostler was? Yup—our very own CEO, the head of our worldwide, or rather *global* as they like to call it, firm.

I laughed, and then I laughed some more when I heard that story.

However, the prize for office freak goes to a woman I dub Frankenstein's widow because she has this awful flapping way of walking, like her feet are zombies and the rest of her is (almost) human. Alice is also a senior client partner and I am extremely angry at Management for keeping her on, because she rips and tears at her assistants. I am convinced it gives her pleasure, but do they address it? No, because she brings money in, you know, and goodness! that's the whole point, isn't it?

One day Helen, the office manager, said, "Susie, Alice needs your help because two of her clients are unhappy with the service they've been getting and we know you could do a great job of fixing it."

I sighed because I was already swamped, and taking on client relations for two more executive searches was the last thing I needed. But I said Fine, and asked Alice's assistant for dates when some meetings could be scheduled, and in a half hour I had everything done. I emailed the client to confirm everything and copied Alice.

Not two minutes later, FLAP, FLAP, FLAP and there she was in person, eyes blazing.

Frankie's widow screamed at me for using the wrong dates, but believe me, I was sure I had used the ones I was given because I had checked and double-checked. (As it turned out, her assistant was responsible for the error, but I did not hold the poor woman culpable—everyone who worked for Alice made a lot of mistakes; you can't operate in an atmosphere of fear and not short out mentally now and then.)

I tried to speak but Alice ran over my several attempts to do so and continued screaming at me. I waited until she was finished and then I got up from my chair and walked out the door. I took the elevator down to the lobby, pushed my way through the loathsome revolving door, and walked around the block, steam rising in billowing waves from my ears.

When I came back I marched to Helen's office and explained what happened. "Keep Alice away from me," I said. "And in the future, I will not deal with her or help her. Are we clear?"

Helen looked stunned because she had never seen that side of me, but I had had just about enough of these abusive types, and all I can say to our corporate office is this: get ready.

This criminal—and that's what I call those types who hurt others for pleasure, *criminal*, because even though they can't get arrested for their behavior, in universe terms, in justice terms, they should be barred from *ever* managing people again— is going to get hers one day.

And Alice, my friends, is a lawsuit about to happen. There are laws in this country about hostile work environments, and while I've never had the guts to go that route, there are those who do. But, of course, the god who watches over these corporate types couldn't let me get away with standing up to Alice, his favorite pet, so when Helen called me into her office one day, I had a sinking sensation in the pit of my stomach.

I knew by the look on her face that it was going to be one of those lectures in a series, from bosses past and present who admired my people skills, my organizational skills, and my writing skills, but had a problem with that something-something beneath the surface, i.e., my frankest, most honest self. I eyed her guardedly. I may sound tough but I'm not, when it comes to authority figures in the workplace. I'm still, after all these years, just a scared little girl sometimes.

"So, Susie," Helen said.

"Yes?"

"I've been hearing some things we need to discuss."

Oh, shit.

"Gary Solanger says you have a bad attitude."

The *tadpole?* That came as such a surprise I was rendered speechless. I may have laughed quietly at the way he crept around the office in that slimy way of his, but I had helped the man more times than I could count. When his assistant was out he usually came to me. Most recently he'd needed help with a document "right now" and I had inwardly groaned but said Fine, I'll help, and stepped over to his haunt.

"Gary," I said, "I'm happy to help you, but I think we could do this most efficiently if you dictate to me while I type."

That was my kind way of saying that I, and everyone else except his assistant, could not read his handwriting. The last time I'd been hit with a request for help it almost put me over the edge trying to decipher his squiggles and curlicues.

He looked up with his pale, bulging blue eyes and said, "I'll come to your desk."

I was gracious but crisp, I thought, and slammed that thing out in about 45 minutes, all ten pages of that damn document.

Helen continued, "Yes. His assistant is leaving and when we discussed who would replace her he said he didn't want you, because you have an attitude."

For all my bravado, that hurt. I had put my heart into that assignment, and done a spectacular job in a short amount of time. What, was he offended I hadn't offered him a blow job too? And this from a man who had said F you to the CEO?

Helen yammered on, citing more examples, until I felt that she was smashing my head repeatedly against a concrete sidewalk. My gut told me Helen was manufacturing most of what she was accusing me of, because I had a reputation for working hard and doing a good job. Regardless, it didn't matter, because the real reason she was angry at me was because I had had the audacity to stand up to Alice. As a member of the administrative staff and not a "rainmaker,"—God, how I hate that term—I was supposed to know that I had no voice at all. And she was going to make sure that I learned my lesson, and learned it well.

Don't you ever wonder how people like the tadpole and Frankenstein's widow learn leadership? In all the years that I've been in the corporate world, I am *amazed* at how idiots like this inherit these types of positions. And while we employees are de-motivated and demoralized, they keep getting promoted to higher and higher positions and making more and more money. Sometimes word gets out—leadership skills are lacking. So Corporate sends their little darlings to workshops or has them read the latest slick book on leadership. Nothing wrong with workshops or books, but you can't teach a person to care about people. Either they do or they don't, and if they don't, their employees will continue to be miserable or eventually find new jobs.

The other thing I've noticed is that if the bottom line is healthy, no complaint from a mere employee will usually move corporate leadership unless a) there is legal action involved, which means some of their precious lucre could be affected, or b) there is the possibility of bad publicity if the employee is vocal enough.

Usually, they will stand firmly behind the boss and make *you*, the employee, look like a troublemaker.

I dedicate this poem to everyone who's been downtrodden in the workplace.

Damn All Beige

I wonder why the fuck
Every wall in Corporate America is beige
        or gray.

Just a thought.

I wonder why in the lobby
        of these same beige/gray tombs
        there is always some work of "Art" (I
use the word loosely) that basically looks like
a brain on crack, but in color.

What if instead they painted
                just one wall yellow

        What if instead of that worthless
        revolving door they installed a real
        one for a change and painted it red.

                What if maybe there was a cat
                in the lobby everyone petted
                and perhaps a rocking chair or
                two.

        What if they ripped down our cubicle
walls (whoever invented those should be
shot no questions asked)

and put in real walls again or hell, just
threw us all in one gigantic warehouse at
least it'd have character, natch.

What if business suits were banned and no
one could ever wear a tie unless it had a
funny animal on it and

What if CEOs were Chief Executive Outsiders and the kids ran the show

What if the janitor were the honored
employee he probably does a hell of a lot
more than the fat cats in the executive suite

> Yeah and what if instead of the
> mandatory appearance at the
> company picnic where everyone gets
> drunk on beer they don't like

They sent us all home to play with our kids
in the park and look up at the sky and
remember what it's all about.

241

Chapter 46

T he other side is that happiness can come when you least expect it, like the morning I was commuting to work with a man who had a high voice and a kind face and a brown mustache. His brown pants were too short and he drove a very old, large car, like the one George Costanza's father drives on *Seinfeld.*

As we crossed the Memorial Bridge I looked up from my book and caught my breath because the sky was all gray and misty and some rays of sun shone down and lit up the Potomac River, and a lone seagull soared up to the heavens. In front of me the Lincoln Memorial looked stately and dignified and beautiful.

DC and I, however, still aren't on speaking terms, really. She is far too power-hungry for me and I am, frankly, too Amish for her. But then occasionally we have our moments.

I like standing in Lafayette Park, across from the White House, and feeling lucky that I have the opportunity to be in the capital of the U.S. where so many historic moments have shaped the courses of our lives.

I enjoy looking at the Washington Monument when I cross the Fourteenth Street Bridge and remembering how I thrilled at the sight of it when I was in eighth grade on a field trip. And I think I feel most grown up when I'm driving in the city, swearing happily along with the other drivers, trying to stay alive.

In springtime DC and I have a romantic fling, when we adore each other so much we forget all about politics and our grudges against each other. If you've never seen Washington

DC in the spring, you've missed out. The cherry blossoms are celebrated and rightfully so, but I usually avoid that area at the peak time because of all the tourists and instead, soak in the rest of the gorgeousness. The flowering trees, the tulips, the daffodils—I'm describing it badly; you'll just have to come see it for yourself, if you can.

There's even something soothing about routine, isn't there? My dream is to one day not work for other people anymore and have the luxury of creating without forcing it into my schedule at crazy hours of the morning, like I do now. But I think there would be elements I'd miss, like walking past the Firehook Bakery on 17th Street and waving to the man with a white mustache sipping a cup of coffee...and hearing the musician on Pennsylvania Avenue who serenades us employees every morning with his beautiful trumpet playing...and getting takeout sushi from Wasabi from the guy who is always so kind to me...

I don't think I'll miss my cubicle, though. My first week on the job I tacked up a gigantic sunflower poster, which helped, and I brought a few plants and photos and that sort of thing, but eventually I took everything home except the poster, because the universe seemed to say *Be ready to leave at a moment's notice*. So now it's just me and the poster and the employees I love and laugh with every day.

Even inside the beige walls I hate so much, I've had moments of sweetness, like the morning when our receptionist Mohamed offered to buy me a yogurt when I mentioned that I was hungry and didn't have time to eat. I'm sure he had no idea how much that simple act of kindness touched my heart.

Then there's my friend Claire, a black woman who has a backbone of steel and at whose feet I listen and learn, because just when I think I'm doing well in the courage department, she one-ups me and I adore her.

And just when I had thought that there were no bosses in the corporate world I could tolerate—ever—a year ago I started working for a man named Sloan in our CFO practice who, while not perfect—no one is—showed me that not all authority figures in the workplace are spawns of the devil. He and I got along just fine, and when he left for a position at another firm he wrote a reference letter for me that I need to frame, to remind me that not all my corporate bosses have hated me.

Then, if all else fails, there's my favorite Greek restaurant in DC, Kellari, located next to our office. I feel like I'm going to a different country when I'm there, a place where there is color and life and good food and conversation. I love sitting at the bar with one of my coworkers, noshing on the excellent aged parmesan cheese, melba toast, and olives they always keep on the counter...and then there is one of my other favorite escapes, Finemondo, a restaurant on F Street that brings all that is best of Italy—its warmth, charm, good food, and wine—to our capital city.

And how could I fail to mention the time I was carried across one of those grates that wreaks such hell on a girl's stiletto heels? It was a rainy night and I was walking to the Old Ebbitt Grill with a Secret Service friend of mine. I didn't have an umbrella and neither did he, and I guess he felt a girl should only suffer so much. Suddenly he picked me up and carried me across, and honey, if you've never had a Secret Service agent with strong biceps pick you up and carry you, well, you should if you can. It is a lovely experience.

Chapter 47

I worry sometimes that I've departed too far from my roots. There is a glaring dichotomy in me, two forces diametrically opposed—the Amish and English parts.

The Amish one is a caped-and-aproned sweetheart who sees the world through innocent eyes. She often feels out of place and is not quite sure she's comfortable with herself or anyone else, for that matter. She likes to read, enjoys nature, and wants to be left alone a lot.

My English side, on the other hand, adores attention. She likes red and pink and makeup and blond hair and stilettos and would rather shop and chat with girlfriends than read. She drinks and (occasionally) wishes she'd smoke if it weren't bad for her health. She demands that she make up for lost time because the caped-and-aproned Susie got the first 20 years. So, she says, she'd like the last however many years she's given on the planet to express herself on a grand scale.

My goal is to bring these two sides together, like little girls who don't speak the same language and yet share toys and smiles and occasionally even hugs. But I don't think I'm doing a very good job. I attribute this to the multiple layers of my psyche, layers that were developed almost independently of each other. My development was different from the average American's, if there is such an animal, who typically does the whole elementary school thing, then middle, then high school where he/she might have the odd bit of rebellion or what not and then college, if that's the plan, and then the career and, if inclined, the marriage and babies. All morphed together, all evolving into one (hopefully beautiful) mature adult.

I have this list: Amish. Sheltered. Innocent teenager. Virgin bride, married to crack-addict husband. Hymn-singing Christian. Move to the city. Shed a few religious layers.

And so on.

I went to San Diego with my sister Anne not too long ago and we were returning from dinner one evening and had almost reached our hotel when a couple of Marines hailed us and asked if we'd like to join them for a night out on the town. They had just returned from Afghanistan the day before and were, by the looks of it, ready to party on a grand scale.

Heck, no was basically Anne's correct (married-woman) response and she toddled back to the room. I, on the other hand, hesitated not at all.

"Sure!" I said.

The quieter of the two Marines slinked off toward the beach and I studied the long, cool glass of water standing in front of me. He was wearing jeans and a white shirt, and didn't have an ounce of spare flesh on his body. He was wreathed in smiles and had clearly started the celebrating early.

His name was Robert and I told him mine was Susie, and he seemed as delighted with me as I was with him. San Diego seemed pretty happy with all its inhabitants, if the weather was any indication. Granted, I hear it's like that most of the time, but it was a soft, velvety kind of night with a playful breeze and it seemed specially designed for adventure.

"What are you doing in San Diego?" Robert said.

"My sister and I are here for a quick getaway weekend and I'm celebrating finishing a book."

"Susan!" he exclaimed. "This calls for a bottle of '96 Dom Pérignon!"

I laughed and said, "Thank you very much, but I can't possibly let you buy me a bottle of expensive champagne."

"Not to worry, my dad is a retired executive and he's taking care of everything tonight." He took my hand and we ran to the street, hailed a cab, and found a bar on Pacific Beach that had wood floors and a hard yet endearing edge.

Robert whipped out a credit card and shouted to the bartender, "A bottle of Dom Pérignon, '96 if you have it, for Susan!"

The bartender said, "Sorry, I don't have '96 Dom but will '97 do?"

"Sure!" Robert said, and when it came, those two perfect flutes of champagne, the bubbles reflected in the light, we drank Dom Pérignon, and kissed, and shared some of our champagne with a lonely-looking bearded man sitting at the end of the bar.

Afterwards we went to yet another place that had a bar in the front and a group of empty tables in the back room. Robert and I found a group of people who immediately became our new best friends, but after a while I needed space and wandered to the back room alone, where those empty tables were huddled together, snoozing in spite of the loud music. The bare table tops looked like they could use some jazzing up.

Hmmm! I thought. *Dare I?*

My inner two-year-old, the little girl who had sung Jolly Old St. Nicholas for the Esh aunts and uncles from the vantage point of a table, thought it an *excellent* idea. However, the teenage girl who had been preached to by the Bearded Ones wasn't so sure. And then, naturally, I thought about my two Amish grandmothers. What would they do?

In my mind's eye I saw my Grandma Esh, and even as a ghost she looked overweight and unhappy in a shawl and bonnet. She shook her finger at me and said, "Don't do it, Susie! What will people think?"

Then I imagined Grandma Susanna Fisher, and she didn't waste time in chit-chat. She shucked off her (Amish) shoes, grabbed my hand, and we danced on top of the tables until a gray-haired man with a stern expression looked up at me and said, "If you don't get down from there I'm going to have to ask you to leave."

I can't describe the quiet thrill of pride I felt at those words. And that's what I mean by a sense of compass—where others might have felt ashamed at the threat of being kicked out of a bar, for me it was the ultimate sign that I had come about as far as it gets for an Amish girl from Lancaster County.

Chapter 48

Since I moved to the Washington DC area I have met some horrible human specimens, true; but I have also had the good fortune to meet some delicious men, some fabulous men, some simply outstanding men.

There's a book out that I have not read but I understand the principle is this: if you believe in God, and Jesus, well—you should not date. Hmm! Wonder where they got that? Well, biblical or not, here's the (interesting) theme: you should trust God to bring your Chosen Mate to you and then marry him (or her) quick.

To which I say Bravo! Bravo! How cool is that, for those special people for whom this works? No drama, no fuss. Just: here you go. You two belong together, and off you go. Marry, children. Have babies. Live the dream.

It is said God never sleeps. Well, in my case maybe I'm so much work the Divine Being finds it necessary to take the occasional nap because obviously I didn't go this route. Or maybe he chose Husband #1 but, since we're all free agents, the dude decided drugs were the answer. And so God had to get a little creative, but he seemed to be taking his time, so my sister Anne suggested I try the computer dating thing.

"Nope!" I said. "Try it," she said, and added that one of her friends had done so with some success, and why shouldn't I?

So I did, and wow! What a world! You've never seen so many *fantastic* men, a group who, collectively, want nothing more than to dance with me on the beach at sunset. They have impeccable children, if any, and they all work out and live innocent, beautiful, lives, which would only be enhanced if they spent the rest of it with me, the unattached female for whom they pine.

Then, alas, comes the face-to-face meeting. It may be my imagination but the few times I met anyone live, I felt that they were a little disappointed in me, too, at least at first. I mean, my pics were current, and I'd be foolishly modest if I said I wasn't attractive by most standards, but still, photo-gazing on-line and meeting a human is strikingly different. The photo is so easy, you know—just a face and a body—but that human you're sizing up and shaking hands with is rife with flaws, simply rife, and it's jarring isn't it?

I met Lance at a restaurant in Bethesda, Maryland. I was heading to Lancaster County afterwards so I only had an hour, and when I walked into the restaurant he had chosen I felt that exhausted sense of Oh God, what am I getting myself into now? I know there are people who love this sort of thing, but I find the thought of dating a stranger overwhelming.

The restaurant smelled good, like there were excellent cuts of beef sizzling in the kitchen, and there was a happy bustling energy about the place. A basket of oranges sat on the hostess station and it added a cheerful, wholesome touch.

And then there he was! The potential dancing-at-sunset man of my dreams.

He wore khaki pants and a nice shirt, and I liked the proud way he held his balding head, as if to say, Yes I'm an older man, get over it because I have, and life is good, baby, good. He beamed at me and seemed quite delighted with my company, but here's the other thing about the whole internet dating thing—it makes you feel a little less special when you realize that he had probably beamed at dozens of women before me, you know?

Still, he exuded warmth and ordered a glass of wine for each of us, and by the time my salad came I found I wasn't having a terrible time. He was easy to talk to and when we parted ways, I to Pennsylvania, he to a golf game, I congratulated myself on going through with it.

Our next date was karaoke night at his country club. He introduced me to his friends, a trio who had clearly started celebrating early, but I was still reeling from two things: one, that the security guard at the gate to the country club estate had been in a tuxedo—a tuxedo!—and two, from the tour Lance had given me of his house.

The universe likes its jokes, doesn't it? My second ex had driven me nuts with his hoarding tendencies and it had been a constant battle not to lose my temper, not to mention my mind, because of all the clutter and mess he created. But Lance's house was so impeccable, so spotless, so devoid of anything human that I was sure even the dog asked first if he could shed a hair or two.

So there I sat in that fancy bar with Lance and three inebriated rich guys while someone screeched Aerosmith's "Sweet Emotion" into the microphone.

"My friends think you're hot!" Lance whispered in my ear when I returned from a trip to the ladies room. I smiled and nodded my thanks and he invited me to a Valentine's Day dinner at the Club with a couple he knew and I said Okay, sure.

Next I met him after work one night. Two of his colleagues joined us for drinks, and afterwards we hopped into Lance's BMW and went to Legal Seafood for a bite to eat. I was exhausted from my work day and when the conversation turned to politics I wished it hadn't—I get so sick of the whole Republican/Democrat thing. I think it's insane, the whole hate-filled rhetoric that fuels so many talk shows these days. But then, that's just me. Some people love it; I just happen not to.

Even the food didn't cheer me up. Normally, I enjoy New England clam chowder, but somehow the smell of it mixed with whatever cologne Lance was wearing was making me feel a little sick. All I wanted to do was go home, take a hot bath, and go to bed.

Lance sat on the booth next to me and an arm snaked across my shoulders.

"I could marry you," he said.

I am always happy when I make a good impression on my fellow humans. Always. But I reeled a good bit, not sure my ears had received the right information from the mother ship, i.e. my stunned brain.

"You don't even know me!" I managed after a fortifying sip of wine.

"Forget I said anything," he said curtly and ate the rest of his salmon in a rather cold, distraught manner.

When he dropped me off at my car he grabbed me and kissed me, hard. I hated that kiss; it felt like he was trying to own me, and when I drove off I felt a little queasy, emotionally speaking.

I called him when I got home and tried to explain how I felt—that the marriage conversation seemed premature (!) at this stage, and also that his kiss had made me uncomfortable.

"I'm a very independent woman," I said as gently as I could. "I am sure there are women out there who would be happy to move at this pace, but I'm afraid I'm just not one of them."

"But I was thinking you could sell your house and then you and your son could move in with me!" he said. "You wouldn't have to work anymore!"

And I'd be dead in a year.

I've never been the kind of woman who can be bought by a rich guy, and maybe that was the problem—Lance thought if he showed me his BMW and his house and his fancy club, I'd fall at his feet and beg him to take care of me and mine. I've been pursued by wealthy men before and while I am all for a fluffy bank account, the guy has to show he wants to get to know me first, and truly love me, before I say yes to anything. You can't make love to a car or a house or a dollar bill, for God's sake.

"Lance," I said, "Let's just take this slow, okay?"

His response told me he didn't like that statement, at all, and I hung up the phone feeling really upset.

The next day when I turned on my computer I saw an email from Lance. I opened it and there was a Word attachment, a full-page letter where, basically, he uninvited me to the Valentine's Day dinner and informed me how misunderstood he felt and on and on. That night he called me and apologized for the letter and said he wanted to take it all back and would I please go out with him again. As gently as I could, I said, No thank you, at which point he burst into tears. I hung up the phone feeling slightly tattered from the experience but decided, in the spirit of openness, to give another candidate a shot.

I found Alvin attractive from the first moment I laid eyes on him. We met on a sunny December day in Old Town Alexandria, in front of the Torpedo Factory Art Center. He wore a faded black coat, and seemed like an athletic type but not to the extreme of being a gym rat. And there was something about the expression in his hazel eyes that I found interesting.

Over lunch he told me he had an MBA, was a director at a nonprofit in DC, believed in Jesus, and was a staunch Democrat. A (tiny) red flag waved when he talked about his ex-wife who, he said, had cheated on him with the house painter and gotten pregnant. Now he (Alvin) was supporting the kid and her, as well as the children they'd had together because the painter was long gone. His ex-wife had gotten Fat and had no interest in finding a job. This was all said in a spirit of great bitterness, justifiably I suppose, but not really what a girl wants to hear while eating Ahi Tuna on a first date.

Another off moment was when we talked about places we'd been, and then we discussed art, and I told him how, during a tour of the Vatican, I'd been moved to tears by Michelangelo's sculpture of Mary holding the crucified Jesus. Then he said in what I can only call a scornful manner, "Oh, you mean the *Pietà,*" and I said "Oh, is that what it's called?" and when I glanced up from my salad I saw he was looking at me in the most demeaning manner.

Other than that, and his rather officious way of discussing his political views, I liked him and looked forward with great anticipation to our dinner date the following Saturday night at a French restaurant of his choosing in Alexandria. For that occasion, I donned a cocktail dress and high heels and showed up on time, not being a female who believes in Grand Entrances. I was seated by a lovely man with a French accent at a corner table in the upstairs dining room.

Fifteen minutes went by, then ten more. Two waiters buzzed about and I felt smaller and smaller as I sipped wine. Finally, in desperation, I ordered escargot to feel less like I was taking up the table in vain.

My cell phone rang before the appetizer came. "I'm running late," Alvin said and gave no reason why, just *I'm running late.* When he walked in he was wearing a sour expression and a blue shirt, tan pants, and no jacket. He had dropped a few degrees in my estimation by that time but still, hope clung—I had really been looking forward to this date and we all have off nights, don't we, and that Northern Virginia traffic could be a bear.

He sat down and scanned the menu with a frown. The gracious waiter who had been so sweet to me while I sat alone brought the escargot and placed the plate on the table with a flourish.

"Do you like escargot?" I said to Alvin.

He squinted at the menu and said, "Not enough to pay fifteen dollars for them."

Dude! If you're going to be twenty-five minutes late for a date with no explanation, I am not going to sit there and twiddle my thumbs. I sort of went numb at that point and ate a few (delicious) bites of escargot and sipped my wine and ordered a moderately-priced entrée, no salad, nothing else, just an entrée, and he did the same.

He continued throughout the meal to seem like a brooding carbon copy of the man I'd conversed with the week prior, and when the check came I said, "Do you want me to contribute?"

He picked up the check and his eyebrows shot up. "Yes!" he said. "This is a lot!"

I thought it reasonable for a French restaurant in Alexandria, especially one that he had chosen, but I forked over some cash and he snapped it up and put it into the black leather holder.

I was quiet as we walked to the next place for coffee. Hope had pretty much gurgled to death that this was going to be anything but a disaster, but there was some small part of me that could not believe that this man to whom I had been so attracted at first could behave so badly.

And here's the thing, guys—you may consider it unfair that you are expected to pay on the first several dates, but what you probably don't realize is the amount of money we spend because we want to be Lovely for you. This feminine trait is inherent in most of us women, I suspect, and we do it gladly— we get our nails done, and our eyebrows waxed, and buy a new shade of lip gloss and maybe even a new outfit, and perhaps get our hair professionally blown out and why? Because we think so highly of *you*. We probably spend more money on a date than you do, just for the preparation, so please—we might chip in later, but for the first dates at least, don't be mad if you're expected to pay. And if you can't afford a fancy restaurant, we don't care; suggest one you can and pay attention to us and be a gentleman, okay?

At the next place, my date ordered a piece of chocolate cake with two forks and coffee for us both. He seemed better now, maybe because I had helped with dinner, and I was sort of over it, so I relaxed and we had a decent conversation until I put my fork down after a couple of bites of cake—it was all I needed or wanted, at which point he said, "Is that all the cake you're eating?"

The question startled me, but I said yes it was, and then he said, "I don't know what the point is of buying you food if you don't eat it anyway."

Okay. That did it. That just damn well did it. He *hadn't* bought my dinner and he was the one who had complained about his heavy ex-wife. What, had he shoved cake down her throat, too?

I let him pay for the cake.

By that time I needed something just a little stronger than wine, so when we passed this darling place of which I am very fond, a restaurant on King Street called Two Nineteen, I said, "Let's go in here." Sort of like a woman who's eaten a very bad lunch and needs a spot of ice cream to banish the memory.

Alvin followed me up the stairs to the nightclub, a room that exudes old-style glamour and where I always feel like a reincarnation of Marilyn Monroe. I was about to open the door when he said, "I don't want to spend any money on drinks!"

I said not to worry, I'd buy, at which point you would not *believe* the change in that man. He exuded joy and entered the room with me in a spirit of jovial camaraderie. We sat down at a small round table and I sighed with pleasure at the surroundings in spite of the lemon seated next to me.

A waiter strolled over, pad in hand. "Something to drink?" he said and my date frowned in concentration as he studied the drinks menu.

"I'd like something frozen," he said to me. "A daiquiri, perhaps."

A woman can only be tried so far. I'd handled his no-excuse tardiness, his lack of a jacket in a romantic French restaurant, his petulance during dinner, his request for cash, his cake comment, and his announcement about not paying for drinks with elegance, but girly frozen drinks? No way, honey. Only men who've been behaving *very* well can get away with that, but never on first dates and never, ever, after bad behavior.

"We'll have two margaritas on the rocks," I said crisply, thinking that might be a compromise.

"What kind of tequila?" the waiter said and looked at Alvin.

Alvin shrugged helplessly so I took a breath and said, "Milagro would be great, if you have it," and waited for it, waited for it, and when that beautiful drink came I licked a little salt off the rim and drank.

My date and I talked, we even danced, and that lovely room soothed me and said "Darling, don't worry, there are Other Men out there. Chin up, Sweetheart."

We left and were almost at our cars when I glanced over at Alvin, who was frowning in a deep, disgruntled sort of way—the kind of frown that usually means heartburn or dyspepsia. I asked him what was wrong and he said in one of those If-Only tones that make life so morbid, "I still wish that drink had been frozen."

Computer dating is great for some, but not for me. I'll have to trust my good angels to bring me the right man at the right time and hope the dude drinks Scotch or Bourbon when the occasion calls for it.

Chapter 49

T he conversation with Alvin reminded me, yet again, what an ignoramus I am when it comes to art appreciation.

I had been to Italy in 2006 with a coworker. I did not see the Sistine Chapel because I was part of a tour that had gone on for hours and hours, touring the Vatican, which I hugely enjoyed, especially *La Pietà* which, as I said, brought tears to my eyes, but eventually I needed to find a ladies room, fast.

So while everyone else in the tour was admiring Michelangelo's beautiful work in the Sistine Chapel, the crème de la crème of the Vatican, I stalked the halls trying to explain to the security guards what I needed. But they only shrugged their shoulders and I realized later that the crasser world "toilet" rather than restroom might have done away with the language barrier. Suffice it to say that by the time I finally reached the ladies/*toilette*/*gabinetto* at the front entrance I was in quite a state. The tour was by then over so the Sistine Chapel and I have a date to meet sometime in the future. I can't wait.

Sometimes when I go to an art museum I feel so...*unsophisticated.* I realize I need to take an art history class, but from what I understand it involves a lot of viewing of slides and memorizing of dates and while there is nothing wrong with that, it makes me feel old and sad to contemplate it.

I prefer to create things myself, and I guess I'm like a quarterback who'd rather throw the damn ball than view slides of the one Joe Montana threw in Super Bowl XXIV. Having said that, one of my favorite things, art-wise, is visiting local art galleries, small-time places that always grab at my heart, because while the names of the artists might not be recognizable to the average person, there is usually some really good stuff, treasures actually, to be found in those kinds of galleries.

I struggle a lot with the things I *should* like because everyone else does. For example: I have a grudge against Shakespeare. I don't know why. Jealous, probably. Oh, I've tried. I struggled through the thee's and thou's until my brain hurt from the effort of understanding why everyone raved about him so, but I never did get it.

However, I kick myself to this day for hurting a Shakespeare-lover's feelings.

I was married to Morton at the time and we were invited to a post-christening brunch one Sunday afternoon at a mansion in Middleburg, Virginia. Horse country, old money, wineries. Lovely countryside. For some reason Morton couldn't go so I said I'd show the flag for both of us. I donned a summer dress and a hat and off I went.

My red Honda Civic, the car I was driving at the time, asked me if I was sure we were at the right place, what with all the BMWs and Mercedes in the driveway, and I said Hold your head high, darling, they're cars just like you.

This couple had a butler—a butler!—and a house that was professionally decorated to the point of excruciating perfection.

My hat and I were greeted warmly by our hostess, who had gone to college with Morton. I oohed and aahed over the just-christened little princess in an off-white gown and helped myself to a few goodies from the fabulous spread the caterers had laid out. And then I did as I so often do in gatherings like this when I've exhausted my supply of small talk and enjoyed the company of a new batch of entertaining humans: wandered off in search of solitude and found myself in a room facing the gardens. I looked out the screen door at the spectacular day.

Fluffy clouds...blue sky...elegant bees buzzing...flowers blooming...Middleburg at its best, and I silently applauded the creator who dreamed up such gorgeousness for our pleasure.

Then I felt rather than saw a person standing a few yards away from me to my right. At first it irked me that someone had intruded on my space. Then I turned and adjusted my hat and gosh! was he handsome. The bluest eyes I've maybe ever seen. He had dark hair and was impeccably dressed in a white shirt and black pants and was even wearing suspenders, and a man who can make suspenders look sexy is quite a stud, in my opinion. In short, he could have played understudy to Hugh Jackman in the movie *Kate and Leopold*.

He said hello, and I said hello back, and we chatted of this and that, but mostly I was enjoying the sight of those unfathomable blue eyes. How we got onto the subject of Shakespeare I do not remember. His fault I'm sure, I usually try to avoid that topic if I can help it, and then, of course, I had to open my mouth and say I didn't really get what all the fuss was about.

He looked hurt, as if I had personally insulted him, and said, "I did my thesis on Shakespeare."

Ouch. As I said, I'm still kicking myself for my thoughtless remark, and am trying hard these days to keep at least some of my opinions on art and other things as well to myself. And here's where I come to a kink in my personality which I've had ever since I left the Amish. It's a good and bad thing at the same time, I suppose, and I suspect I'll just have to live with it because it's only gotten stronger over the years rather than weaker. I suspect my antipathy to Shakespeare has nothing to do with him at all. In fact, when one of my creative writing professors, Robert Bausch, read him to us in class one night, I was almost carried away with the cadence and magic of those amazing words. No, it's not the Bard that troubles me, it's this incessant fear I have of being a follower, one of many, swallowed up by the group until I'm faceless and nameless, dressing just like everyone else and not thinking for myself. In short, I didn't suffer excommunication to become a lemming. Even the word lemming, which dictionary.com describes as "a rodent known for periodic mass migrations that occasionally end in drowning," grosses me out. So I choose random things that everyone else thinks are wonderful and go the other way just to remind myself I have a mind of my own.

I am sure I have offended other people without wanting to with this stubborn streak in my nature, and I apologize. However, as Shakespeare himself says, "To thine own self be true."

Hoo Ha!

(P.S. Sistine Chapel, maybe it was good I didn't see you last time. Timing, as they say, is everything and I'd like to think next time we meet I'll have taken an art appreciation course and know a lot more about you. Then again, maybe not...)

Chapter 50

W hen my sister Ruth Ann called me in April of 2010 and told me about the traffic accident that had taken the lives of my Uncle John Esh, his wife Sadie, and four of their children, I could not at first comprehend it. It was not until I spoke with my mother later that night that it began to sink in. Mom sounded like she hadn't slept, hadn't eaten, and hadn't stopped crying since she heard the news and it was at that moment that I decided to go to Kentucky, not only to attend the funeral, but also to show my love and support for her.

It's always a difficult decision for me during these times, i.e., will my presence cause my parents, and the Amish, more pain than comfort? Will the very sight of my non-Amish self twist the knife in their already grieving hearts? So I go by my instincts in those situations and hope that they know whether I attend or not, my heart is always with them.

I called Helen, the office manager, to let her know I would be out for a few days and explained to her what had happened.

"They were your relatives?" Helen exclaimed. I could hear the incredulousness in her tone, i.e.: *you, of all people, have plain relatives?*

I didn't say anything. Why should I? My cultural background was none of her business. I had hidden it from her for a very good reason—I didn't trust her with something so intimate.

Then she cleared her throat and said, "By the way, you might want to go shoe shopping. Something in a ballet flat might be nice."

I laughed in spite of myself. "I promise not to wear stilettos, Helen," I said.

I can't begin to tell you how hard it is to shop for clothes to wear to an Amish, or in this case conservative Mennonite, gathering. I needed a dress. It was Sunday afternoon and we were heading to Kentucky very early the following morning, and it was now or never, I thought as I rifled through dresses at a local Fashion Bug. I finally found a black dress with a few humble flowers scattered here and there on the skirt. Not too fancy, not too bright, and yet not trying too hard either.

"You could wear some pink beads with that!" the salesclerk enthused as she rang it up.

I shook my head and smiled.

Shoes were next on the list, and I went to Wal-Mart because I didn't want to spend a lot on shoes I'd likely never wear again, but every time I looked at ballet shoes, with their flat heels and round toes, my inner child, that precocious Susie who is so very particular about her footwear, made a sound similar to the one my cat makes when he's coughing up a hairball.

She (little Susie) and I finally agreed on a pair of shoes that had a thicker heel than we were accustomed to, but it was 3" high and there was some metallic gold stuff scattered around the toe area. The shoes Tina Turner might wear to a funeral, about sums it up.

Five bucks, too, radically on sale.

Happy with my purchases, and feeling ashamed I was thinking about clothes at a time like this, I drove home and packed for the trip.

I left early the next morning and met my brothers Junior and Merv at an exit off I-81, where we breakfasted at Denny's and met up with my brother Steve who was bringing my sister Sally and her husband Mel.

We reached Albany, Kentucky in the evening and checked into the hotel, and then drove the twelve or so miles to the viewing.

I had pictured that it would be similar to Amish viewings—i.e., everything is subdued with low lighting and there is very little noise except for the murmured conversation of the mourners. The body in the open casket is in one of the rooms of the house with only a kerosene lamp for light, and one views the body and then exits to allow space for others. There is a lot of shaking of hands and everything is very organized.

The chaos we encountered at the viewing in Kentucky was as jarring as it was unexpected. I had never seen so many buses and vans in my life, and a policeman directed us to a parking area where a local man with a charming accent shuttled us to the viewing, which was being held in a warehouse-like building that my uncle John and some of the church members had completed shortly before his death.

"About a two-hour wait," our driver said as he waved and drove off.

Two hours? We collectively groaned as we saw the long line of people waiting to get in. It was almost dark and chilly out, and none of us had eaten dinner. But we stood in line and after what felt like a very long time, finally entered the building.

Instead of the softly-lit, subdued atmosphere of Amish viewings, there was harsh fluorescent lighting and a concrete floor. There were no windows and the sound of hundreds of conversations being held simultaneously ricocheted off the bare walls.

We followed the line to the open caskets and I almost could not bear to look at the bodies of those dear people whose lives had been taken so suddenly. We exited the building and went back out to the parking lot where there were still hordes of people milling about. I hadn't seen my parents and while I wanted badly to see my mother and comfort her, there was a part of me that was worried about how she'd feel about seeing me in the presence of her family, a group who could be a tough crowd, spiritually speaking. They like to have fun, they're great if you're "in" with them, but if you're shunned like I am they sometimes don't bother to hide the coldness they feel toward you.

The ironic thing is that some of my mother's siblings are also excommunicated and the churches they belong to are even plainer than the Amish in some ways. The dresses are longer, the prayer coverings bigger, the expressions meeker; but the Amish don't differentiate—if you leave for another church, no matter how conservative, you're delivered to Satan for the destruction of the flesh, and that is that.

My deceased uncle John was a preacher when he left the Amish church which made the scandal that much greater. But he and his wife Sadie felt they were called to a different church and they left along with their children many years ago.

"Look," my brother Junior said. "There's the bus Mom and Dad rode down on."

"I'm going to see if I can find Mom," I said, and as I walked toward the bus in the darkened parking lot, my Tina Turner funeral shoes hurting me now, I suddenly spied her.

I rushed over to her and saw nothing but welcome on her face.

Maybe grief has a way of washing us clean of the trivialities of life, I don't know, but my heart rejoiced when she opened her arms, and I hugged her, hard.

"I'm so sorry, Mom," I said as I held her close and she nodded and looked drained and tired. Dad looked weary too; he had organized the bus ride for my mother's relatives, not an easy task when not everyone has telephones.

My brothers and I ate dinner at a local restaurant and afterwards, in the lonely confines of my hotel room, I felt that disquieting guilt I always feel after I'm with the Amish and Mennonites, because they put most of us to shame. They give their time and money to those in need, and I am convinced that no group on the planet does community as well as the Amish and Mennonites.

I think about that sometimes when I'm paying my Verizon bill. The Amish don't need that expensive three-in-one plan I have—TV, phone, internet—so they have that extra to help when others are in need.

I tried to shake off how I was feeling and wanted a distraction, but television held no appeal and neither did the book I had brought, because I continued to struggle with the feeling that I'm a terrible person compared to my relatives.

While they avoid worldly activities, I listen to rock music, enjoy the occasional movie, and drive a car. My child plays videogames and not only listens to rock music but also plays it during his weekly guitar lessons.

When I'm at home in Northern Virginia where everyone else considers those activities normal, I'm fine; but when my life appears in stark contrast to the lives of my plain relatives, wretched pretty much sums up how I feel.

But here's the thing—for me, religion, the external kind that puts man's rules on a par with God, is cyanide in my well. Spiritually speaking, I am like an alcoholic who can't take even one sip without spiraling out of control until I am puking in a gutter somewhere.

It seems that some people can handle going to those kinds of churches. I am sure there are Amish women right now who can don a cape and apron and not feel it's anything but a smart fashion choice. I am certain there are plain Mennonites, like my late Uncle John, who can grow their beards and know it is just a thing they've chosen to do as a group and has nothing to do with their right standing with God.

Then I remembered a parable Jesus had told his disciples, about how there were two men praying in the temple, the first a religious man who thanked God he was not like other men, and the second who said, "God be merciful to me a sinner," and how God was much more pleased with the latter's prayer than the former.

That cheered me up, so I took a hot shower, put on my pajamas, and went to bed.

The next morning, I woke up early and couldn't go back to sleep, so I headed to the gym to exercise before it was time to get ready for the funeral. In the hotel lobby I saw an Amish couple sitting ramrod straight on the sofa. The woman's white organdy covering strings were tied in a neat little bow and her husband's white hair was combed and his beard sternly obedient. It was quarter till six in the morning and they probably were used to rising at an early hour to milk the cows or whatever in Lancaster County, Pennsylvania, so why should they dawdle at a Best Western in Albany, Kentucky?

I hesitated. Should I talk to them? My hair hung in messy waves around my head, and I was wearing a black hoodie with a pink design on the front and black exercise pants. Not an outfit I would have chosen for such an occasion, but I summoned up my courage and walked over to them.

"Vie bish du?" I said, and they could not have looked more surprised if a Korean man—one they had actually seen get off the boat—started speaking in perfect Shakespearean English.

To their great credit, they recovered and I explained in Pennsylvania Dutch who I was, i.e., Manie L. Fisher's daughter.

The husband—who had the cheerful expression of a man who, if not Amish, would definitely have a boat, drink Coors Light, and drive a blue Chevy—said, "Oh! Manie L's!"

"Yes. I'm Susie," I said as I shook their hands and continued chatting with them in my somewhat rusty Pennsylvania Dutch until it got to be too much for me and I switched to English.

"We live close to your parents," the woman said.

"Oh? And what is your name?"

She told me and then said, "I'm Sadie's sister."

Her expression I could not at first understand—there was grief, yes, but there was horror also, understandable given the violent nature of her sister's death, but I wondered about the relationship—had she shunned her sister and regretted it now?

I didn't hesitate for a moment. Grief was grief, and I hugged her and said, "I'm so sorry."

She nodded and sat back down on the sofa.

I said goodbye and walked down the hallway to the gym and opened the door with my key card. I frowned at the treadmill and it scowled back. I hate treadmills, preferring fresh air and sky to some contraption that rumbles and has that irritating habit of measuring my heartbeat. If I want my heartbeat measured I'll ask, thanks!

I considered briefly heading outdoors but it was dark and unfamiliar outside so I stepped up onto the gray machine, pressed Start, and walked to the sound of CNN broadcasting quietly in the corner of the small room.

I thought again about all those caskets as tears trickled down my face. And then, unexpectedly, I flashed back to when I had left the Amish church at age twenty. I had lost everyone then—my cousins, my uncles, aunts, grandparents, and for a while, my parents too.

All that pain, all that grief; however, I had lost my loved ones not from a car accident, but from rejection.

I went back to my room and showered, and then joined my siblings in the lobby for a light continental breakfast. Afterwards we headed to our cars and drove to the funeral.

It was a gloomy morning. Fog clung to the Kentucky landscape like particles of gray mythical spores, comforting us in our grief because sunshine would have been unbearable. In short, the weather was weeping with those who weep, and I was grateful.

There was again a long line of people waiting to get in, and suddenly I exclaimed to my sister Sally, "There's Cousin Sheryl!"

I hurried toward where she was standing in the parking lot with some of her children. Sheryl had eight children by now, I thought, or maybe more, and as I greeted her I noticed how tired she looked. Her green eyes were as lovely as they had been as a child but if a woman ever deserved a spa day, it was this one, starting with a massage by a hottie named Lars (although maybe her husband would have a problem with that, come to think of it, so in that case by a gal named Bertha with large hands and a kindly spirit).

I hugged Sheryl and she introduced me to her children.

One of the girls, who wore a large prayer covering and a dress that reached almost to the ground, nonetheless sported a cute purse on her shoulder, a snappy number adorned with colorful faux gemstones.

"Bethany," her mother scolded. "You don't need to bring your purse into the service."

I looked at Bethany and her eyes sparkled back at me, a look I recognized because it had been in my eyes as a child and still was anytime purses or shoes were discussed.

Then like an idiot I said, "It's okay! I'm bringing mine in, too."

Sheryl shot me a glance that I can only describe as sardonic and shrugged her shoulders. The purses won the day, I'm afraid.

I felt a little guilty as I walked back to where Sally, Mel, and my brothers stood in line. Finally we were inside, but had almost an hour to wait before the service began and I looked around to see if I could find any more of my cousins.

To my delight I saw Lena, my late Uncle Stephen's daughter. She was only a few rows ahead of me and I discreetly made my way to where she was sitting next to her husband. I noticed that she still had beautiful skin, with no artificial help whatsoever. Her lips were full even though they had never been injected with a foreign substance or glossed with lip plumper. I sat down next to her and whispered, "Lena! How are you!" I hugged her, but her shoulders were stiff and her face expressionless.

I toiled on but it was clear she didn't want to make small talk so I joined my sister Sally, who was sitting behind my parents. I hesitated because my encounter the night before with Mom had been so positive, but today she was sitting next to her siblings and I knew there was a very good chance I'd see that look, the one that scanned me head to toe and called it not good. To my great relief she greeted me warmly, and when Sally and I together placed our arms around our parents' shoulders, I knew she felt the same way I did at that moment, that Mom and Dad were too precious for words.

Next I saw my cousin Lydia Ann! My experience with Lena notwithstanding, I hurried over to where she was sitting next to her husband.

"Lydia Ann!" I cried in a hushed tone.

"Susie!" she said.   No rejection here; just pure, unadulterated delight at the sight of a childhood friend.

Her eyes tilted up at the corners giving her a slightly exotic look, and she still had that same mischievous gleam in them she'd always had. I slipped onto the empty chair to her right and settled in for a good chat. We giggled quietly together which felt comfortable even in that sober setting, because she and I had always laughed together. We'd worked together at market and hadn't waited for things to laugh at, but rather created them with our collective fertile imaginations.

"Did you know Uncle John called my mother the day before he died and said he wanted the Esh reunion in Kentucky this summer?" I said.

"I heard," she said, and looked around at all the uncles, aunts, and cousins gathered together in that huge building. "I guess he got his wish, didn't he?"

We both got a little teary-eyed at that, and I said goodbye to her and went back to my seat and waited for the service to begin.

Leroy Kauffman, Sheryl's husband, preached the sermon and how he got through it I do not know; he and my Uncle John had not only been in the same church but had also been close friends. He struggled a few times to fight the tears and then soldiered on.

That morning felt surreal to me. There I was in a sea of plain people, my uncovered head feeling conspicuous indeed in the midst of all those prayer coverings, and through the open door I could see the media trucks that would carry the news of the funeral to the outside world.

When the service was over, the music the Esh family had recorded flooded the room and my eyes filled with tears as I listened to the many songs they sang about heaven.

As the ushers guided us toward the door, I felt sad because I had not yet visited with my cousin Anna. I had seen all my other female Esh cousins closest to me in age, but Anna would complete it for me, the Anna who had scared me with ghost stories and acted in the plays we made up to entertain our uncles and aunts at Christmastime.

I was almost at the door when I looked to my left and saw her! I couldn't speak to her because she was still seated and three rows of people separated us, but she waved her hand and smiled at me with that impish grin she's always had and I mouthed, "I wanted to talk to you!"

She nodded and my heart was full.

Those moments with my cousins were beautiful for me in spite of the solemn occasion, and I wished with all my heart I could see them more. Sheryl and Anna are plain Mennonites and excommunicated like I am, while Lena and Lydia Ann are still Old Order Amish, but why should that stop us from having a relationship?

Why couldn't we all go to lunch together some day? We could squeeze two tables side by side, with the requisite few inches apart and the Mennonites and me at one table and the Amish at the other, and since the Amish aren't supposed to take anything from the hands of the shunned, we could set the salt and pepper shakers on the table instead of handing them directly to Lena and Lydia Ann.

And what about transportation since the Amish ladies aren't supposed to ride in a car driven by Anna, Sheryl, or me? Well, heck. There are no Amish rules that say you can't hire a limo. I say we get a big black limo and go to lunch, darling cousins, and I'll drink champagne while the rest of you drink grape juice. But if my champagne offends you, I'll have grape juice too—bubbles mean nothing to me compared to a relationship with you.

In short, even though we have a slightly different interpretation of what constitutes a good outfit, I believe love can and should remove any barriers between us.

Even the Amish have no laws against love.

After the funeral the sun shone brightly, and my brother Steve and I drove out of the small town of Burkesville. We had a light lunch and continued on through the lovely countryside. I said to him, "Can't you feel it? Kentucky. Daniel Boone country."

He smiled and nodded and we continued to enjoy the landscape of the small yet charming towns we passed. There was an edge of derring-do, a freedom and sense of adventure that big cities like Washington, D.C. sometimes lacked.

After a comfortable silence I asked Steve what he thought about the service.

"I thought the preacher harped a little too much on being saved," Steve said. "It's like one plus one equals two. We get it, salvation is a gift. But what about maintenance? It's like a car, if you neglect it, it gets rusty and then what good does it do you?"

I grinned at him. This was Steve to the core—challenge everything. He can be a pain, frankly, and yet we need people like him in the world, don't we?

We chatted about it some more and before I knew it I was confiding all kinds of things to him, like I had as a teenager, and somewhere in Tennessee my friend Jude called and invited me to a party the following Friday night at the marina where he keeps his boat.

"Yes!" I said. "Yes! After what I've been through the last couple of days, I can't wait to party."

When I hung up Steve was looking at me with a quizzical expression on his face. "Didn't that service have any impact on you whatsoever?" he said.

"I know, Steve, I know. But I can't live that narrow of a lifestyle, I just can't! I admire them tremendously, but I couldn't do it."

"Yeah, me either."

A few minutes later he said, "So, what's your drink of choice when you go out?"

"You couldn't have asked me a single question I'd like more!" I said, and we discussed wine versus beer versus martinis with great aplomb.

It was getting dark now and as we drove through the mountains of West Virginia, the moon rose and bathed everything in a holy light, and I thanked God for his creation, and prayed for my cousins, the surviving children of John and Sadie Esh, who would be left to pick up the pieces of their lives long after the rest of us had gone home.

Be at peace, my dears, and know that I will not forget you in my prayers.

Chapter 51

T he day after I came back from the funeral I knew some elemental part of me had shifted and changed, and that evening I sat on my bed crying, feeling like an orphaned child, lost in a cold world where there was no comfort.

I had spoken with my mother earlier to check on her and while we were chatting, Dad interrupted and said she had to get off the phone because three couples had just arrived to visit them. I could picture them, consoling as only they can, in their sweet unassuming way. I miss that so much sometimes—with the Amish, there's no pressure, no protocol, no you-have-to-bring-flowers-or-wine rule when you visit someone's house. No, *you* are the gift. There are no baby showers or bridal showers which is a whole other subject! Rather, the Amish visit the parents of a newborn baby and bring unwrapped presents along, and when a couple marries they visit all the relatives, a beautiful practice in my opinion, and yes the newlyweds get gifts but they are accompanied by relationship.

After my conversation with Mom I felt more alone than I think I've ever felt since leaving the Amish church. I had again witnessed the beauty of what happens when a community gathers around the bereaved. I had just lost an uncle and aunt, and four cousins, and who, in this Northern Virginia suburb, was there to comfort me? Josh was with my ex and my siblings were all back in Lancaster County, and I felt their absence keenly.

I had no church people to turn to—my fault, of course, for not currently attending one—and my girlfriends all had their own lives and would find it odd, indeed, if I called and asked one of them to sit with me while I cried. Besides, none of them lived in my immediate area but rather in parts of Fairfax, Alexandria, and Washington DC.

It was one of those empty, raw, lonely places of the soul—knowing I did not have what the Amish had, community-wise, and had never really replaced it with anything either.

I dressed for work the next morning in a kind of stupor, putting on the same dress I had worn to the funeral, the black one with the humble flowers scattered over it, and the Tina Turner shoes. The funeral scenes still fresh in my mind, I endured the long trek on I-95, the landscape looking more commercial and soulless than usual and the drivers whizzing by more aggressive and rude than ever.

I slid my card over the security key pad and when the office door clanged shut behind me and I entered that beige hallway, my soul cringed inside itself and asked, *I left the Amish for this?*

There was a staff meeting that morning, our once-monthly report from our managing director as to how we were doing financially, etc. When everyone clapped because we had just had the most profitable month in the firm's history, I clapped along with the rest, but at the same time felt numb to it all. We had had months like that before, when we blew all previous profit records out of the water. And that is exactly why I get angry at these captains of industry—as soon as profits go down, they toss people overboard. They call it smart. They call it protecting the company's assets. To which I say *bullshit.* Guess who got them those profits? The very people they tossed overboard.

I know sometimes layoffs are necessary and that companies need to get creative, financially, during the slow times. However, if the CEOs and CFOs of these companies would save some money during the boom times instead of pocketing so much of the profit, maybe we'd all be better off.

And if, collectively, these decision-makers would hang in there *just a little* during the slow times, which are normal cycles for any company, maybe the economy wouldn't tank to such an extreme.

To me, it's like a crew that takes a gigantic boat out to sea. They load up caviar, and the finest wines, and all kinds of delicacies. They go island to island, country to country, and the crew work their asses off loading and reloading, sweat pouring down their faces. The captain does his job too—i.e., lounging in his luxurious perch giving orders, which as we all know is crucial to success too.

And then! Suddenly, for some inexplicable reason, one of the islands cuts down on their order and, while the captain is still making a profit, it's not as much as he expected so he calls the First Mate, a man who kisses the shoes of the captain every morning so to speak, and says, "If we toss three men overboard we won't have to pay them this week and that way we can make up for the profit we didn't get at the last island."

"Great idea, Boss!" the First Mate says, and throws to the sharks the last three men he hired.

And then there's blood in the water, and the whole crew gets scared, and suddenly what started as a profitable, glorious venture becomes hell for everyone but the captain and his first mate, who pocket the profits and eat caviar and swill champagne till they bulge.

So forgive me if I don't clap too hard this morning.

Then a female partner stood up to speak and it sounded like her jaw was weary from carrying all those teeth in her mouth, and as I listened to her, not really absorbing the words, I realized she was close to my age and maybe even a few years younger. When I was in my twenties and thirties, being an assistant seemed okay but now that I was in my forties I was beginning to realize how successful, in the world's terms at least, some of my female peers were.

Had I been fooling myself when, years earlier, I had chosen not to go down the hardcore business route because I wanted to be true to my creative side and do something that would pay the bills but not lure me down a path that, while right for some, would smash my soul to bits? Was I, in short, a joke—not Amish anymore but not successful in the outside world either? None of my artistic dreams had come true and I was a single mother, twice divorced. I had a motley group of friends of whom I was fond but they had their core group of girlfriends and then…me, sort of stuck on, and I knew none of them considered me a best friend, high school as that sounds.

I don't often allow myself to look at life through such a bitter microscope, but that morning the green-slimed doughnut framed in greasy immortality on the conference room wall and I agreed that while life could be good, and there was much for which to be thankful at all times, sometimes it hurt too.

I dreaded going back to my computer and the hundreds of emails that had stacked up in my absence, because none of it mattered to me that day. As I read the first one with glazed eyes—a conference call that needed to be scheduled—Teressa, one of my coworkers, showed up at my desk holding a gorgeous bunch of flowers! Lilies, roses, daisies…I almost cried when she handed them to me.

Teressa has high cheekbones and a playful spirit. She has long shiny dark hair and mischievous eyes, and we take the occasional walk that sometimes finds us at our favorite candy store, Chocolate Chocolate, and when we walk back to work swinging little bags of candy in our hands, sneaking the occasional nibble, I feel like I'm back in the first grade with a fun new friend, and this time my shoes are pretty too.

I placed the vase of flowers on my desk and they brightened up my cubicle even more than my trusty sunflower poster. Then Teressa said, "And I'm taking you to lunch today."

Tears welled up in my eyes again and throughout the morning other coworkers, partners included, expressed their condolences. I noticed the curious looks because it was probably the first time most of them had heard about my Amish background, but I didn't care anymore who knew about my plain past.

For lunch Teressa took me to the BlackFinn, an upscale sports bar/restaurant close to the White House.

"Drink?" she said, and I was considering a glass of wine when she exclaimed, "Oh! We have to get this!" and I agreed that yes indeed we did—it was a "cherrytini"—a martini that came out looking like a thin strawberry milkshake with that little extra something-something that goes down so well in the middle of a workday after attending a funeral filled with plain people.

As we sipped the frothy pink stuff I thought, *I highly doubt if anyone is buying cherrytinis for my cousins Lena, Lydia Ann, Sheryl, or Anna today* and the thought cheered me up a little.

Lunch was fantastic—scallops grilled to perfection, garlic mashed potatoes, and snow peas.

I came back to work feeling much less like an orphaned child than I had the night before, and then that afternoon I got condolences and emails from some of my girlfriends. I may be the random outsider on my friends' respective rosters but it no longer mattered that day. Who needs to be part of a roster when one can be Susie E. Fisher, beloved in spite of her Amish background?

And when I watched *American Idol* on TV that night, and Katie, one of the contestants, sang the Beatles song "Let it Be," I cried all the tears I had held back at the funeral.

The following Friday night I attended the party my friend Jude had invited me to, which took "comfort" to a whole new level.

I felt subdued as I sipped a cosmopolitan and looked out at the Occoquan River, the bar behind me and flickering tiki torches cheering up the dreary April night.

I shivered in my sleeveless blue dress. A dress had seemed like the right choice rather than jeans, maybe in honor of my heritage I don't know. It was a soft electric blue, a comfortable number that had seemed just right for the occasion, but I was kicking myself for not bringing a jacket or pashmina to drape around my shoulders when Jude sat down next to me.

"Cold?" he said.

"A little," I replied and he trotted off to his boat and came back with a windbreaker emblazoned with the red Ferrari logo. I was about to slip it on when Lanny, one of the bar's owners, walked in lugging one of those giant outdoor heaters.

"I couldn't let the lady in the blue dress be cold!" he said as he wheeled it next to me.

Something about those kind words had me tearing up, and then the DJ started the music and I hoped it wasn't inappropriate to dance because dance I did, in my blue dress, until close to midnight.

Chapter 52

I ache, still, for the *rhythm* of Amish life. The closest I get to describing it is how you feel when you watch a movie adaptation of a Jane Austen novel, where the pace is slower, the outfits simpler, the conversation humbler...and when you're finished, it feels like you're wrapped in comfort for a while.

I realize that with the choices I have made comes a great deal of loss. That was driven home to me one Saturday afternoon when I was visiting Lancaster County and decided, spontaneously, to visit one of my Amish friends. I knocked on the door and her daughter answered. She didn't know who I was and looked startled when I spoke to her in Pennsylvania Dutch. I explained, and asked if her mother was home.

"No," she said. "She and Dad went to the grocery store with another couple and won't be home until later."

My heart lurched a little. These were my old friends, women who had married once, just once, and had settled lives, versus my drama-filled life full of yes, excitement, but a goodish amount of wear and tear too.

The Amish have gorgeous social lives because heck, what else can they do on a Saturday night? Watch *Saturday Night Live?* Nope. No TV. Play videogames? Nope! No TV. Go to the movies? Nope. No car, and not allowed to. Go clothes shopping at the mall? Nope. They sew their own clothes. Read the latest gossip magazine? Nope. They couldn't care less what Jessica/Kim/Jennifer/Angelina have been up to and indeed probably don't even know who they are.

So they get together, and talk, and eat, and act like humans who care about each other, and sometimes I feel my life is a little isolated in comparison.

On the other hand, I can't complain.

One day when spring finally shoved winter out of the way with a manicured hand and said Get out of here you blizzard-dealing son of a bitch! and delivered a day in May that was created for pleasure, 70's, sunny, perfect, I was gifted with a day I shall never forget.

It was one of those times that make a girl glad she left the Amish, frankly, and goodness was it a day of celebrating my freedom!

If you had to pick a car that is about as opposite a horse and buggy as it gets, what would you choose? I don't know about you, but I think the Italians know what they're doing when they dream up sports cars. My friend Jude owns a Ferrari, a red one at that.

So—he gave me a ride in it, top down, and I felt like a celebrity in that thing. I don't know if it's possible, really, to fall in love with a car, but the growl of that engine will stay with me to my dying day.

We went to a Mexican restaurant where Jude bought me a margarita and guacamole and chips. Heaven, sweetheart, heaven! However, that was the *end* of my Saturday night, the icing so to speak.

When I had met Jude at the marina earlier and the hello's were out of the way, and I had socialized with the neighboring boater's German Shepherd named Schatzi (means "little sweetheart" in German, which I think is darling), Jude untied his boat and off we went.

There was a lot of debris in the water due to all the rain and snow we'd gotten during the winter, but Jude skillfully avoided it all. We docked at a restaurant called Tim's

Rivershore and I'll tell you this—my Amish friends may have a better social life than I do, but I defy anyone to find a more delightfully eclectic group of people than you'll find at Tim's on a sunny Saturday afternoon.

We saw a group of three guys wearing sunglasses who looked like they might be FBI types. I was polite and didn't scrutinize them too closely, although I sneaked glances now and then.

There was a woman wearing black kitten heels, which I found a fascinating choice of footwear, and black capris and a pea-green top that hugged her bulges.

There was a dude wearing a bandana and a leather vest, with a long ponytail hanging down his back.

Then there was the owner, Tim himself, a gentlemanly yet appropriately roughneck guy who helped with the boat and made us feel royally welcome.

My happy place, one could say—in teeming humanity, drink in hand, soaking in the sun.

On the way back to the marina I stood at the back of the boat sipping a glass of pink champagne and as I watched the debris floating by I thought—hmm. Maybe this is a picture of life. Letting the old behind, all the hurts, all the challenges. Sure, there would be more to face ahead, but I toasted the universe, and God, for that magical moment.

Summer flew by and then it was a hot August evening, the kind where you feel the humidity more than the heat, and I felt sorry for my mother in her purple dress, black apron, black shoes, and thick stockings as we trekked down the hill toward a store that the locals call Amish Wal-Mart. We passed the field I had raced by the day I left home and I glanced over at the ditch where my black Sunday shoe had fallen out of the garbage bag.

Dad looked cool, casual and even elegant in the heat, but then, he's a dapper guy. Even his beard looked well-behaved.

My Golden Retriever, Angel, trotted along beside me. I had brought her along with me this trip because my ex announced at the last minute he couldn't keep her. Angel was thrilled, of course—she loves car rides above all things.

Dad gave me a hard look when Angel and I rollicked in together and Mom fussed about the dog hair, a legitimate complaint considering how Goldens shed, but I didn't care. *Love me, love my dog* about sums up how I felt. However, Angel didn't like my parents' house because at some level I think she knew she wasn't wanted, and was clingy and skittish as a result.

Earlier that day my mother had asked me to take her and Dad to Costco's. I cringed because I don't like that place, no offense to the good people who shop there and love it. But frankly it overwhelms me—all those vats and cartons and oversized bags of things make me feel like a bloated American with no sense of perspective.

However! Mother loves it, it's one of her favorite places to go, so I fired up my car and settled my parents in the back seat. When we got to Costco's my mother said to me, "You'll have to pretend to be someone else today."

Hurt stabbed through me because I knew exactly what she meant, that they could get in trouble if someone saw them riding in a car with me, but I pretended to be confused so I said lightly, "Why? For the Costco people or the Amish?"

"The Amish," she said darkly as we trudged our way across Costco's massive parking lot.

Usually I wear a skirt when I'm with Mom and Dad, but I had helped clean their house that day so I was wearing black sweatpants, the ones I should have tossed a long time ago, and sneakers, footwear I usually reserve for exercising, so I wasn't exactly at my stellar best.

We entered the store. Senses assaulted by the cavernous energy that is special to Costco's, I was trotting after my parents while they shopped when suddenly Mom said, "Hide!"

Oh, my God. *Really?* I thought as we lurked behind the frozen food section until the Amish couple, who were perusing hams, had passed.

In real life it's not ever perfect, is it? If this were fiction, I could write a great ending that would include a mother who would accept me completely, shunned or not, and not ask me to hide behind the freezer section when she sees someone Amish coming.

The perfect ending would also include a father who remembers my birthday and tells me he loves me, words I've never heard from him, and maybe even installs some of his fabulous cabinets in my house rather than in everyone else's.

But this isn't fiction, it's life, and we don't get to write our own endings. And in a way, I wouldn't change anything because I love my parents just the way they are.

"I'll stay outside with Angel while the two of you shop," I said and they nodded, unable to hide their relief that they wouldn't have to worry about an Amish sighting while they were with their English daughter.

The Golden and I sat on the grass outside the store and suddenly I remembered—August! My leaving-the-Amish anniversary month. I took off my shoes and felt that sensation I'd loved so much as a child, of the warm grass tickling my feet.

Feet...journeys...all those years since that fateful August when I'd left home...and *gosh*! I thought, some of the awful choices I'd made. I had trusted the wrong people, fallen in love with the wrong men, worn the wrong clothes on more than one occasion, worked for wrong bosses, worshipped at wrong churches, and wronged Shakespeare.

And yet, I survived. *And maybe going forward I'll be smarter*, I thought. *At least I know how to use chopsticks and that's saying something.*

"It's been quite a ride, hasn't it darling?" I said to my dog as I stroked her blond hair.

"Ride!" Angel said. "Did someone say ride? Speaking of, can we get the H out of this burg? I want to go home."

"Don't swear, Angel," I said. "I never do."

She looked up when she saw Mom and Dad coming out of the store and snuggled closer to me.

"Angel and I are jogging up the road because she needs exercise before the car ride home," I said, and hugged and kissed my parents goodbye. "I love you."

Mom said, "I love you, too," and while Dad didn't say anything, I knew he loved me because I could see it in his eyes.

"Come on, Angel!" I said. "Car ride?"

We ran up the hill, bounded into the car, and got, as Angel would have said, the H out of Lancaster County.

And this time, I had a car, a dog, and the knowledge that I was loved.

Take that, August.

SUSIE FISHER

To the Amish

What does being "separate from the world"
really mean?

    Is it outside,
        what we do,
            the clothes we wear,
                how we get around?

    Or is it love not greed,
        humility not pride,
  trusting in that which can set us free
      from ourselves?

    Is color defined not so much by individuality
        or groups, but rather
            that whole snowflake thing,
  Each of us different
    and yet caring,
        yet helping.

  My Amish tree,
      my mother,
           teach us how to do this.

  Teach us how you love.
        And maybe love can
        wash this planet clean
            until we're all little children…
            Just little children.

Acknowledgements

I feel like such a pipsqueak when I think of the beautiful acknowledgements that have been written by gifted authors that include things like "To my sister Penny without whom this book could not have been written." Sad thing is, I don't have a sister Penny!

I have also noticed that writers never thank themselves. Truth is, writing is hard. Wait, no; the writing itself is glorious, it's the other stuff that's difficult, like earning a living and other irritating trifles. And sometimes folks don't like us much because when we're writing, we're mean. We tend to stare off into space during meetings because we're writing in our heads, which makes us look unfocused and uncaring. So I thank myself for hanging in there, and acknowledge that against all odds, I kept scribbling.

Authors often thank/honor their parents. Can I? Should I? Yes. I can and am. Manie and Katie, I honor you for helping me see things I would not otherwise have seen.

There are some special people I'd like to mention. Axl Rose, for one. I could not have survived the writing of this book without two songs: "Don't Cry" and "November Rain." My three a.m. writing sessions before work were often accompanied by tears and those two songs on my iPod.

Someone once said to me that people would consider me a bimbo if I told them that I am a Bon Jovi fan. Well, color me bimbo, then. "It's my Life" blasting on my stereo in Lancaster County helped me remember that even when I was cleaning houses for the Amish who shunned me, I did it because it was my choice.

Eminem, thank you for the song "Cinderella Man." I realize that a few people might hesitate to vote you Most Likely

Candidate for Keynote Speaker at the annual Baptist convention. (Personally, I think you'd be great.) Regardless, I dined off that song during some mighty bleak days in Corporate America.

To the band Cage the Elephant for the song "Shake me Down." I soaked it in, as I do all your music, like a flower turning toward the sun.

To Luke of the Luke Mulholland Band, whom Josh and I heard in concert on George's Island in Massachusetts. Luke, thank you for chatting with us and for giving me an extra CD just because!

There are so many more musicians I'd like to thank. However, some of you are not on my son's List of Bands Mother is Allowed to Listen to. He ran a censorial eye over my iTunes list one day and said, "You're a mom! You shouldn't be listening to Metallica and Alice in Chains!" Well, hell. I've never professed to be your average Mother (ask my son, he has stories), so: Thank you to Alice in Chains for the song "Again." How else would I have survived the van-pool ladies with whom I currently commute to DC? They voted me off the suburban mom fat-ass club. How dare they, because here's the thing—I try! I eat as much butter as the next girl! (More, in some cases! We're not all Gwyneth Paltrow!) So I huddle sadly in my corner while they chatter away and treat me like I don't exist. The cadence and harmony of "Again" and other songs are great company when I'm feeling like I did with the Amish—shunned for no damn reason. (Layne Stayley, I can hear you singing and making new music in heaven. I look forward to hearing it when I get there!)

Metallica, thank you for the song "Justice for All." You know the old saw, Be angry and sin not and don't let the sun go down on your wrath? Justice for All in my ear kept me from sin on several extremely important occasions. Got some good old-fashioned wrath in there before the sun went down and then went home and slept like the proverbial baby. You might not ever make a mom-friendly playlist, but you'll always be special to me.

Kudos to the band Zebra for the song, "Take your Fingers from my Hair." Love the mad vocals and if you ever want to collaborate with me, just say the word. I don't have your skills but I can warble a little.

To Mike Tramp of White Lion, for the song "Kid of 1000 Faces." I've had to wear a lot of different hats, not all of them comfortable, and when I heard that song it made me cry.

I would also like to thank some truckers. Trucker A, thank you for all the coffee you brought to my local store. I could not have written this book without you. Truckers B, C, D, E, F, G, H...for all the shoes you brought to my door that kept life (somewhat) bearable. I no longer envy Sally and Jane of my first-grade days their patent-leather shoes. (Recently, a woman introduced me to a new coworker as "The girl with the fabulous shoes." Not a bad title. I accept.) Truckers everywhere, thank you for the liquor you deliver to various establishments. How would I live without champagne and the rest of the gang? I consider all of you truckers my dear friends.

To Professor and Author Bob Bausch, for hope and inspiration, and for the laughter in class. Humor should always accompany learning.

That's it! Oh wait, not quite. To my son Josh: you are the only one who was there for me when I didn't get published the many times I hoped I would. You never stopped believing in me as a writer, and for that, I will always be grateful. And of course, you're a great kid. I'm so lucky. Thanks also for writing the bio on the back cover of this book. You wrote it when you were eleven years old and it's not your average bio, which makes it special, and of course, you and only you know how very much I loathe washing the dishes.

To the dear friend who recently adventured with me to my beloved Tilghman's Island on the Eastern Shore of Maryland. Thanks for the Corona, the conversation (especially the scintillating Dodge Challenger versus Charger debate), and for encouraging me to speak my dreams. You'll always "fly me high through the starry skies..."

Finally, to my faithful Golden Retriever Angel and affectionate (albeit thug-like) cat Zack. Who but you kept watch over me and blinked your sleepy eyes when I wrote at ungodly hours of the morning? Well, not ungodly, who came up with that? God is present in the still small hours, and to you, my darling Almighty, I lift up my soul in thanksgiving.

Made in the USA
Middletown, DE
29 October 2015